Vagabond Voyaging

THE AUTHOR OF *Vagabond Voyaging*

VAGABOND VOYAGING

THE STORY OF FREIGHTER TRAVEL

BY LARRY NIXON

BOSTON
LITTLE, BROWN AND COMPANY
1938

TO
ROY AND INEZ

Foreword

BACK in 1926 a press agent named Larry Nixon became the publisher of a magazine for the travel industry, *Travel Trade*. This momentous occasion had one particularly unlooked-for result. Newspapermen have long memories. Here was a friend of other days, a press agent who had always been very much in evidence whenever one of his clients had a story to plant. Turn about being fair play, the newspapermen immediately jumped to the conclusion that their old pal Larry could "fix it up" for a vacation at sea on very, very low rates.

Steamship lines don't give rates. Except for special occasions, such as trial runs when reporters are guests of the line, steamship companies make no distinction between newspaper people and the rest of the herd.

The press-agent-turned-publisher had to deliver. His friends wanted to journey far and wide — and had only the money their wives could save out of Friday-night pay-checks. Larry did a lot of running around until, presto, he suddenly discovered *Freighters!* Magic word — three dollars a day, around the world. (That, of course, was when the dollar was on gold.)

Larry introduced the chief copy-reader of a big New York daily to the captain of a West Indian freight boat. The C.C.R. found Scotch-and-soda at fifteen cents a delightful variation from fifty-cent bootleg on Forty-second Street. He came back from the trip praising the captain, the drinks, freighters, and the publisher of *Travel Trade*.

Including the latter in the kudos was basest ingratitude. Before long Larry was spending more time arranging trips for reporters than in *bona fide* editorial pursuits. The return of every delighted voyager contributed another brick to the structure of Larry's growing reputation for knowing "all about tramp steamers." Friends journeying on the far seas wrote grateful (and sometimes blistering) letters to the former press agent who had canvassed the streets of lower Manhattan to find agents, rates and sailing dates for their vagabond voyages.

Right there, if Larry had been smart, he'd have gone into the business. Freighter lines had little or no literature, but by dint of much questioning, visiting, letter writing, and telephoning, he had accumulated considerable information.

Friends told friends and these in turn told others. Soon perfect strangers were writing letters asking about the lowest fare between Boston and Burma. Others would drop in on press day to find out why foreign boats were afraid to violate the law against carrying passengers between American ports.

Larry eventually sold *Travel Trade*. I suspect he did it largely to get away from what had become an onerous task; if so, he was unsuccessful because the information seekers continued to attach themselves to him like barnacles. It gave Larry what fancy writers call considerable pause. "Surely," he told himself, "if so many people are interested in freighter travel there must be a market for an article on the subject. Perhaps some national magazine . . ." He made the mistake of writing it.

This first manuscript should have been sufficient warning in itself, but Larry was not then aware of the correspondence habits of our great nation.

The first fan letter came from the stenographer who typed the manuscript. She wanted to go to Cuba, where few if any freighters carry women passengers. The Author was flattered. (If you want to flatter a press agent address him as "Author.") The Author took a half-day off, made numerous telephone calls, carefully typed out all the available information for the edification of the typist.

The manuscript passed into the hands of a literary agent who had an assistant who wanted a vacation at sea. Fan letter Number Two followed. Before the magazine check was cashed, one of the publication staff asked Larry to figure out a schedule for her. Up to this point it was fun.

But when letters were still coming in a year after the article had been published, Larry sat down and took stock. It developed that the cost in stamps, stationery, telephone calls and a secretary's time spent in answering readers' questions was more than twice the amount he had been paid for writing the article.

At this point Octavus Roy Cohen enters the picture. "Why don't you write another article answering the questions readers have asked," he suggested. "I know an editor . . ." Larry fell for it. *Cosmopolitan,* under the title "Vagabond Vacationing," printed it. He thought he had answered every conceivable question the most inquisitive could ask.

Again the letters poured in. The very first one began: "I note you say that freighter travel is not for the two-week vacationist, but that's all the time I have — so where can I go?" But perhaps the prize was from a maiden who was planning her honeymoon. Freighter travel offered her the opportunity she had dreamed of all her life — a romantic ocean voyage at the start of the new life she and her husband were to enjoy. "A trip we can remember forever," she wrote. It brought tears to the eyes of the Author — particularly the last paragraph: —

"We want to go to Honolulu or Hawaii," she wrote. "Freighters are cheap and we haven't a lot of money, but we have to be back home two weeks after we're married."

It broke Larry's heart to write her that the fastest ship to Honolulu makes the trip in eighteen days — *one way*.

This book has been written out of sheer desperation. Larry has hopes it will bring his mail back to normal proportions. It contains as much data on freighter services, schedules, fares, sailing frequency and other such information as it is humanly possible to conceive and compile. More than 3,000 letters have been written to obtain it. Where letters were inadequate Larry has personally seen freight agents, Chambers of Commerce, and the like in many ports. To make the viewpoint as universal as possible more than a hundred freighter travelers have been pressed into service for their contributions. Approximately sixty freighters of varying classes have been visited and inspected. Then the material has been checked and re-checked.

The result? To me, it is one of the most fascinating

books I have ever had the pleasure to read. It gives you the primordial itch to get back to the sea, to take the pennies you have carefully garnered and blow them on the kind of trip that freighters make possible.

He has even unearthed some trips for poor people like me who have only two weeks in which to get the taste of salt air in their teeth.

And if provocation is not enough, Larry has provided the vicarious thrill of languorous nights under an Oriental moon with Sarawak off the port bow somewhere. His account of Sparks and the World's Series is something that will make you glow inside.

Last but far from least, turn to the tables at the back of the book where ports of call are listed. Roll these off your tongue: Cebu, Samarang, Belawan-Deli, Penang, Rangoon. Magic names. Magic places. Resist them if you can.

ANDREW STEWART

New York
1938

Contents

CONTENTS

CONTENTS

Illustrations

Original photographs by Harold Stein
Pen and ink drawings by Paul Quinn

Vagabond Voyaging

1 · Let's Go Vagabond Vacationing

LET'S go Vagabond Voyaging; down to Rio and the River Plate; off on the Road to Mandalay, where the famous flying fishes play. Take a Tramp Trip!

There's an empty bed in an outside stateroom on a ship that's ready to take you to strange harbors, to strange lands. Your place is set at the Captain's table. The outports of the world are calling! Can you spare four dollars a day for a tour of the globe? It's as cheap to go traveling now as it is to stay at home.

Is the wanderlust upon you? Follow the trail of those wise in leisure, the experienced vacationers who travel this new way.

At the start your path leads you to a dingy pier; a huge cavern of a warehouse with the smell of spices and tea pleasantly saluting your nostrils; a long quiet warehouse into which your taxicab boldly charges. At the far end you find an old chap wearing a faded uniform cap and coat, adorned with tarnished gold braid. In a cane-bottomed armchair he leans against the warehouse wall.

He stirs a little as the motor echoes die away in the vast expanses of this modern Ali Baba's cave. The driver goes around the car and starts pulling at the ropes that bind your trunk; you reach in the cab for your luggage, wondering if, after all, this is the right place.

"Are you the passenger?" the uniformed one inquires in a mild tone.

Your identity confirmed, he leads the way to a door half-hidden in the wall. "The boys will get your things," he says.

You follow into the bright sunlight, onto a narrow passageway; a platform around the pier — now like a crack in a rock. On one side the dingy warehouse, on the other, rubbing against the dock, a towering white wall, the side of a giant vessel. The *River Takow* is truly a monarch of the seas — no toy boat this. Following your guide of the armchair, who pauses to introduce himself as the Captain of the ship, you reach the gangplank.

As you prepare to mount the steps up the side, another officer appears at the ship's rail to inquire, "Are you the passenger?" That query is the password that says you've found your way to the prosaic cargo carrier that for you is now transformed into a private yacht, ready to sail on the voyage of your dreams.

Malay sailors, wee and weak, swarm down the ladder at the order of an officer. Your typewriter, books and other bits of light luggage will be brought up the gangplank with much tugging and puffing. Your trunk and the heavy bag you packed with winter clothes will be rolled away on a truck to be hoisted aboard.

The cab driver finds you standing on the forward deck looking back along the outer rail. You pay him with a substantial tip, but he lingers for a final word. "Gee, I never knew they were so big."

"We go around the world," you say in the tones of one imparting a great pearl of truth, just as if you hadn't talked to him about the projected journey all the way from Manhattan.

The driver represents your last tie with mundane

things. He's a friend of yours. You've been lost in Brooklyn with him, worried over missing the boat; together you've sworn at the strange Brooklynites who never seem to know anything about their own city, and you've rejoiced at eventually having found the proper pier. You almost wish he were going along too.

"We go around the world," you repeat. Already it's "we" — for the rest of your journey on the *Takow* it will always be "we" — you are now a part of the company of adventurers who accompany this majestic vessel on its circumnavigation of the globe.

"Tomorrow we'll be in the Gulf Stream," you'll explain.

"I went to Florida once," he offers.

You follow the cabbie to the rail. "Have a good time," is his inane parting word. Like all visitors to a freighter, he is loath to leave. You're glad to see him off.

He goes down the ladder; your last shore tie is broken. No longer are you the assistant to the purchasing agent, or the instructor in Math; no longer do you occupy some sad, dull, shore job. You are an explorer, a voyager, a vagabond vacationer. You are looking towards the west, the whole wide world before you; the path of the setting sun is your road to romance, your highway on a pilgrimage of pleasure.

A soft-voiced steward stops beside you. "The Captain" — he hesitates, leaving the sentence in the air. He turns away and you realize you are expected to follow.

You wonder if you have wandered to some forbidden part of the ship, then you remember that no deck is *verboten*. This is your boat — the man who sold you the ticket, and that chap you met in the steamship office, both emphasized the point. That chap — meeting him in the steamship office was a bit of luck — told you lots of things about what to take on board, about what to see in various ports. He was nice to give you so much good advice, to tell you what he learned on his voyage around the world. Another day and another steamship office, and you'll discover him again. You'll find his counterpart everywhere. Some day you, too, will haunt the shipping office, lying in wait for a new passenger so you can talk about your trip. That's something you haven't discovered yet. You're surprised at the meeting, but the astonishing thing would have been for you not to run into a previous passenger in your booking and planning days.

You follow your guide to the salon. Several people are gathered there. The Captain, a couple of other officers, and two ladies who look like schoolteachers; perhaps other passengers.

The steward manages to get the whole sentence out this time. "The Captain says: 'Will you have a drink?'" Freighter captains all over the world will say that to you in the future; it's almost a custom of the sea.

You drink with the party. The steward notes your taste; tomorrow, at sea, he'll discuss drinks. Before you leave the Atlantic, arrangements will be made to stock your favorite beverage for the world voyage. Today the cocktails that accompany the *canapés* are served from the Captain's private stock. Past the twelve-mile limit the steward will open his custom-sealed stores, and post the ship's wine list in the smoking room.

The others are introduced as former passengers. "We made the trip from Singapore in 1930," the tall girl

Cool, Clean, and Comfortable Quarters

says. You count back rapidly to 1930. . . . Eight
years . . .

"We always come down to see our boat sail," the other
one explains. "We're going again next trip."

Eight years, you think. Eight years, three times a year,
the boat is in port; at most twenty-four sailing-day
visits . . . And still . . . to keep memory green . . .
"*We* always come down to see *our* boat sail."

Every traveler cherishes pictures of past voyages.
There may be a spot by the Number Four lifeboat on
the *Champlain* where you stood and looked at the moon.
Some folks enjoy telling their friends about the accent
of the dining-room steward on the *Hamburg*, others do
imitations of the old salt on the old *Majestic*. One may
recall with a sigh the food on the *Île de France*. But
these are only tiny memories — freighter passengers store
much more in their hearts. You remember not one spot,
but every nook and corner of the vessel; not one officer,
but every member of the crew; not one port, but every
landfall.

Aboard the 8400-ton Norwegian motor vessel *Bronxville* (three passengers, Boston to Manila); or in one
of the six cabins on the giant McCormick Line *West
Mahwah* (Oregon to Brazil); no matter what cargo
boat you ride, you'll find one thing that's universal —
the ship you are on is your ship. You have the freedom
of the vessel, you are part of the ship's company. Instead of being the Mate, or Third Engineer, your rating
is Passenger — but you belong.

Lloyd's register may show the *Chinese Prince* as the
property of the Furness Lines, but there's a Los Angeles
newspaper man who will never call her anything but his

own. He made half a world cruise on the *Chinese* in 1931 and talks about it to this day. You have to buy a yacht to own one — a freighter is yours forever, after just one trip.

Freighter travel is different from any other form of vacationing. The cargo-boat passenger has more privacy than those aboard a giant liner, and all the freedom of a picnic in the north woods; more to say about the food than the average residential hotel guest; meals superior to those served in the better class foreign pensions. Accommodations are often far more modern than tourist class on the biggest of boats, the outside cabins large and usually equipped with beds. There's never been a report of an inside cabin on a freighter.

Passenger boats make regular voyages from and to the larger ports. Freight boats follow beaten trails too, reaching all the big harbors of the world, but they also go to the lesser-known shores, constantly varying their circuits to follow the call of cargo. A freighter journey is a voyage of exploration, coupled with the safety of a big ship and the security of a regular route of travel.

But the fact that they go places no other boats go, and the rule that travel on them is cheaper, are only two of the reasons for the hold one of these ships takes on the heart of the customer. It's not because the paying guest has the freedom of the ship, nor because he is thrown in close contact with the officers, eating with them, playing with them, occasionally even taking over one of their cabins while junior officers double up. There's more than all this. There's something about a long ocean voyage, something about the allure of the sea, the comradeship brought about by sharing things together, braving the elements in a storm, facing the rabble at dockside after a riotous shore excursion in some foreign port: there's a tie that binds the passenger to his ship, a tie that binds while traveling, and that keeps memory bright throughout the years.

This newest way of travel is the oldest. Long before giant ocean liners carried cruise passengers to the four corners of the earth, clipper ships sailed from New England for China, bearing the merchandise of the New World to the Far East, returning laden with silks and other wares of the Orient. Freight boats have always gone with the trend of the trade, coffee from Brazil, cotton from Galveston, tea from Ceylon, spices from the Islands of the Eastern Seas, coal from Manchester, and manufactured products from the centers of industry. Where there is cargo, sailors will go; where ships sail, there also go Yankee voyagers.

Five years ago only one or two freight-boat lines had anything even remotely approaching a travel folder. People who wanted to go somewhere went down to the docks, looked up the Captain of a ship bound for their destination, and made a deal. The fares varied with the ability of the passenger to bargain, and the desire of the officers for company on the voyage. The idea of tramp tripping for pleasure was rarely mentioned. But now Americans are discovering freighter travel as offering something different from cruise-liner journeying, and operators are discovering American vacationists.

Today, two busy travel bureaus on the Atlantic and one in Los Angeles devote their entire efforts to booking passengers aboard cargo vessels, and more than a hundred different pieces of descriptive literature have been published. So popular is the appeal that several lines operating on regular routes that formerly called their ships "passenger liners" now boldly break out in print and talk about the "romance of vagabond voyaging."

The rates are probably the chief attraction. Next in importance is the matter of seeing the out-ports of the world. There was a day when the traveler bound for Sarawak was either a businessman off for trade, a missionary setting out to carry the word of his religion, or someone returning to the isolation of work in the jungles after a vacation at home.

Today things are different. Yankee school professors and college students, married women and high-school girls, vacationing stenographers and truckmen who have just won a prize in a lottery, have changed it all around. American travelers want to go everywhere — to see what there is to see. The demand is not "Is the dance floor good?" but "What different ports are visited?" Yankee curiosity, British inquisitiveness, German thoroughness in demanding *all* the information first hand, have combined to make travel for pleasure more important to the transportation companies than travel for trade.

A few years ago one of the steamship lines proposed a cruise calling at Little America, from which land the Byrd expedition had just returned. Several hundred American women hurried to inquire as to details, each eager to be the first to set foot on the icy shore where only men had been before. The idea was abandoned, but not from lack of cash customers. Americans want to see!

Ships carrying merchandise offer the best opportunity to go places that are off the beaten track — where the sight-seeing is not complicated by "dives" that are merely traps for the tourist's dollar. Freighters reach points not available by any other form of transportation.

Rates and romance have their appeal, but there's another important factor, one that probably moves most tramp trippers to take their second journey: the absolute freedom for the passenger, the absence of pre-tense, show-off, or fol-de-rol. Freighters are work boats, not show ships. Stewards are polite, but they are aboard to work, to care for the needs of the officers (and passengers if any), and their livelihood is not dependent on tips, nor do they rely on the passenger's praise of their perfect servant manners to hold their jobs.

Americans have become just a little bored with over-done politeness, with overdecorated hotels and bars, with too elaborate entertainments. The night club era is past. We all demand a more substantial fare in our fun. The vagabond voyage offers just that. Millions still seek the most expensive watering places as being the only spot for a perfect vacation, but other millions don old clothes and wander off into forests to camps and farms for their rest periods.

Passenger liners are great floating hotels — freighters are country homes afloat. You find slacks and sweaters rather than tails and evening gowns; reasonably priced liquors in place of cocktails and vintage wines; food that is substantial — no fluffy, delicately prepared dishes with expensive French sauces and hard-to-pronounce names.

The companies that carry the cotton from Ethiopia to

the mills of Manchester, that move the sugar of Santiago to the markets of Memphis, are headed by smart business-men. Keen competition has sharpened their wits. They know that their boats must move cargo from port to port if profits are to be made. There's plenty of room for a few extra cabins. The demands of the shippers who provide the merchandise require that occasionally some effort be made to carry passengers. The same stewards and cooks that care for the officers can attend to the wants of a few more people. The vacationist wants to ride, so freighters now take a few paying guests on every sailing.

Old freighters have been overhauled, storerooms cleaned out, extra plumbing installed, and beds built in. New boats have the passenger cabins planned when the keel is laid. Smoking rooms are being made a little larger, refrigeration compartments for foods placed a little more conveniently to the galleys, and decks planned to allow room for games.

So today we have passengers on cargo carriers. Pas-sengers that mean profit to the owners; passengers who furnish entertainment for the officers; passengers who have found in this form of vacationing the gratification of the ambition of a lifetime at a price they can afford to pay.

2 · How Much?

Some years back when the pound was quoted around three dollars and something, freight boat travel was offered freely at three dollars a day. Today the easy way to figure costs is to say six dollars a day for almost any voyage you want to make.

This doesn't mean there aren't lots of cheaper trips. The more days at sea the lower the cost. A few coastwise services give you berth, meals and transportation from Seattle to New York, at twenty dollars per week. A number of services can be found at three dollars to four dollars per day; an appealing one is the Wilhelmsen Line tour from New Orleans to Dunkirk, Oslo, Gothenburg, Copenhagen, Savannah, Havana, Vera Cruz, Tampico and New Orleans — two and a half to three months for $250.

At five dollars a day you find a wide range of the longer trips at your command. New Orleans to Europe, 21 days, $85; around the world, 130 days, $550 (175-day globe tour, $700). These are fair samples.

But six dollars a day is the price to quote your friends. There practically the whole field of travel is open. Almost every trip of more than thirty days figures out just under that figure.

Sixty cargo vessels leave New York each year on world cruises. Silver, Prince, Barber and Blue Funnel send boats around the globe. Fares range from $550 to $784 — with no ups. There's another wonderful thing about freighter travel: prices are the same for everyone, the low rates quoted are not merely bait to attract interest. Passengers book and pay the price they hear quoted when first they begin to discuss a trip. Silver-Pacific-Java has an eastbound service out of New Orleans, five and a half months, $700 fare around the globe. This sets the world journey at four to five dollars a day, depending on the route.

Charges are fairly stable. New York to California, for example, runs $106 to $130; the faster the line, the higher the fee. McCormick takes twenty-five days, Shepard twenty-one and Luckenbach fifteen. Brazil from New York calls for a seventy-five to ninety days round-trip cruise. Fares start at $315 and run as high as $385 (for the Booth Line's sixty to eighty days' cruise). Some of these tours include a thousand-mile sail up the Amazon. Booth boats stop once a month at Barbados, Pará, Maranham, Tutoya, Ceará, Natal, Cabedello, Pernambuco, Maceió, Manaos, Iquitos, and Bahia. Essco-Brodin boats make most of these stops sailing every month, while Wilhelmsen charges $285 and covers the round trip to Rio and Buenos Aires in seventy-five days.

Service from New York to Central and South America, and to the West Indies, is heavily patronized by Eastern vacationers. The trips are shorter and costs are higher. Most of the boats are cargo liners rather than true freighters. Fares range around ten dollars a day for the shorter trips, down to five or six dollars a day for the longer voyages like the two-month tour of the West Indies and South America, which winds up with a week at Madeira off the coast of Africa before starting home.

Transatlantic costs are something else again. Cargo

boats offer room with bath for $100 one way, and other lines, from time to time, advertise service "for men only" as low as sixty-five dollars for an eleven-day voyage.

Transatlantic is where the real freighter travel business started, and where tramp trips are still available. You can ride on many ships that do not ordinarily carry passengers — if you go down to the docks and make your deal yourself. Agents will write you "we have no facilities for passengers," but if the Captain happens to like your looks you suddenly find yourself aboard and on your way — with charges as low as thirty dollars for the crossing.

This is one booking you have to make for yourself. No one can handle this kind of deal for you. Fares are rather stable, being thirty to fifty dollars from New York, Philadelphia or Boston to Belgium, France or Germany. From San Francisco to these countries, the charge is usually around sixty-five to ninety dollars. Physicians will be asked to sign the articles as "ship doctor," and others sign on as "supercargo," but no actual duties are required.

Norwegian ships are more likely to accept passengers, but everything depends on the Captain's desire to take on paying guests. These vessels may be owned by the company operating them, or they may be real tramps, chartered for a specific voyage.

Sailing dates are always a bit uncertain and accommodations and food are not always up to the standard set by lines regularly carrying passengers. Women are often taken on these trips, especially if accompanied by their husbands, and once in a great while a couple of girls together make the journey across the Atlantic — the only females with a load of mules.

All prices are based on information current at publication date and are subject to change. Fares were stable for several years; but increasing interest in freighter travel may send rates up on long voyages as they have already been raised on shorter trips.

Don't let some smart salesman fool you about this tramp tripping business. Not every ship that advertises Vagabond Voyaging is a freighter in the true sense of the word. A recent "tramp-tripping" list presented by an agent shows fares running as high as ten or fifteen dollars a day — with plenty of ups.

Close checking of this list shows ships like the *Monarch of Bermuda* included. The *Monarch* is as proud a passenger luxury liner as ever cruised the seas; there's a bath with every room and the service is the best offered on the Atlantic, with cruise directors and dance bands and all the trimmings that any top-hat vacation fan could possibly ask. But the *Monarch* is no freighter, nor does the Furness Company advertise her as such, and her rates are not freighter rates either. A trip to Bermuda is reasonable enough for almost any limited income vacationer — but for long voyages, freighters are cheapest.

Many, many lines operating cargo vessels carrying fifty to two or three hundred passengers have tried to get on the band wagon of public interest in tramp tripping, so called. But these lines depend too much on passenger revenue to cut rates down to the level of the charges on the vessels that make profits from cargo, and carry passengers only as an accommodation.

When some friend tells you about a "freighter" trip at ten dollars a day, investigate and you'll find it's a cargo boat with two hundred rooms.

Freight lines are selling out every trip. Lines have waiting lists a year in advance. Only a limited number of rooms are available six months before sailing, particularly on cruises of less than two months. If the demand is more than the supply, prices will certainly rise to equalize things; perhaps they will be raised until they are above the level of the current cargo-boat imitators of true home-at-sea vacationing.

3 · What Is a Freighter?

ALL boats are freight boats in one sense of the word. The *Queen Mary* and the *Normandie* carry cargo, but they're a far cry from the *Carmell Fjell* of 2,500 tons. The main business of the *Mary* is carrying passengers, rapidly and comfortably, the quickest way across the Atlantic. Only in that service is there enough traffic volume to justify her operation. The *Carmell Fjell* starts at Duluth and wanders around the Great Lakes for a week or so, accumulating cargo at every port before she starts across the Atlantic. The three passengers who may embark at Montreal will spend three weeks on the voyage and have every bit as much fun as the folks in the de luxe cabins on the *Normandie,* though of a different sort — and the fare is under $100 for the trip.

It's easy to say that the *Mary* is a passenger boat and the *Carmell* is a freighter, but in some other cases the distinction is not so apparent. The Maritime Laws have developed classifications. A "freighter" is a boat carrying freight mainly, with space for twelve passengers or less. The boats that carry a larger number freighter travel agents classify as "cargo liners." Here decks for passengers have been added and space for public rooms set aside. The cargo liners carry as many as 150 passengers in a few instances, but usually many less, forty to sixty being a fair average.

Freighters run from 2,500 to 15,500 tons. Cargo vessels are rarely much larger, but more space is devoted to passengers and a little less to freight. Freighter cabins are always amidships and outside, with the cabins centered on one or two decks. Cargo liners occasionally have inside rooms and also have public rooms for the passengers in addition to the lounge rooms for the officers. On the freighter you smoke in the officers' smoking room, order your drinks from the ship stores provided for the officers, and eat in the officers' dining room. Tables for two rarely exist — you just have to be a part of the party at meal times.

You may think of freight vessels as dingy, dirty, and ancient. "Take a trip on a tramp steamer," someone will say, and immediately you have a vision of a tramp, an unkempt individual begging a handout at kitchen doors. Well, just as the hobo of yesteryear has vanished, there are no old-fashioned tramp steamers; owners don't find them profitable. A few old ships are available for one trip charter, but they're rapidly being junked. Nowadays cargo moves on regular routes in freighters, modern, fast, clean freighters that go everywhere. Samarang, Sourabaya, Sumatra, Singapore, and Shanghai; Jaffa, Haifa, Beirut, and Malaga; Port Said, Colombo, Madras, and Calcutta; names that ring with the romance of the crossroads of the far oceans. Every day from American shores some freighter puts her nose down to the seas and starts her journey to ports like these; a huge clean vessel off on her scheduled route; her twelve passengers lining the rail as the shore fades from view.

Most of the newer ships are Diesel-motored, practically all of them burn oil instead of coal. It costs too much to move slowly, only swift vessels can profitably operate in these days of keen competition.

A freighter plies a regular route; a tramp steamer is a vessel that seeks odd loads, for one or more voyages. Very few tramps remain afloat. The freighters rule the seas.

A freighter relies on cargo for its income, carrying two to twelve passengers, moving on a route that, while not completely known in advance, at least has a starting point and an ending place.

A cargo vessel is a vessel that relies on cargo for its main income, but carries fifteen to a hundred and fifty passengers in cabins maintained for passenger service. The route is a bit more definite.

Cargo vessels occasionally have steerage or third-class accommodations. Freighters are always one-class. Cargo boats almost always carry a doctor, usually a stewardess. Neither is to be expected on a freighter.

"But aren't these freighters small, only five thousand tons?" someone will ask. It seems there are lots of different kinds of tons when you start talking about ships.

First there's the question of "net" tonnage, which indicates how many tons of freight the boat will carry when fully loaded. It actually refers only to space.

Then comes the tonnage classification that is most used: "gross" tonnage means the total capacity of the ship, the total of cubic feet of enclosed space divided by 100.

And then we have the classification "displacement" tonnage, which indicates the weight of the vessel and her contents.

"Deadweight" tonnage is the difference between the displacement tonnage loaded and unloaded.

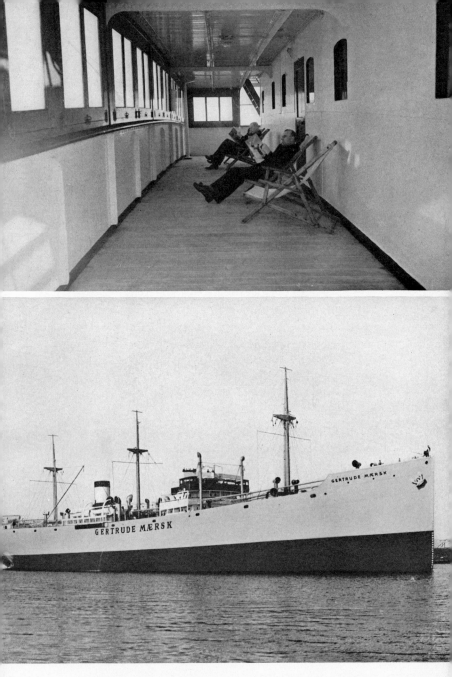

THERE'S A LOT OF DECK SPACE ON THE *Gertrude*

The only way to arrive at a proper understanding of tonnage figures is to make some comparisons.

The *Queen Mary,* newest giant liner of the seas, is 80,773 gross tonnage, with displacement of 77,500. The *Margaret Lykes* (Gulf to West Indies), gross tonnage register is 3,537 tons. That should make the *Mary* 20 times as big as the *Margaret.* But look at the other specifications.

The *Mary* is 1,004 feet long at the water line. If the *Margaret* were one twentieth as long, she would only measure fifty feet from stern to stern; but the *Margaret Lykes* stretches 335 feet. In other words, she is one third as long as the *Queen Mary.*

The Waterman Line *Kenowis* boasts of 11,450 tons displacement. She measures over 400 feet in length and is 54 feet wide as compared to the *Queen Mary's* width of 117 feet and her 1000-foot length. The tonnage may be eight times greater, but surely no one would say one boat is eight times larger than the other!

The Cunard *Georgic* gross tonnage is 27,759; displacement tonnage 39,380. She measures 712 feet in length and stands 43 feet, 9 inches from keel to deck. This cabin-class liner has carried thousands of passengers across the Atlantic in great comfort. The Booth liner *Clement* is exceptionally stable, she carries fourteen passengers to the Amazon and measures 420 feet in length and 53 feet in width and 28 feet from keel to deck. Her gross tonnage is listed at 5,051, or only one fifth that of the *Georgic.* Net tonnage of the *Clement* is 3,082, one seventh of the *Georgic's* figure; yet she is four sevenths as long as the *Georgic,* not one seventh.

Tonnage figures are used throughout this volume

only because there's no easier way to indicate size. Most of the figures are *gross* tonnage. When lines have reported *displacement,* figures are listed as such.

Don't let tonnage figures throw you off. A 10,000-ton freighter is a mighty good-sized ship, plenty capable of meeting the storms of the seven seas on a journey around the world.

4 · Where Do They Go?

FREIGHTERS go wherever there is something to haul. Seven times a month there's a sailing from New York for the Honduras; twice a month one line sends a ship on a cruise of the world, other lines swell the total of globe-circling freighters so that on the average of every five days there's a ship heading away from North America to return on the other side of the continent four or five months later. There's always merchandise for some far land, always a freighter putting out, and if you wait long enough you'll find one to any place you choose to name. They sail from and into every port of the seven seas.

Four lines regularly call at St. Thomas, Virgin Islands. The largest boat has a passenger capacity of around a hundred, the others arrive with from four to sixteen passengers aboard. A cruise liner may come into the harbor at Cebu in the Philippines once a year, but there's always a freighter loading cargo there, with eight or nine companies listing Cebu as a regular port of call.

Freighters go to small as well as to large ports; to landings where the sea is so shallow that passengers awaken to find the anchor down with the shore almost out of sight, and native stevedores aboard flat-bottomed lighters loading and unloading on both sides of the ship. Passengers get an opportunity to make excursions at many places not listed in the family atlas; little communities that live from one ship's arrival to the next. The Ivory and

Gold Coasts of West Africa are far from the beaten track of civilization, tiny ports there with native produce being fed down from the back country. Carrying goods to traders and returning with the products of the country, freighters schedule only a few regular stops on the Dark Continent, but dozens of ports are listed for "calling if sufficient inducement offers."

Freighters go to ports undreamed of, that's part of the allure of such travel. Miragoane, Petit Goave, St. Marc, Jacmel, Aux Cayes; strange ports and probably ones you've never met in print before. Freighters go into the Haitian outports several times a month, three or four lines list them as possible ports of call.

Your departure may be postponed for a day or even two or three when sudden bookings divert the *Black Osprey* from Baltimore to Chester, or send the transatlantic *Edam* up the Hudson to load at Albany. Your arrival may even be delayed at the end of your cruise. It's mighty rare for a boat to start off from Milwaukee with passengers and deliver them in Africa instead of Southampton — but one such case has been reported. If the facts were checked, however, you'd probably find that the passengers stuck with the ship because they wanted to stick, not because there was no chance to leave when the new route was announced. It's rare for your course to be changed in a major particular; but oftentimes routes vary, and almost always some small port or other is added to the list only a few days before sailing.

On the most prosaic routes of commerce the operators reserve the right to vary schedules without warning. American Gulf Orient ships leave Houston for the

Philippines with a fairly well-defined route; but, homeward bound, only a few days before you sail you may learn Philadelphia is to be the first port in America — when Galveston is the normal terminal. Mobile Oceanic ships (Gulf ports to Europe) operate with clocklike regularity, but the destination in Europe is not announced until shortly before sailing. Every cabin connects with a bath; the twelve passengers on these 400-foot oil-burning ships sleep in real beds with innerspring mattresses; there are long promenades and plenty of steamer chairs at no extra cost, but the *S.S. Maiden Creek* is a freighter first, a passenger carrier second. If the goods come aboard so that the Holland shipments come out easiest, Rotterdam will be the first port of call on the Continent. If wares for Le Havre are to unload first, the French port is the first landing at the end of the fourteen-day voyage. Passengers usually go ashore at the first stop — they're in the way when cargo's unloading.

Incidentally, while mentioning the Mobile Oceanic, it might be well to add that the fare is $85 [1] one way, or $150 round trip, whether you journey in the fourteen-day vessels, or on the twenty-one day ships. Only one or two passenger cabins are available, on most of their slower boats.

Freighters go everywhere. The smallest waterfronts are reached by boats of one size or another carrying cargo. A list of the ports touched would be a list of the ports of the world.

[1] Most lines increased fares, Gulf to Europe, in the spring of 1938. This fare may be higher soon.

5 · *Where Do We Sleep?*

You'll like the places you go, and you'll like the way you go too, but you'll find the accommodations as varied as the ships.

The majority of passengers nowadays choose new boats. Ride freighter class and you find it easier to follow this inclination. Shipowners think a long time before they replace a cabin boat; in doing so there's a tremendous investment for a small possible profit. Freight operators find it more profitable to build. Ten-thousand-tonners cost less to build and are cheaper to operate; and there's more profit from freight. Most cargo vessels are much more up-to-date than the average liner. Many of them were built last year. Ten or twenty new freighters slide down the ways for every new passenger ship launched.

The man in the street rarely hears about it. Freighters don't get newspaper space such as was given the first arrival of the *Normandie;* but then owners don't build for newspaper mention, their job is to carry merchandise swiftly, safely and economically. There are lots of new oil-burners on the seas. The Kawasaki Kisen Kaisha will soon have eight new Diesel-motored silk-carrying vessels. They'll go as fast as the *Katakawa Maru,* first of the lot — twenty-three knots an hour. Mitsui has half a dozen new motorships; they make the trip from Yokohama to New York in twenty-seven days, crossing the Pacific faster than anything but the *Clipper* plane.

Other lines have new boats just launched, or on the ways, with the passenger sections as up-to-date as the engine rooms.

Most of the freighters that come from the shipyards of the world, week after week, are oil-burners — Diesel-motored, twin propeller vessels, capable of good speeds and fitted inside and out in the most modern manner.

Your outside staterooms on a modern freighter are built without worry about space. Rooms are larger than most first-class conference-ship cubicles, and fitted with all conveniences. There's usually running water, always electricity, and oftentimes individual showers.

There's a room with private bath on the Gypsum Line; the charge is only two dollars extra for each three-day leg of the voyage to Nova Scotia. On the Barber Line world cruise the suite costs twenty-five per cent. extra. Blue Funnel has rooms with bath. They are only fifty dollars over the regular fare for the three-month Amazon tour. There are five cabins on the *M.S. Berganger,* Interocean Line (Seattle to Europe), and there's no extra charge because every one has a private toilet and shower. The single stateroom on the Newfoundland Paper Company *S.S. Hunbrian* was furnished for the directors of the company. It's really a suite rather than a cabin and it compares favorably with any yacht on the seas.

Owners' cabins are found on a number of ships that carry only two or four passengers. The space on some boats, of course, is strangely reminiscent of tales of immigrants' voyages, particularly in the case of one line that used to advertise "cabins for men only." Even with the row of eight bunks in a single long room, however, there is plenty of space to dress, great lockers for clothes, and a shower with both salt and fresh water connected with the dormitory. You'll find beds on practically all freighters in preference to bunks, windows instead of portholes. There's no need for inside rooms on a freighter.

Not all freighters are modern, not all are fast. Once in a while you'll find one, with a slovenly Captain or a work-dodging steward, where a bit more cleaning could be done; but as a class the quarters are clean. Sailors are naturally neat.

The average cabin is as attractive as transatlantic tourist class — and much larger. There's more square feet of deck space per passenger than on our first-class liners and the decorations are simple but usually pleasing. In any event they are refreshingly simple in contrast to the glitter of many of the big passenger boats.

The public rooms do not compare with those on the first-class transatlantic ocean palaces, yet there are enough corners for rest, plenty of space at table, a lounge with a radio and a phonograph as a rule, a smoking room indoors and deck space outside where you can sit in the cool of a summer evening, sipping your favorite beverage. The modern freighters are neatly finished! The smoking rooms of the Port Line remind you of yachts, and the appointments of some of the newer Castle boats equal an American's idea of a better-class London club. The deck space set aside for recreation is usually more than sufficient. Once the cargo is stowed, swimming pools and tennis cages are set on hatch covers. Under the bridge there is a spot to sling a hammock. Sleeping outdoors in the South Seas is a real experience.

There's no band to direct your march around the decks, but you can get your morning's mile on the Motor Vessel *Annie Johnson* en route for Europe as effectively as on the *Hamburg* and there's always plenty of room for your deck chair — no fighting for position or bribing stewards for choice spots.

6 · What Do We Eat?

WHAT about the food? That question is always among the first asked by those who have never taken a Vagabond Voyage. With memories of the seven elaborate meals served daily on transatlantic vessels, travelers immediately begin to wonder about freighter fare.

It's as hard (and as easy) to explain as it is to generalize on the meals served in the homes of your friends. Freighters are homes, and as in the average home, the meals are prepared to suit the head of the house. At home Dad or Mother sets the food style; aboard ship it's the Captain.

If the skipper likes garlic, garlic you'll find in many, many dishes. On a Dutch boat you'll get Dutch food, and you'll eat it in preference to American specialties, too, if you're smart. On a Japanese line you'll find the Japanese dishes far superior to the chef's idea of American cooking; on English ships you'll find the menu running to roasts — and how they can cook them!

On the more pretentious vessels, Blue Funnel, Java, Waterman Line and others, serious efforts are made to please the passengers, and you'll find the food of fairly high standard. Where only one or two cabins are set aside for paying guests you may discover your menu built more or less on a catch-as-catch-can basis. If you have any real preferences in the matter of diet, discuss the proposition with the Captain and the Steward.

Every cargo boat that accepts passengers has cold storage space for foodstuffs. Fresh vegetables and meat are always available. Order milk in advance, otherwise you get canned cream for your coffee. Not every boat has a coop of hens aboard, but some ships raise some of their own food. There's one Captain who grows mint in a pot in his cabin window — or is mint a drink?

Of course you can take along your specialties, it's sometimes safer than asking for them. The story of the chap who soundly praised the marshmallow sweet-potato pie comes to mind. It was served aboard ship at a meal he enjoyed as a visitor when the ship was in port. As a voyager he found it on the menu three times a week. Obviously, if you like olives and they are not to the taste of the officers, the olives will become a drug in the storeroom unless you consume the stock laid in at your request. So, in placing your orders, be sure you know what you want.

Dining with the Captain has its drawbacks as well as its advantages. Most freighter officers are so anxious to please that they sometimes get involved in peculiar situations. If you ask for special dishes you may find yourself in the spot occupied by the girl who once liked fried chicken. The steward was a literal fellow and laid in enough fowl to serve it seven times a week on a sixty-day trip. Have you ever tried eating chicken daily for a month? Even the most confirmed professional Southerner gets weary of "chicken à la Maryland, à la China boy chef" after a few weeks' steady diet.

Don't be too positive with your likes and dislikes until you have sampled the fare, but be prepared for a lot better food than you could get ashore at any resort hotel or even a country boarding house for anywhere near the same cost per day.

If possible, eat the native food of the vessel. German cooks do best with German dishes; Japanese cooks serving their officers with home foods bring you the Orient before the Brooklyn shore fades from view.

No two freighters feed the same, just as no two homes have identical menus. The larger companies stick rather closely to form, and a passenger with anything like a decent morning disposition can be fairly well assured of things to his own taste as long as that taste doesn't run too heavily to pheasant and caviar — not that both aren't available from time to time, but at five dollars a day you can't make a steady diet of hothouse grapes.

The menus quoted here are good representative menus, not the best seen, and not the skimpiest. Perhaps they answer the question: "What about the food?"

On the Chilean liner *Angol,* with cabin space for only six customers, these were typical menus: —

Breakfast

FRESH FRUIT

OATMEAL   CORNFLAKES

HAM   BACON   EGGS

BOILED OR FRIED POTATOES

TOASTED BREAD

JELLY   MARMALADE

COFFEE, TEA

Luncheon

CHICKEN SOUP

STEAK

[*And what a steak!*]

FRENCH FRIED POTATOES

ASSORTED COLD CUTS

EGGS TO ORDER

GREEN PEAS   CREAMED SPINACH

TOMATO SALAD

FRESH FRUIT

COFFEE, TEA, MILK

Dinner

HORS D'ŒUVRES

[*Very French*]

STUFFED CELERY

HOT ROLLS

POTATO SOUP

[*Almost as good as the chef's lentil soup*]

BAKED NATIVE FISH

[*A giant, name unknown*]

MEAT LOAF

EGGS TO ORDER, ANY STYLE

BOILED OR FRIED POTATOES

CORN   PEAS

ROMAINE SALAD

PIE

[*Hot from the galley*]

FRUIT

CHEESE AND CRACKERS

COFFEE   TEA

Peaches, oranges, bananas, and grapes were the fruit north bound. South bound there was grapefruit at breakfast, too. This vessel had a French cook who delighted in concocting strange native dishes. He had an entrée in honor of every port visited. Pastry was served only rarely on this ship, but the vegetables were fresh and there was an abundance of fresh fruit at meals and between meals as well — apparently a native custom.

Here's the regular dinner served on the *Javanese Prince* one day last spring. It's nothing out of the ordinary, but it's typical of the service on that particular ship: —

TOMATO JUICE COCKTAIL

STUFFED OLIVES

CONSOMMÉ CELESTINE

FRIED SOLE   TARTAR SAUCE

BREADED PORK CUTLET

BEEFSTEAK AND KIDNEY PUDDING

ROAST MUTTON   RED CURRANT JELLY

COLD: PRESSED BEEF   HAM

BAKED OR BOILED POTATOES

MARROW BEANS   VICHY   SUGAR CORN

GOLDEN PUDDING AND SYRUP

CALIFORNIA FRUIT SALAD

CRACKERS   CHEESE   FRUIT

COFFEE

And here's an American meal on an American-owned and operated schedule: —

MOBILE OCEANIC LINE
On Board *S.S. Afoundria*

Dinner

SHRIMP COCKTAIL

ICED HEART OF CELERY   STUFFED OLIVES

HOT CONSOMMÉ À LA CHIFFONADE

MINCED CHICKEN ON TOAST   LAMB CHOP

BROILED SIRLOIN STEAK À LA BORDELAISE

O'BRIEN POTATOES   FRENCH FRIED POTATOES

MACARONI AU GRATIN   SPINACH WITH BOILED EGG

COLD BUFFET

BOLOGNA   BAKED HAM   ASSORTED CUTS

LIVER CHEESE   HEAD CHEESE

SALAD

HEAD LETTUCE   THOUSAND ISLAND DRESSING

DESSERT

PEACH SHORT CAKE   SLICED PEARS

VANILLA ICE CREAM   NEAPOLITAN ICE CREAM

ENGLISH CREAM CHEESE   SALTINES

COFFEE   COCOA

TEA, HOT OR ICED

Every ship seems to pride itself on a farewell dinner — on the last meal before entering port. It's the "Captain's Dinner," and the steward tries to do himself proud.

No listing of food offerings would be complete without showing at least one such.

Here's the Captain's offering on the twenty-fourth voyage of the *Afoundria:* —

Captain's Farewell Dinner

MANHATTAN COCKTAIL

CAVIAR & ANCHOVIES   CANAPÉS

LOBSTER COCKTAIL

QUEEN OLIVES   ASSORTED PICKLES

ORIENTAL CHICKEN SOUP

FRIED RED SNAPPERS   FLEMISH SAUCE

ROAST YOUNG TURKEY   GIBLET GRAVY

OYSTER STUFFING   CRANBERRY JELLY

CHATEAU AND DUCHESSE POTATOES

ASPARAGUS TIPS IN BUTTER

PETITE GREEN PEAS

STEAMED RICE

———

SAUTERNE WINE

NEAPOLITAN ICE CREAM   PRESERVED PINEAPPLE

COCONUT LAYER CAKE   ASSORTED BISCUITS

COFFEE   ICED TEA   LEMONADE   COCOA

ASSORTED COLD MEATS AND CHEESE

The only printed menu collected from over a hundred freighter calls is the one used aboard the *S.S. Tyndareus* for her Christmas Dinner, 1935.

Where it was printed and how the gold ink in which it appears was secured is a mystery, but as noble a job of printing appears as ever graced the card at any groaning board on a transatlantic floating palace.

The three pages of the folder showed: —

[OUTSIDE COVER]

MENU

With the Compliments of the Season

S. S. *Tyndareus*

Commander P. Y. Pycraft D.S.O.

X'mas 1935

[INSIDE LEFT-HAND PAGE]

Officers

Chief Officer	P. J. Makepeace
2nd	A. Pope
3rd	M. G. Turner
4th	C. H. McKno
Chief Engineer	A. Robertson
2nd Engineer	W. M. Thom
3rd	J. N. Stephenson
4th	D. Robb
5th	R. McAllister
6th	F. Milsom
7th Engineer	T. W. Appleton
Wireless Operator	C. L. Gardner
Junior Wireless Operator	K. Icke
Surgeon	T. L. Tan

[INSIDE RIGHT-HAND PAGE]

Le Dîner

HORS D'ŒUVRES   VARIÉS
OLYMPIA OYSTER COCKTAIL
GRAPEFRUIT   LA BOHÊME
POTAGE MARIE LOUISE   CONSOMMÉ MINESTRONE
FRIED LOBSTER   AUX CREVETTES
ASPARAGUS HOLLANDAISE
LAMB CUTLETS   RÉFORME
BOILED YORK HAM   MADÈRE
ROAST TURKEY   CHIP OLATA
GARDEN PEAS   CAULIFLOWER
ROAST & BOILED POTATOES

Cold Buffet:

SALMON À LA RÉGENCE
MELTON MOWBRAY PIE
JELLIED OX TONGUE   ROAST RIBS BEEF
ROAST SURREY CAPON
ROAST LEG LAMB   MENTHE
SALAD IN SEASON   SALADE DAUPHINE

Sweet:

PLUM PUDDING   BRANDY SAUCE
GLACE FANTASIA
MINCE PIES   X'MAS CAKE   YULE LOG

Savoury:

CROÛTES DU PORTUGAL
BISCUITS   CHEESE

DESSERT   COFFEE

A Table Richly Spread in Regal Modes
With Dishes Piled
And Meat of Noble Sort and Savour.

And no account of freighter literature would be complete without something in the so-called "humorous vein." Long hours at sea stir stewards to efforts to win the applause of the passengers. The following menu undoubtedly was intelligent to the *Silverash* passengers, eight in number; today it is prized by each of the eight, no doubt, and it certainly adds a bit of mystery to this chapter: —

M. V. *Silverash*
The Hobo's Jungle Party
Suggested by and by kind permission of
COMMDR R. L. Pallett.
This Menu is taken from Hebrews
13th Chapter 8th Verse

———

TELL US A FEW   SOUR GRAPES
DIRECT FROM THE TRENCHES
ADAM'S ALE
TWO EYED STEAK
SPARROW GRASS   COW'S MUDGUARD
FLOATING BEEF
HER HERO — A BIT OF BULL
BAKED & BEAT SPUDS   GREENHOUSE ORCHIDS
A BIT OF SWEET STUFF THE LADIES
STOP ME & BUY ONE   CURDLED COW'S JUICE
WEEVILS' MANSIONS   NATURE'S DOWNFALL   JAVA MUD

———

A TRAVELER'S LETTER ABOUT FREIGHTER MEALS

Here's a report, one that gives a picture of life aboard a world cruise freighter with emphasis on the meals.
The name of the ship has been taken out in fairness

to other vessels. Not every freighter is the vagabond's paradise this ship turned out to be, yet the story is fairly typical of all the world cruise cargo boats. Read it and let your mouth water a bit; read it in stiff shirt and high collar, with traffic noises coming up through the window, while telephones ring and buzzers hum. Read and understand the lure of freighter voyages.

DEAR LARRY: —

About the menus! Sorry, but the dinners were usually eaten in the soft haze of afternoon's highballs and a pre-dinner collection of cocktails. Breakfasts, aside from a few inevitables such as a rather soggy corn bread, and a plate of half a dozen assorted jams and conserves, usually meant ordering what you want, but having it prepared by a cook who quickly learned whether you liked your eggs well done, wanted a rasher of bacon or a bit of ham beside them, and otherwise was able to get each passenger about what he or she wanted. Midday meals were usually rather full. Tea in the afternoon (after the siesta) was served in the state-rooms for most passengers, and the early morning coffee, with banana or other fruit, was always brought around at getting-up time, before you took your bath.

Meals were served in the "salon," which served as a library and lounge when not used for eating. Tables (two large round ones) topped with a flowered red oilcloth were covered over with the conventional white linen for all meals except afternoon tea. Tea in the salon was for the men when the ladies didn't come out of their staterooms in the afternoon the first two or three days, and the men looked on that as a promise never to do so. At teatime we sat around in sarongs twisted, towel-like, around our waists, perhaps pajama tops, unbuttoned, the flimsy "chenalis" or Philippine straw slippers, on our feet.

A. P. MOLLER   COPENHAGEN

M. S. "M A R C H E N   M Æ R S K"

Nov. 18. 1937.

M e n u.

Consomme Laitue aux Quenelles.

Filets de Carrelet, a l'Indienne.

Bœuf a la Mode.

Epinards, Choux - Fleurs.

Haricots verts, Pom - Sautees.

Pommes d'Terre au Four.

Poires, Creme a la Vanille

C a f e.

TYPICAL MENU

Typical breakfast: half a grapefruit (or papaya, in the parts of the world where they could be had fresh) or other fruits. Some were the conventional breakfast fruits of "home" and others the strange little or big fruits of the tropics. Also, a choice of stewed fruit of one sort or another. And quite often prunes. Hot corn bread (always, it seemed) and soda biscuits, toast, and our choice of short orders — small breakfast steaks, omelettes, eggs any style, with or without real Westphalian ham (with a fine smoky taste), bacon, etc., soups, salads, drinks.

"Buddy," the cook or steward, (or what) — did most of the breakfast cooking in the butler's pantry adjoining the dining room. He is a Portuguese East Indian, Gawnee his race (that's the phonetic spelling). Other, heavier cooking, done below decks.

At each port, new food supplies are taken on, particularly fresh things, so there are nearly always fresh vegetables and something specially characteristic of the part of the world that the ship left just behind.

Big stocking-up on supplies is done in Singapore, Shanghai, Port Said, and in the U.S. Liquor stores are heavily taken on at Shanghai and Singapore — two free ports. Also, at Singapore, the ship takes on great stores of ginger ale (I think the finest in the world) and sparkling water. These are in "split" bottles, and cost two cents each, or less if you save your bottles and bring them in to be refilled. On the ship, the icebox always has these cold for passengers, and nobody ever thought of charging a passenger for such a thing as all the ginger ale needed. Liquor prices also were well down. Johnny Walker, red label, the big drink: ten consumed to one of all other whiskies combined — and some ales and stouts (gosh-awful stuff so far as I was concerned).

Of the two dining salon tables, one was presided over by the Captain, and the other by the Chief Engineer. Captain and Chief Engineer have equal rank, but the Chief draws more pay and is really more punkins as an officer.

Lunch, the Captain nearly always stayed above, and the Chief Engineer often missed. But both came on for dinner.

Dinner was not served in very elaborate style. Few courses and not much hooey, but plenty to eat, always five or six meat choices — including very regular appearance of good, rare roast beef, *au jus*. Always dessert, lots of ice cream, and for dinner, always fruit and black coffee — and once in a while someone sets the habit of taking coffee up on the Captain's "Porch" under awnings and sunshades, where the ship radio or phonograph could play soft music — even dance music.

Luncheons very much like the dinners, except slightly more restricted choice of meat orders. Soups, of course, and usually a fruit or other cocktail.

Whenever we were to lose a passenger at a port, there was always the Captain's farewell dinner, with the Captain opening champagne for all concerned, and usually at other dinners there was someone who would provide wine for some sort of trumped-up occasion.

Need I say more of this eats question?

Tea consisted of coffee — and cakes, and fruits if wanted. Always served at four o'clock, which marked the end of siesta time. Then dinner was around seven-thirty or eight, and the butler (or steward) would always get you anything you wanted between meals, especially at night when sandwiches were made up, and coffee ready if there was anyone on the ship that was hungry. Our crowd usually had heavy duties near a Scotch bottle, and so we didn't deign to look at the sandwiches, and in due time our man got tired of making them and eating them himself — and just gave it up. And I suppose the same thing happened about the morning ten-o'clock broth, customary on so many ships.

Different on the boats going out. All food tasted like Chinese cooking, which in fact it was. Roast beaf and roast mutton both hid their flavors beneath a load of allspice, and although there were always elaborate menus and nine courses, the food got dreadfully tiresome after a few days. On the freighter, things always taste good. I ate like a pig, and really enjoyed meals, both as to cooking, and as to the company and atmosphere in which they were served.

Plenty of storage space for fresh vegetables and meats on these freighters. And most always something green and crunchy — like head lettuce, celery, etc., which taste better in the tropics than anywhere else. Milk was fairly scarce, but not unobtainable, especially if the crew knows there is to be a child aboard, as was the case a part of our trip.

Oh, yes, the water. Heard of the "limeys"? Well, the contraction for "lime-juicers" came into use because the British ships have a rule that between certain latitudes, lime juice must be put in the water to prevent scurvy or something. And when the ship gets into the lime-juice zone, the two familiar (and never used) water bottles on the serving shelves are doped, daily, with lime. I tasted it once just to see what it was like. Brackish, warm and just there for tradition's sweet sake.

WALLY

7 · Drinks

VERY few freighters boast of a bar, but who wants a brass rail at sea? One boat has a room devoted to drinking, but the ship phonograph and piano are in there too, and it's a rather sizable vessel carrying twenty-two passengers coast-to-coast. Another line shows a bar in its plans, but it's only a counter from a stateroom opening into the salon.

A few of the larger boats have wine lists; on a number of other ships the steward types or writes by hand a single copy of the drink list, but nobody pays any attention. Drinking aboard freighters is either something neglected or a daily rite that calls for certain drinks at certain hours; the steward stocks to meet the demand.

Regardless of whether or not there is a bar, the officers' steward on the smaller boats and the passengers' steward on the larger ones always manages to provide a drink unless, of course, the line is one of the few teetotaler organizations still afloat. Scotch-and-soda used to be a dime on most freighters. It's not much higher now. Liquor stocks come aboard at ports where there is no duty, or where the taxes are low. The lines don't try to make a big profit on the stores sold to passengers. You pay for wine with your meals, but the charges are reasonable enough.

There's a story about drink prices that, while not guaranteed, is certainly worth repeating. The heads of one famous line were strict white-ribbon men, belong-

ing to temperance societies and all that, but business
demanded that they carry liquor aboard to entertain
shippers, and for the occasional passengers.

"Put in stocks," the managing director is quoted,
"but be sure we have the very best, and that it is sold
at prices that do not give us a profit. We'll take no revenue from the rum trade. I'd rather lose money."

That's what "they say," and the prices on this line
are a shade under those of competitive companies. We
have not been able to get a printed wine list from them;
the prices are set by the stewards rather than by the
home office.

The *A. P. Moller,* one of the Maersk Line motorships
in the Far East service, has a printed wine card and the
prices are tempting when compared with Broadway.
Read these samples! Hennessy Three Star Brandy,
$2.50 a bottle, ten cents a drink; Canadian Club
Whiskey, $2.00 a bottle; Haut Sauternes, $2.00. Very dry
sherry, $2.00 a quart. Old Jamaica Rum, $1.50 a bottle.

On the Silver boats the ginger ale is put aboard at
Singapore where prices are low. On many boats the
steward never thinks of charging for soda, if you remember to bring the bottles back.

Native wines are often found. Especially recommended is the native vintage on vessels between Europe
and Australia. Prices vary with the rate of exchange,
but they're always far, far below American tavern costs.

There's always beer in bottles — and now American
beer in cans — at prices sometimes lower than the chain
stores, too. The heavy brews on the Dutch boats are
something to write home about if you like German
beer.

The real answer to the liquor problem on a long trip, however, is to buy your own at some port where the duty is low. But don't make the mistake reported by a New Yorker. He ordered a case of Scotch in Barbados and got 144 bottles delivered just as the ship sailed. It seems that's the Barbados idea of a case. He had to enlist a lot of help for the job of consuming the stock on the run from Bridgetown to Brooklyn.

Wine Lists

Not many freighters have wine cards, you'll hardly see a steward in the dining room with a chain around his neck as a symbol that he carries the key to the cellar. On most trips the dining room steward will produce bottles when they are required, occasionally selling single drinks, but as a rule recommending to passengers that they take a full quart and pour their own drinks.

But like everything else in vagabond vacationing, the rules are marked by the exceptions. Some wine lists have been printed, and to be sure there is no question about *all* the details, they are reproduced, in full.

The most pretentious card at hand is that of the Booth Line. These four-hundred-foot steamers carry ten to sixteen passengers in considerable comfort on a cruise that covers nearly three months from New York to New York. And here's the printed card: —

Right table:

	1/1 Bot. Dollars	1/2 Bot. Dollars	Glass Cents
BRANDY Jas. Hennessy & Co. ***	2.50	1.25	10
Martell ***	2.50	1.25	10
Courvoisier Napoleon	2.50		10
RUM Old Jamaica Rum No. 1	1.50		15
Old Nigritta	2.00		20
LIQUEURS D.O.M. Benedictiner		2.50	15
Cherry Brandy		2.00	20
C.L.O.C.		2.00	15
Aquavit	2.00		10
Gordens Dry Gin	2.00		20
VERMOUTH Vermouth, italien	2.00		15
Vermouth, french	2.00		15
BITTER Angostura	2.00		
COCKTAILS Cocktails	2.50		20
BEER Lager		0.15	
Pilsner		0.15	
MINERAL-WATER Sodawater		0.10	
Lemonade		0.15	
Ginger Ale		0.15	
Tansan pint		0.15	
Tansan split		0.10	

Left table:

	1/1 Bot. Dollars	1/2 Bot. Dollars	Glass Cents
CLARET Chateau Beychevelle	2.00		
St. Emilion	1.50		
St. Julien	1.50		
Medoc	1.50		
BURGUNDY Macon	2.00		
Pommard	2.00		
WHITE WINES Haut Sauternes	2.00		
Hochheimer	1.50		
CHAMPAGNE Pommery & Greno, carte blanche sec	4.00	2.25	
Louis Roederer, grand vin sec	4.00	2.25	
OPORTO WINE Oporto white sup.	2.00		20
Oporto Sandemann	2.00		20
» Invalide	1.50		
SHERRY Sherry, very dry	2.00		20
MADEIRA Madeira, fine old	2.00		20
WHISKY Black & White	2.50		20
Canadian Club	2.50		20
Johnnie Walker R. L.	2.50		20

TYPICAL WINE LIST

Wine List

Sherry		BOTT.	PER GLASS
Very Fine, Pale		6/–	8 *d*
Claret			$\frac{1}{2}$-BOTT.
St. Julien		4/–	2/3
Margaux		5/–	—
Sauterne		4/–	—
Port			GLASS
Dow's " Royal Dry " Old Tawny		6/9	9 *d*
Whisky	HALF-GLASS		
" White Label " (Dewar's)	5 *d*	7/6	9 *d*
" White Horse "	5 *d*	7/6	9 *d*
Brandy			
Cognac *** (Antonio Frères)		10/	1/–
Gin			
Three Mast		5/–	6 *d*
Burkes' Gordon's Old Tom		5/–	6 *d*
Rum			
Jamaica (Wedderburn's)		5/–	6 *d*
Champagnes			$\frac{1}{2}$-BOTT.
Pommery & Greno		17/–	9/–
Portuguese Wines			
Amarante, Red and White		1/9	—
Evel		1/6	—
Lisbon Red Wine		1/–	—
Bucellas		1/9	—
Collares		1/6	—
Liqueurs			GLASS
Benedictine		—	6 *d*
Crème de Menthe		—	6 *d*
Cointreau		—	6 *d*
Vermouth			
French and Italian		—	6 *d*
Malt Liquors			
Bass' Ale		9 *d*	—
Guinness' Stout		9 *d*	—

Lager Beer (Dutch) Light & Dark		9 *d*	—
Do. (English) *Do.*		8 *d*	
Mineral Waters	SPLIT		
Lemon Squash, with Soda		7 *d*	—
Do. Do. Do.	5 *d*	—	—
Do. Do. With Water		—	3 *d*
Soda Water	4 *d*	6 *d*	—
Ginger Beer		6 *d*	—
Ginger Ale		6 *d*	—
Lemonade		6 *d*	—
Quinine Tonic		6 *d*	—
Kola		6 *d*	—
Champagne Cider		6 *d*	—
Cider-Herefordshire Medium S	6 *d*	8 *d*	—
Vichy Water ½ bot. 1/		1/6	—

Cigars

Havana	" Petit Coronas "	each	1/–
Brazilian	" Sem Rival "	"	4 *d*
	" Mocca "	"	3 *d*

Cigarettes

Virginian	" State Express "	555	per tin of 50	2/6
	" Three Castles "		" " " "	2/6
	" Gold Flake "		" " " "	2/–
	" Capstan "		" " " "	2/–
	" Plus Two "		" " " 60	1/3
	" State Express "	777	" " " 50	1/3
Brazilian	" Aristocratas "		pkt. " 20	6 *d*

Tobacco

" Waverley " Mixture	per 1/4 lb. tin	2/–
" Capstan " Navy Cut	" 1/2 lb. "	4/3
Rich Dark Honey Dew	" 2-oz. "	1/–
" Cavendish " Plug	" lb.	5/–

Chocolates

Cadbury's

| " King George " (In Airtight Tins) | 1-lb. ea. | 4/– |
| *Do.*   ("   "   ") | ½ lb. " | 2/– |

" Best Selected " ("	"	")	1-lb. "	3/6
Do. ("	"	")	½ lb. "	1/9
Bournville Neapolitans			packets	1/–
Do.			"	6 *d*

Sundries

Safety Matches	per box	1 *d*
Playing Cards	per pack	1/6
Novels	each	2/–
"	"	6 *d*
Bridge Scorers	"	9 *d*

Currency Rates *

Franc	3 pence	Peseta	5 pence
Escudo	2 pence	Milreis	2½ pence
U.S. Dollar	44 pence		

* These changed from time to time.

The Silver Line also has printed cards showing the price of beverages, cigarettes and tobaccos. These cards are used on all Silver boats, both those in the around-Africa service and the world-cruise ships.

The full card offers: —

Wine List

Wines	PER BOTT.	Spirits	PER BOTT.
Sauterne	5/–	Brandy	7/6
Beaune	5/–	Whisky	6/6
Port	6/–	Gin	4/–
Vermouth (Italian)	4/6	Beer	
Vermouth (French)	4/6	Lager	7 *d*

Minerals

Soda Water Splits	3 *d*	Ginger Ale	4 *d*	Lemonade	3 *d*

Cigarettes	PER 50	Tobaccos	PER ¼ LB.
Capstan Medium	1/3		
Players	1/3	Capstan Medium	2/2

Gold Flake	1/3	Capstan Full	2/2
Bachelor C.T.	9 d	Players Navy Cut	
Camel	9 d	Medium	1/10
Lucky Strike	9 d	St. Bruno Flake	1/9
Chesterfield	9 d	Fair Maid Plug	1/2

Playing Cards 1/6 per pack

The American owned and operated Mobile Oceanic
Line (Gulf to Europe) shows the influence of American
laws in the warning on the bottom of the typewritten
list of "Bar Suggestions." *"Checks will not be accepted"*
is reminiscent of the corner saloon — but the service
and quality of the beverages are more like the Waldorf-
Astoria.

The list shown passengers on the Waterman Steamship Company operated vessels reads like this: —

Bar Suggestions

Bass Ale	.25	Eagle Beer			.15
Budweiser Beer	.25	Jax Beer			.15
		Regal Beer			.15
		Piels			.15
Scotch Whisky	.25 per drink		$3.00 per bottle
Gin	.25 " "		2.00 " "
Vermouth	.25 " "		2.00 " "
Benedictine	.25 " "		2.00 " "
Sauterne	.25 " "		1.00 " "
Sherry	.25 " "		2.50 " "
Cocktails	.25 " "		3.00 " "
Brandies	.25 " "		3.00 " "

All Mixed Drinks	.25 per drink
Coca Cola	.05 " bottle
Soda Water	.20 " "
Cascade Ginger Ale	.10 " "

Camel Cigarettes	.75	per carton
Lucky Strike Cigarettes	.75	" "
Chesterfield "	.75	" "
Prince Albert Tobacco	.60	" can
Bull Durham "	.06	" bag
Matches	.10	" package

Checks Will Not Be Accepted for Bar Service

8 · The People You Meet !

"But, the people you meet!" the uninitiated will exclaim when you start talking about Vagabond Voyages.

That, you'll discover, is one of the nicest things about freighter travel. To paraphrase a line overworked in the newspaper world: it doesn't *cost* so much money, and you do "meet such interesting people."

Freighters, by their very limitations, serve to protect the carefree adventurer from most of the pests of ocean travel. Your fellows are those who have leisure, men and women who are able to give the time for a long trip. Starting with the full knowledge that days will pass in lazy sequence means that high-pressure hustlers and supernervous people are left behind.

Newlyweds with more time than money get the best break from tramp tripping. Two weeks at a resort hotel cost as much as two months of this kind of cruising to the Windward and Leeward Islands. Honeymooners are good company because they're so much interested in each other that they rarely get underfoot, yet when you need someone for bridge or an extra pair for a moonlight dance on deck, as "old married folk" they think they must be ready to join the party on request. Not all your fellow passengers will be loving couples, naturally, but you'll find a larger percentage of them on freighters than on other ships.

There's rarely a doctor, so invalids and the talkative aged stay at home, or book on the larger liners. This gives you a more interesting group of passengers — you need not listen to symptoms all day long.

You may be startled by finding a wrestling bear snoring outside your cabin window — as was the experience of an automobile salesman on a coastwise German boat off South America (a circus troupe had shipped overnight); but when you awaken in your outside stateroom on the Motorship *Tabian,* the chances are about seventy to one there'll be no plaintive voices of little children from the cabin next to you. Almost always you'll find plenty of fresh fruit and vegetables in the giant refrigerator compartments, but somehow fond mothers prefer the more orderly life of a conference liner for their journeyings *en famille.* You'll have a lot of trouble hearing anyone in the next room on the *Tabian,* for that matter, as this Nederland Line motor-driven speedster carries only sixteen passengers on its world cruise — and the cabin walls are soundly built, another merit of modern construction.

Freighters are easy on pocketbooks, and while they're not slow as a rule, they do not appeal to the chap who is in a hurry. Third-class costs little more, once in a while even less, on some of the more popular passenger routes where sailings are adapted to passenger convenience, not to cargo. Freighter travel does not interest people who are satisfied to be cooped up in second or third. With rates the same, the returning immigrants will ride far down in third class in a big boat in preference to traveling on a freighter of the same line, even though on the latter they have the run of the vessel and midships outside cabins. The passenger boat saves two days, they'll explain.

People who expect to spend a lot of time on a sea trip are rarely nervous, seldom ill, and not often barflies. Officials always announce that because of the small number carried they reserve the right to discharge those who are objectionable. The occasional nuisance who braves the possibility of a trip of three months or so may suddenly find himself ashore waiting for another ship, a wiser man and likely to be good company the next time.

You'll usually find more men than women, but when groups go out like one motorship on a recent world cruise, with two men passengers and ten women aboard, it's quite easy for the six officers to entertain the ladies and prevent the tour from being too much like a twelve-day vacation to Bermuda, Nassau and Havana. The girls will never outnumber the men so radically as to make the dances tag affairs, à la leap year, with the ladies doing the partner chasing.

You'll find authors and writers, artists and college professors. You may not meet Noel Coward on a world cruise writing "Design for Living." He's already done that; but others just as famous are proudly proclaimed by the shipping lines as among their patrons. Claudette Colbert, if the agents are to be believed, would rather vacation on a freighter than any other way, and practically every travel agent in Southern California can tell of some cargo boat cruise on which he has booked a major picture star or executive.

Folks back for a second or third trip will often be found on freighters. You may not run into the chap who has made eighteen transatlantic crossings with the same Captain out of Philadelphia, but you're practically certain to meet at least one "second tripper" if you see more than a dozen freighter passengers in your travels.

Close personal friends of the officers are almost sure to be aboard too, either former passengers, or friends made ashore, or friends of friends. Every traveler likes to ride with braid-wearers he has met before. Most voyagers are so impressed with the personalities of the ship executives they meet that their friends are hounded unless they book on that identical ship, once the route is accepted as worth traveling.

At the dinner table, especially on boats serving ports in South and Central America, you hear talk about previous meetings. Does the owner of a plantation near Pará, Brazil, go to London on a Booth liner? All his sons and daughters must travel the same way between New York and Pará thereafter. The Captain's a guest at the plantation on his visits to Brazil's greatest port. What's more natural than that the travelers should be guests aboard the Captain's ship?

You're bound to meet friends of friends when you vacation by freighter; the spirit of home is present there all the time.

On Japanese boats you see almond-eyed students returning to their native land, or managers of foreign branch offices on their way to new posts. Nederland Line boats oftentimes carry executives of the government or planters going out for their vacations at home. On almost any route you are likely to meet students who have finished four years at American universities, wives and daughters of plantation owners off to New York for their bi-annual shopping sprees; or an aviation mechanic shepherding a new war-training airplane.

Painters and photographers, printers and princes, retired businessmen and women, schoolteachers and scholars, almost always adults, and as far as can be checked, always interesting people — these make up the passenger lists of the freight boats of today. From every walk of life come the vacationers, all ready for variegated excursions ashore and restful days aboard ship to lull them into the easygoing life that is part of the charm of freighter travel.

It's getting to be quite the thing, with "society people" more and more taking up the tramp steamer as the smart way to travel. "Interesting little ships digging their way into interesting little harbors," is the way one socialite expressed her opinion to a gossip-writer recently.

Lady Geddes, wife of the former British Ambassador to the United States, arriving at New York on the Colombian Liner *Martinique* from a tour of the Haitian outports, told ship news reporters: "I've traveled lots of times in giant liners but this was the most magnificent trip I've ever taken. We slipped in and out of little ports, Cap Haitien, Gonaïves, Port de Paix . . . , never knowing quite what was coming next. All these places are lovely, I'm surprised more Americans don't go down there on cruises."

Lady Geddes was accompanied by a party of four debutantes, society girls from Toronto, all of whom reported a wonderful time. Whether it was her interview or merely the allure of the voyages, I'm sure Lady Geddes will be glad to know that bookings on the *Martinique* have been made for more than a year in advance and that only once in the year following her return was there a single empty berth.

You Eat with the Officers and Use Their Lounge

Your Friends the Officers

The people aboard a freighter you get to know best are the officers who operate the ship. You'll find up to eight of them, the Captain and three Mates, and the Chief Engineer and his three assistants. Two or more are always off duty, so there's someone around nearly all the time to make a fourth at bridge, or to challenge you to a chess match. Some ships have young cadets, boys just out of school or college who are studying to be officers in the Merchant Marine.

Occasionally a wireless operator or two will be found on a cargo boat, but on most freighters one officer is experienced at the radio — rarely is there a special operator unless the line so advertises in its literature. But if there is an operator, he'll eat with the passengers and be available for deck tennis, or join in the swimming parties in the canvas pool. Once in a great while there will be a purser, or some chap accompanying a special shipment of merchandise, perhaps one of Frank Buck's men with a flock of animals. In a blue moon you'll book with a Captain who has his wife aboard for a cruise, listing her as stewardess in the crew roster, but stewardess and supercargoes are the exception rather than the rule.

Sometimes you'll find a dozen officers, but even the boats with only four or five to entertain the passengers present a decided advantage over the average cruise liner. On a de luxe cruise you have twenty officers and two hundred to a thousand passengers, or ten passengers to one executive at the best. On a freighter there are never more than twice as many passengers and usually the official family outnumbers the paying guests. Anyone with the money to buy a ticket may sit next to you at dinner on a cruise to Nassau, but when you go to meals on the *Samuel Bakke,* enroute from Vancouver to London, you'll be next to or opposite one of the officers. You know he'll be an interesting chap. The braid on his coat means he has worked hard to get where he is — no handsome cruise director, expert at inventing games, but a real he-man. Executives on freighters spend years climbing to their jobs; the weaklings, the dullards and the inefficient are lost on the way up.

Taken as a class you'll agree that freighter officers are the grandest of people, and individually the odds are ten to one that after a single voyage you'll develop some strong close friendships. At a cocktail party the other day a prominent advertising man introduced an up-standing young Merchant Marine officer as "one of our best friends." His wife started talking about the sailor's new wife. To overhear the conversation you would be sure they had at least gone to college together. Close investigation brought out the fact that the advertising man and his wife met the salt a year before on a six-week cruise, and since had seen him once every two months, when the ship got into port.

You never need be afraid to introduce the officers to your acquaintances. The Captains may not be sprightly young blades, and occasionally the Chief Engineer will have a burr in his speech, but they're real men, men who have climbed to the top through their own efforts, men who face difficulties and conquer them, men who know themselves as well as they know the people of the world.

On one boat in three you'll meet a yarn-spinner, a salty old seagoing chap of the fiction type, but these fellows are rapidly passing out of the picture. The average ship Captain today is first a businessman, second a sailor. To call them "diamonds in the rough" is unfair. Some of the most polished diplomats in the world sail the seven seas for lines like Kokusai, Maersk, and N.Y.K.

They aren't all salty, and they aren't all bowing and scraping polite young naval reserve officers. You can't classify the commanders you meet on boats, any more than you classify the men you meet at the heads of other business enterprises. That's one of the interesting things about tramp tripping. Each set of officers is as different as the line for whom they work, each ship is as different as the men who operate her. There are still a lot of old-fashioned "characters" among the seafaring men of the maritime nations, but more and more a new race is coming to the fore. Once practically every ship had a buckaroo Mate and a tale-spinning Captain; today you will have to travel on two or three freighters before you find one of the old-fashioned characters out of Dana's *Two Years Before the Mast.*

There's a chance you may meet the Captain who keeps the olives in a special locked case. Ah, there *is* a man! He doles out his olives at the beginning of every meal, one to a passenger, skipping over the wife of one of the paying guests because when the first can was opened she inadvertently said she didn't like them very much.

Or again your voyage may be aboard the Norwegian boat where the skipper banished his officers from the dining table as not being of sufficiently high caliber to eat with the passengers. This Captain sat in shirt-sleeved splendor with his three guests, explaining that the other men were fine fellows, but he didn't think they had "quite the table manners" for passenger service. With all his dignity this old chap took extreme pains to see to his customers' comfort, even going so far as to personally draw the water for their daily baths.

You may see much, or little, of your ship's ruler. Your voyage may be aboard a vessel where the Captain stays very much to himself, retiring because of lack of your language or for other reasons; or he may be a talkative old gent ready to escort you on a tour of the ship, or drive you to your cabin to escape his stories of the proper ways to raise sweet corn. Your officers may be rough and ready chaps, or polished reserve officers scraping and bowing at every opportunity, constantly the soul of politeness, speaking a dozen languages and entertaining in them all. You may find one kind or another, but no matter, of one thing be sure, you'll like them. And they'll like you, unless you go out of your way to be objectionable.

9 · The Chief Steward

A LETTER that tells what one passenger thinks about the crew: —

DEAR LARRY: —

August

I'll never thank you enough for helping me to get aboard this ship. The trip has been complete — and mainly because of one individual, the Chief Steward. Not only the head of a very efficient department, meals served on schedule and all that; but he's the kind of a chap you are mighty glad to know . . . D.S.O., M.C., smart enough to learn to be left-handed after being wounded in the war, and as clever a conversationalist as you'll meet in a lifetime of freighter smoking-room debates.

He has only been with Silver a few months — used to be on the run between Vancouver and Hong Kong. If he's a fair sample of the Blue Funnel staff, they get my next booking.

An Englishman. Until you get used to the burr in his talk it's a little slow, but he picks up dialect rapidly and before we were at sea two weeks he was catching all my Cleveland slang and occasionally going me one better. A marvelous dancer (if the girls are to be believed), he's also a man's man, and he runs his department with the firm iron hand that rarely shows through the gloved fist; but boy it's there, and how! I'd hate to be Joseph, the second steward, on a day when the soup isn't hot. Of course, I honestly can't say what would happen if things went wrong, because in sixty-three days of travel not one meal was late, nor was there a time when I could truly say that the service fell down anywhere.

I love to argue, you know, and this chap certainly helped me practise. Debating with him I got interested in the officers and crew as a class. Likely, you'd rather hear about them than for me to tell you of the weighty matters we settled under the southern skies.

On a Silver world cruise freighter you have six other officers with whom you are thrown in close association: the Skipper; the Chief Officer; the Second and Third Mates; the Chief Engineer; and Sparks, the wireless man. The cadets (three of them here) and the engineers eat in another mess. The crew is fed some place (I don't know where), and in their hours of recreation wrap themselves in sarongs and sit on their haunches and contemplate.

The cadets, I might say in passing, serve five years on these ships as juniors; at intervals they are examined by the Skipper and the Second Mate. Cadets are not guaranteed jobs, as I understand it, but certainly, if I ran a line, I'd be mighty glad to have one of these bright boys as my Third Officer as soon as he passed his Board of Trade examinations.

Our steward's gang consisted of Joseph, the "second," who seemed to be always Johnny on the spot when anything was wanted. Joseph, like the rest of the steward's crew, comes from Portuguese East India, has a Portuguese last name and speaks rather good English — although with something of an accent. Henry was the passengers' steward, and Joachim did the honors for the officers with an assistant called Zed who was another of those ever-present people when you wanted him, yet never underfoot, if you know what I mean.

There was a chief cook, Fernandez; a second cook; and a pantry boy. The final member of the steward's crew was the bath boy — he cleaned the baths and toilets, Albir bin Jasmuth is the way his name went down on the books. The *bin*, I understand, indicates that he is the son of Jasmuth

MONTH 1/4/38	SOUNDINGS			DAY FRIDAY		
BILGE				**BALLAST**		
	PORT	STARR	CARGO HOLD		PORT	STARR
Nº 1	5"	7"		FORE PEAK		LATEX
Nº 2	4	7		Nº 1		7
Nº 3	0	0		Nº 2	2·6	0
F.O TANK	0	OIL		Nº 3	2·3	4
C.O. TANK	OIL	OIL		FORE COFFERDAM	5"	1"
Nº 5	2 0 0			Nº 4	0	4
Nº 6	0			CENTRE COFFERDAM		
F.W. TANK	3·11 4·5			Nº 5	6 0	0
TUNNEL WELL	1·2			Nº 6	7 0	0
FEED WATER	4·8 4			Nº 7	0	0
BILT HEE	2			AFT PEAK	7	
A.D T ml	1 0			COFFERDAM AFT	2	2

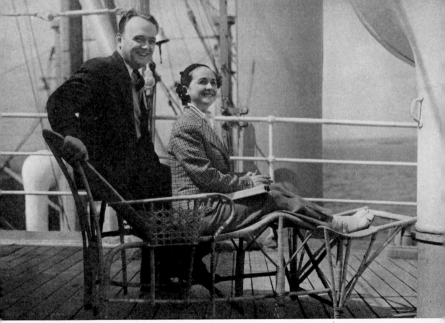

BETWEEN THE CAPTAIN AND FELLOW PASSENGERS YOU CAN FIND OUT ANYTHING

— all the Malay crew but one poor chap had a *bin* in their names. Anyway, Albir, or Albert for short, was a low-caste, as you might judge from his occupation. None of the rest of the crew would speak to him, although I don't quite know how they gave him orders. He not only was shunned on the ship, but ate entirely to himself. I forgot to ask if he had to cook his own food, but it wouldn't have surprised me, the caste system is strong.

The crew names fascinated me. Amat bin Kadir; Yaleb bin Mat; Mohomed Sala bin Patroson — he was a quarter-master; Ismael bin Rafani; Dawee bin Ablula; Sidoori bin Gardangboy, can't you see how the poor chap without any *bin* must have felt? I didn't get any of the crew identified to me particularly, except for the quartermaster — he always had a shy smile for stray passengers when he saw them — so I can't guarantee that there was any discrimination on the name proposition, at that. Perhaps Malay sailors are broad-minded.

These sailors go around the world, and at half the stops they can't go ashore; immigration laws prevent. Some sea law prohibits them being carried above a certain degree latitude, so now and then they are parked in an isolation camp in East Boston or New York while a special crew carries the boat to some northward port to load or unload.

Some of our officers have their wives living in the States and the Line is nice about letting the wives book on as stewardesses for the time the ship is running around American ports loading and unloading. Occasionally, a wife will make the circuit, but as a rule families get to see their men one trip in six; four months at home every two years.

All the officers have pictures of their wives and homes in their cabins. They'll show the photos at the first possible moment and thereafter at the slightest provocation; but what the heck, I carried snaps of Junior along with me, and our lady passenger had a dozen pictures of her dog air-mailed to us in Naples.

The passengers you get on these world-cruise boats are not a bad class of people. About half of them are women, but not always the aged kind — far, far, from it. Recently the entire service was thrown into a turmoil while a party of six college girls tried to make up their minds between four vessels. I don't know which they selected, but if they got the one I'm just leaving, I'll wager they learned something about the law of supply and demand and the gold theory. This Chief Steward of ours makes even that subject sound interesting.

Sincerely,
TONY

10 · Occupations at Sea

WHAT do you do? That question often comes to light in discussing cargo-boat voyaging.

The answer is simple: You do as you please. The freighters are sailing, the cabins are there, the food is ready, the price is low, but whether or not the journey is enjoyable depends entirely on the passenger. The voyage is absolutely what you make it.

You can be friendly with the officers, or stand-offish. Let them alone and they'll let you alone. Be polite to them and they'll stand on their heads to make your vacation enjoyable. If you want to retire to the fastness of your cabin to sit and think, or just to sit, there's no dissenting voice raised; no dapper young man in white pants with a carnation in his blue coat will grab your arm and plead with you to act as jockey in the horse races, no bustling purser will annoy you with requests to join in a fancy-dress ball.

There won't be a round-up of passengers to gather in the Grand Salon for a lecture on Tahiti, and no motion picture shows will darken up one of the public rooms on an evening when you feel like reading. Organized entertainment is for entertainment ships. Freighter folk haven't time to plan pleasure — they just have it.

Passengers are a welcome break in the monotony of the daily routine of a ship's operation, and there'll be cocktail parties in various staterooms every day. You'll be host for tea-time gatherings yourself, if you like that kind of thing, but there's no cruise director shouting up and down corridors, begging your attendance at fashion shows, beauty contests or other such daily doings.

If you like to wander, you have the run of the ship, provided you demonstrate you have brains enough not to sit in the paint bucket; but if you choose to rusticate in the quiet and seclusion of your cabin you'll find it big enough, comfortable enough and quiet enough to really rest there, away from all bothers and annoyances of things to do. If you are interested in machinery the chief engineer will take great pleasure in showing the motors that drive you ahead at liner speed, and if you happen to be aboard a world-cruising British boat, you can sit in the navigation school with the cadets studying to be officers in England's Merchant Marine.

If you are an amateur wireless operator with a license and everything, you can soon put up a short-wave receiving set and copy radio press news in half a dozen languages at varying hours of the day. The bridge is for the navigating officers, but unless you make a pest of yourself you'll be as welcome there as anywhere else on the boat. You are part of the outfit. You belong!

Most passengers really participate in the movements of their ship. When the lines are cast off as the S.S. *Falcon* prepares to leave the dock at Curaçao, practically all the *Falcon's* dozen customers will be on deck to see things done right. The picking up of the pilot at the harbor entrance at San Juan; the transhipping of mail for the residents of some remote island; the shooting of the sun to locate the vessel's noonday position — all the

"You Cover So Much with a Big Brush"

daily routine of the ship's operation is part of your routine too.

You'll find things to do all the time. Many passengers soon attach themselves to one officer or another, grow to be close friends, and when his watch on deck comes around manage to stand the watch too. Of course you may not actively participate in the work to be done (not the first week), but you have an interest in it all and an eye to efficiency. Sailors teach you accuracy as well as neatness. A few weeks and you are an old salt, too.

Would you have been one of Tom Sawyer's customers on the fence job? If so you can appreciate the thrill of helping paint the ship. Not every vessel will permit you to don overalls and climb masts, but once you have proven your ability there's little complaint if you undertake some of the harder manual labor aboard ship — and there's nothing like it to loosen up muscles (and strengthen them too) while relaxing taut nerves.

There's a girl who does fashion drawings for a New York advertising agency. All day she labors at a drawing board making short, fine strokes with a fine pen. Her broadest line will never be more than an ordinary pencil mark. There isn't even a brush on her desk. She might almost be said to be working in miniature. Once a year she leaves her drawing board under the skylight, turns off the harsh electric lights, and hies herself to Montreal. There, aboard a freighter where she is more than well known, she embarks on a round-trip voyage to England. As soon as the last farewells are said and the boat casts off for the journey through the beautiful Saint Lawrence, she climbs into dungarees, grabs a bucket and a four-inch brush, and starts to give the ship a dose of painting as painting should be done. With great broad strokes she goes over superstructure, over the decks, over the outside of the cabins. "You cover so much surface with a big brush," she'll exclaim in reporting progress to the Chief Officer. "You get something done this way," she'll tell any passenger who happens to grow inquisitive about her feverish activity.

Are you so busy you find it impossible to read all the books you've bought during the winter? Take a bundle of them aboard ship and follow the shade around the deck with your chair. If you expect to read be sure to take your own books to supplement the ship's library. Seamen's organizations make a brave effort to supply the crews of merchant marine vessels with reading matter, but while some intelligent person eliminates the Elsie Dinsmore volumes before the boxes of books go to sea, what are left are not always the latest best sellers, and sometimes not in the best of condition. Don't carry valuable first editions or autographed copies. The odds are you'll want to give the books to some officer friend when you finish your trip.

There's always plenty to do besides sunning in a deck chair or watching the waves over the rail. Once the cargo is stowed and you're out to sea, most captains erect a canvas swimming pool over one of the hatch covers. A New York publishing executive and his wife spent their afternoons playing games in the swimming tank with the young officers from the engine room on their first voyage, and introduced all the tank games to the cadets on a second trip aboard another ship. He's thinking of writing a book on "Fun in a Ten-Foot Tank."

Your sun bath is just as effective from the top deck of the *Sorvangen* en route from New Orleans as it is on the Lido deck of the mightiest of Italian liners.

Foreign freighters are truly foreign vessels. It's easy to learn a new language when it's the common medium of speech of those around you for thirty or forty days. If you don't want to study a language, how about the amusements of some other race? The Japanese have several interesting games that make us wonder why Mah-jongg is the only widely recognized game to come out of the Far East.

Contract bridge has its devotees among ship's officers; you can usually get a fourth without much difficulty. Scotch engineers are said to be the best checker players, the Germans shine at chess, the English at cribbage, and the occasional Texan you meet will gladly give you a daily bout at dominoes.

There's lots to do on a freighter. The wife of a foreign correspondent bound for the East (San Pedro to Yokohama) taught the young officers on the *Asosan Maru* all the American dances. Imagine dancing your way across the Pacific! Perhaps lots of girls think that's a swell way to take a boat to China, even a fast one that does sixteen to eighteen knots an hour. Anyway, Japan now boasts of at least five smiling young ship officers who "truck" in style, and the newspaperman's wife is home again, teaching Japanese dances to all the neighbors in Flushing.

A famous writer studied navigation in the daily sessions of the apprentices' school on a Booth boat to Lisbon, and it's not safe to take him out into Long Island Sound. He immediately starts to show you how to steer by the stars and things; he insists on taking a bearing by the North Star, completely ignoring the light of the Sands Point Yacht Club landing which might be considerably closer at the time.

You won't have a bagpiper to lead the passengers on a parade around the decks for the morning's mile, — as on one of the lake steamers, — but you'll find a brisk walk around the decks of the *Manchester Citizen* bound for Europe as invigorating as a hike on the promenade deck of the *Roma*. It may take more circuits, but you get there just the same.

There's no golf teacher, or athletic instructor, as you'll find on the *Columbus* on a long cruise. There's not even a gym with bicycles and such, like the one on the *Western Prince,* but sailors manage to keep fit; if you are worried, take your own rowing machine and more than likely one of the officers will get so interested you'll at last find someone to take it off your hands.

A young doctor convalescing from a serious illness took a stock of medical books along to study. He found himself tempted to spend more time in the galley than with his books, and he returned from a cruise to South America an accomplished cook — and none the worse a physician either, for that matter. Now he prescribes diets to fat women in an Eastern city and every summer sneaks away for five or six weeks of Vagabond Vacationing where they'll let him experiment in the chef's quarters.

An amateur magician developed a complete routine so that he undertook professional engagements after his return from a voyage from Galveston to Hong Kong; and there's the story about the farmer who learned so much about raising lettuce while journeying to Chile

A Salt Will Criticize Your Putting

that today he's a big shipper of the finest, where once he was content to string along with his neighbors in producing average heads.

The Southern Cross is romantic from the top deck of any vessel — which recalls the story of the two Brooklyn girls who made a coast trip on the *Horace Luckenbach*. You can see their pictures in the staterooms of the Second Officer and the radio man today if you go aboard: "My wife," each officer will say, pointing with pride to the girl *he* met on a freighter.

Some lines, especially one out of New Orleans, like to book groups that take all the available space. Take your own gang along if you like, own the vessel and be sure of your company.

One foursome in a Midwestern city saved the winnings of their weekly bridge game for a number of years. Eventually, the fund was enough to buy four tickets for a long, long tour, and away they went. Aboard ship they kept up the policy of having the bridge losers put the money into the pool, the winners not collecting. Because there was lots of time for bridge crossing the ocean, the two teams got home with a swell start towards another vacation.

A group of eight literary people, not content with the daily wireless news bulletin, edited and published by typewriter a weekly magazine for themselves and the officers and crew of the *Eastern Prince*. An art student on another boat left behind some copies of the daily wireless report which he illustrated; today they're treasured keepsakes of the Chief Officer of the vessel, to be shown at the slightest provocation. That the artist is internationally famous now detracts not a whit from the officer's pride of possession.

You won't find movies, although the chances are you may run into an officer with a home motion picture camera who'll shoot several reels of film to give you an interesting souvenir of the voyage. He'll also have a dozen reels or so of former passengers and former voyages, but he's more likely to show these in port when folks come visiting. If you beg though, he'll run them off on a dull evening.

The piano, if any, may not be perfectly in tune and the phonograph may belong to an officer and therefore be likely to leave the ship with any transfer, or it may be part of the equipment placed aboard the line. Ask when you book if you're interested. Where there is a phonograph you'll always find discs; quite a varied assortment, from swing music to symphony; sailors rarely break records or throw them away.

The radio receiver on the newer boats occasionally is connected to loud speakers on one of the decks, but a little judicial discussion with the Captain should fix it so that those who object to listening to the nostrum peddlers of Mexico's stations can have the speakers get out of order at least until Major Bowes is available again. Many ship officers have private radio sets, and talking machines too, in their cabins, and many a pleasant afternoon has been spent with an officer off watch, as he plays his own collection of native music — records purchased in the shops of the four corners of the world. You can set up a radio in your quarters if you think your taste in entertainment is likely to be at variance with the rest of the company. Your portable phonograph will be helpful if you throw afternoon parties of your own.

Take along some magazines, a game or two, your knitting or sewing, be prepared to entertain yourself a little, but don't worry about ennui; you never need be bored unless you choose to live entirely apart and are tired of your own company.

There's lots to see. You'll find no barriers to keep you in your own part of the ship as on a passenger liner. The officers are always eager to show off their own domains, and most travelers are taken on tours to explore the ship from stem to stern before the second day at sea.

The Captain of the Blue Funnel *Clement* felt that his officers should have some kind of refuge from the dozen passengers aboard this 420-foot liner, so he reserved the deck on which the officers' cabins were located as being forbidden to passengers, figuring the five other decks were enough for their recreation.

After one trip the *Clement* officers took the matter up with the skipper most formally, explaining first that practically every passenger had been entertained by one officer or another, time and time again during the cruise, and then pointing out that this section had more teakwood flooring than any other on the boat, and therefore was the most attractive. "We want our guests to have the best on the ship," was the way the officers presented their petition. Today there's no reserved deck on the *Clement* and likely never will be again.

There's a commander running between New Orleans and Rotterdam who is a real concert pianist. He performs every day at dusk. Another officer on the same line is an expert wood carver (not just a whittler). He gives lessons in this art in his spare time.

Of course, if the passenger is disagreeable, courtesies

will not be forthcoming. If the traveler does not fit into the life aboard ship, he will be as uncomfortable as a West Pointer in Coventry. Officers can get very busy at their daily work, and somehow rules and regulations restricting passengers to certain parts of the ship pop out of nowhere to appear in printed form. But unless you've been put out of good hotels and find yourself frequently blackballed by social clubs, have no fear of your reception by the men of our Merchant Marine.

Go down to the docks with a smile on your face, and you'll find yourself welcomed, entertained, and rapidly taken into the heart of the family who live on the ship you have selected for your home for a Vagabond Vacation.

Going Ashore Is Different

As important as the entertainment at sea, is the question of seeing ports as seaports should be seen.

Instead of in the company of a tired young man from a travel agency with fussy old ladies hanging on his arm screaming stories about how different this scenery is from the time they were here on their honeymoons, you come ashore at deserted docks.

When your vessel does not dock you often are lightered to shore in small boats. Steamship lines sometimes provide tender service, not always as thrilling as the surf boats used by Booth at Cera on the Amazon, but even a flat-bottomed skiff pulled by a single sailor gets you there sooner or later, and what freighter passenger is in a hurry?

There's no badge on your coat, "from world-cruise liner So-and-so," no sign indicating to the shopkeepers that you are fair game ready to pay any price they may be able to ask. There's no flood of cruise trippers to send prices sky-rocketing, you come to town sans ceremony, and see the city in the same fashion.

You'll find that as you near a stop plans are made for shore-going. There will be a golf game to arrange, if the time permits. Certainly there will be things to do.

Ashore, on some freighter trips, you find yourself surrounded by guides just as if you had landed from the *Volendam*. But you get no more attention than the Second Mate would get on a short visit. If they're organized to take the visitor to camp, you'll be faced with screaming interpreters and pulling porters until you shake them off by calling the nearest gendarme, but of one thing be sure: you're more likely to get fair prices and certainly more likely to see the towns with a clear eye when you arrive via freighter than when you come to a city that is all keyed up to collect the month's rent from three hundred world trippers.

On voyages to the more frequented ports where passengers are brought every few weeks, arrangements have been set up to take care of sight-seeing. On the visits to little frequented harbors the agent ashore, as a rule, will take the time out to start the visitor off in proper fashion.

The Second Officer is a lot better guide to the dives of Port Said than any local boy, although you'll likely have not only the Second Officer but the local guide and a chap from the shipping agency as well to tow you around on the excursion planned during the ten-day ride from Colombo.

Unless you want to make your own plans that way, there's no set itinerary laid out for the purpose of giving the greatest amount of education in the least possible time; no schedule designed to impress school-teachers who have a sabbatical year to spend on travel. The freighter voyager makes a lazy visit; a casual visit, accompanied by friends from his floating home, or by newly made acquaintances among the local residents, local people who are part of the organization that sends the ship on its journeyings in search of cargo.

Take Your Camera

By all means take your camera. There may be ports where you have to leave it aboard, sealed by the customs inspector, but there will be enough other places where you can snap to your heart's content. Pictures on a cruise are always worth the trouble it takes to make them.

For a short trip, of course, the matter of special packing need not bother you, but if you are going on any sizable journey go into conference with the film folks before you stock up great quantities. This goes for expensive movie reels as well as for rolls for the fixed-focus three-dollar Brownie.

You can get all your raw stock in special tropical packings, designed to get through heat, to stand up against humidity, if you like, but the smart thing to do is to figure out how much it will cost to buy ashore in preference to taking it with you. In some cases it's cheaper to buy abroad.

Be sure the film you use is fairly common. You may

be able to buy odd-sized rolls in Benares (but will it be fresh?). Don't use freak-sized films.

Practically anywhere you choose to tour throughout the world, you find the amateur finisher waiting for you, returning with your prints just as efficiently as the drugstore on the corner delivers the snaps you took on Aunt Mary's roof last week.

Photography at sea is an interesting occupation. Light conditions are different from anything to which you are accustomed; use a light-meter or get plenty of good advice before you shove off; but don't let difficulties prevent you from having a pictorial record of your vagabonding.

Not many freighters can boast of a studio aboard. On a German boat perhaps you'll find someone who makes photography his hobby. He will not only develop and print your films, but help you with your exposures — but that's a rare case rather than something to expect. If you know the ropes and want to do your own work, the officers will be glad to help you arrange for dark rooms, water and such, but unless you have done that work at home, don't saddle yourself with a lot of expensive equipment. It's not easy to learn how to develop and print pictures while at sea. There's much too much to do aboard to waste your time in stuffy dark rooms anyway.

Don't buy an expensive outfit for a long cruise, expecting to learn how to operate it on the voyage. Take a camera you own now, the one you already know. It's not easy to get your shutter adjusted when you're half-way across the Atlantic.

11 · Clothes

THE answer to the question of clothes for tramp tripping is exactly like the answer for every other question about this form of voyaging. Just as you do exactly as you please in the matter of entertainment, so you wear what you please.

On a freighter you wear what you would at home, if you were not going to the office every day. You have liberty aboard ship to go as you please, do as you please, and dress as you please. This is the closest one can come to setting up an absolute rule for all classes; there are a few exceptions, but so rare they hardly count. Freighters mean freedom. Dressing for dinner has its points, but sailor laundrymen do a poor job on stiff shirts. Take your trip on the *Lafayette* or the *Columbus,* or leave your tail-coat at home.

If your idea of a vacation is to engage in a competition with the gal on B deck to see who can wear the most evening gowns between ports, stay off the cargo runs. Slacks are your costume morning, noon and night, unless you prefer shorts.

Don't take the night part too seriously, now; remember each boat is a different world of its own and each Captain a dictator with a dictator's right to rule. There's a ship — New York to Barcelona — where the Skipper insists you not only wash your face before dinner, but abandon sweat shirts and sweaters, and that the ladies wear real dresses — "with skirts" is the way he puts it. But then he's a good chap, even if a bit of a fuss-budget. Every time you pass another vessel he considers it the occasion for a ceremony, and his idea of a ceremony is the opening of an extra bottle of wine at dinner. Ships that pass in the night don't count, unless you've had trouble spotting one during the day.

Take your old clothes. There's one confirmed freighter traveler in New York who saves all old suits, old shirts, and old socks to wear on a cruise. He throws them away as the trip progresses, landing back in New York with the clothes on his back, and nothing else.

For a while this chap threw his dirty socks out the porthole, until he heard a hullabaloo alongside in a certain West African port. There below were a flock of natives fighting over a discarded pair of sock supporters he had just pitched out. Exactly what they were going to do with these over-strained elastics was never made clear to the passenger, but now he turns his old duds over to the steward when they're too dirty to wear any more, and the steward washes them up and trades 'em with bumboat men in the smaller harbors. Old silk hats have a high trading value in Malaysia, so some travelers say, and thousands of second-hand American clothes are exported to Africa every season.

But getting back to the clothes question: Set out to be comfortable. Take along enough evening clothes to make a society appearance once on the voyage if you are going any real distance, but if you find it convenient to leave the tux at home, don't worry. People who entertain freighter passengers in Brisbane, Australia, don't expect them to appear in the height of fashion as a rule.

Carry enough clothes to change as the climate demands. If you are going into a hot country be sure to have enough suits so the sailor you hire to launder your whites won't have to work overtime catching up with you. If you are going where the weather may be cold take along an overcoat. A light coat is always worth carrying on any cruise, even those to tropical waters. As in California, on freighters "the nights are cool" and the wind whips when you stand on the bridge with nothing but ocean between you and the land a thousand miles away. A real breeze can be built up, especially when you add the speed of your ship to the force of the blow.

Warm sweaters are useful on almost any tour, but most of all be sure to take your bathing suit, if for no other reason than to stand on deck while some sailor plays the salt water hose on you. Plenty of clothes that won't be hurt by getting slept in are also useful; there's many a pleasant afternoon lounging in a deck chair and starchy things somehow haven't that Fifth Avenue look after the laundry at Guadeloupe gets through with them.

Officers have their uniforms cleaned while in port and at almost every harbor you'll find the representative of a tailor or cleaner down at the dock, ready to take the cleaning business of the officers and petty officers. A few shirts belonging to a passenger can be laundered at the same time, and if you need a crease in your white pants, and are not satisfied with the way the steward on ship does the job, turn them over on your next port visit; unless it's a mighty small place you'll have your razor edge ready to step out when you're ready.

There's no royal rule for clothes for freighter travel, just as there is no rule for clothes for any other form of world-wide vacationing. Talk to the man you buy your ticket from, or better still, do a little checking up when you make your inspection visit before you book.

One thing that Dad will enjoy about vagabond vacationing is that it shouldn't be necessary to buy any *new* clothes. "Just bring along what you have, it will be okay," the First Officer advises you.

A FEW years ago the only method of booking aboard a freighter was to handle the deal yourself. Today things are different. Practically every travel agent in the United States knows about tramp tripping now. Several of them specialize: handle only freighter trips.

American Express, Thomas Cook and some of the other larger agencies are exclusive representatives of several cargo lines. They have departments where rather complete data files are maintained. Tramp Trips and Viking Voyages in New York, and Freight Boat Travel Bureau in Los Angeles, handle practically nothing but cargo cruises. General Steamship Company at its several West Coast offices operates a most efficient passenger department handling freighter tickets.

First and simplest, see your travel agent. Second, look for your own freighter and make your deal direct. The travel agent can find more boats, he will get your tickets at no extra cost to you, but the occasional vessel carrying two or three passengers is oftentimes found only by personal search.

If your trip is to be a short one, or if you plan going on one of the more standard cruises, write a travel agent, or write the home office of the line. You'll get folders, literature and deck plans, names of previous passengers and an invitation to inspect the boat.

If you have only the desire to travel, by all means start your correspondence with an agent. Tell the agent *how much money* you want to spend, about *where* you want to go, and about *when* you want to travel. And don't be afraid to make your reservations far in advance. There was one sailing this July — one ship with passenger capacity of 124 paying guests — where nearly 600 names had been placed on the waiting list three months before sailing date.

If you know exactly where you would like to go, and know the fare is within your budget, then you can start to plan your own trip and make your own booking.

Be sure to plan far enough in advance. Remember fares are going to be higher in the months when most people want to travel. Remember travel agents who give business to the freighter lines week in and week out, year in and year out, are a lot closer to the lines than any casual possible customer. If you are in a hurry to travel don't attempt to make your own booking unless you want to go down to the docks and do the deal all by yourself.

Figure out your budget. Allow ten per cent. for tips, and if you're going on a long voyage figure that part of your tip money which will be spent in presents for the officers. You'll discover you'd no more hand them money than you'd give five dollars to your best friend's wife after a week-end visit.

Figure out your budget for shore days. You'll find mighty few freight boats that print a list of shore excursions with prices for each tour. Estimate you'll spend in each day's sight-seeing about what you'd spend in a day's outing either at home or in the near-by big city where you go to see plays and to hear big orchestras.

If a day in New York costs you ten dollars, you'll

likely spend about that much ashore in Singapore.

Then, when your budget is right, start to plan your time.

If your vacation period this year is limited to two weeks, be prepared to compromise on Bermuda, Nassau, or a cargo-boat cruise to Alaska or Newfoundland. Don't expect the shipping companies to start running two-week cruises of ten-thousand-ton ships just to take care of a few thousand passengers willing to pay sixty dollars for ten days at sea.

If you have a long enough vacation period to take a real freighter trip, and if you plan your time far enough in advance — so there's still a chance to book on the cruise you'd like to take — the world is at your doorstep.

Not every freight boat is operated by lines listed in this volume. Not every freight boat operating on regular routes carries passengers, and not every operator of freight boats carrying passengers will answer mail inquiries.

There's one firm in the Midwest that has twice publicly denied all interest in passenger bookings — the volume of mail costs more to handle than the total passenger revenue could run to. One of our larger lines carries passengers on its freight boats — if, when, and as the boats sail; but you'll never get them to say that in writing. If you don't book through one of the regular freighter agents, you'll have to come into their offices to get any information.

The companies who refuse to admit they accept passengers represent only a small percentage of the freighter cabins afloat, but it's a growing percentage at that, and it's caused solely by the refusal of prospective

travelers to consider their own abilities before they start
negotiations for space.

When you have your budget right, both in time and
money, it's rather easy to select the route. Having
selected the route, you can pretty well figure that the
faster boats on this route will sell out before the slower
ones, unless there's a tremendous difference in fares —
another reason for early planning.

With these facts in mind, you can start your contact
with the shipping agencies, either direct, or through
your travel agent.

Once you've contacted the Line, you begin to get
close to booking your trip. When the agent answers your
inquiry and gets you an invitation to inspect a boat,
you're well on your way; from there on, build your own
tour.

Go down to the docks and visit. Look the ship over,
be sure you know what you're buying; it's too late to
change your mind when you're halfway across the
Pacific. Get to know your officers, give the steward a
chance to serve tea or its equivalent in the language
of the vessel. Sailors lead a busy life at sea and usually
enjoy their port contacts. Let them sell you the vessel.

The ships that are most fun for the hardy voyager
are those where no plans are made for passengers, where
the Captain takes an occasional guest for company rather
than for revenue; but don't start your tripping on these
boats, build up to it gradually, it's much more fun.

An advantage of working through a local travel agent
is that often you'll find it possible to book on a line
classed as a passenger service at prices within the range
you want to pay — around the world on the President

boats of the Dollar Line, for example. There's a cruise that's only a little more expensive than freighter class; sailings every two weeks with the regularity of subway trains, yet with a large enough passenger list to give you the special advantages of ocean-liner travel while retaining the lure of Vagabond Voyaging. N.Y.K., the famous Japanese line, has a round-the-world service in conjunction with Cunard that is astonishingly reasonable when you get all the facts. The agent will find many other opportunities of combining freighter and conference-line travel to get your vacation tour into the time you have to spare.

Inspect your ship, meet the officers, sample the food and service. See the cabins for yourself, prove that you do have room to move around aboard a freighter. Meet a few former passengers, read up a bit on the countries you'll visit.

Your Inspection

When you go down to visit your freighter before you sail, see if you can't find someone who knows one of the officers on the boat you want to see; but even if you have to go knocking at gates and doors — look your boat over first.

The proper procedure is to get a letter from the agent. If possible have the letter call for your admission to the pier on a specific day. Then write the Captain a note — and be sure you allow plenty of time for its delivery. Tell him you and so-and-so many people are going to avail yourselves of the opportunity to inspect his ship at such an hour on such a day. Give him a chance to get his dress whites cleaned up.

A Sailor Welcomes You on Board

A telegram is smarter than a letter; it is more certain of being delivered on time.

Having paved the way for your visit, and warned the Captain that you're on the way, be prepared for almost anything.

Take your letter of introduction in your hand and start for the dock. You may not see them, but in the background are customs officials and guards. Somewhere else you'll find a steamship line pier guard. Begin to walk into the wharf shed and you'll meet one or the other of them.

Your letter will be collected, and unless you are young and female and pretty, you'll be directed with a casual wave of the hand towards the other end of the shed.

Pay no attention to your enthusiastic reception. It's typical of freighter life. If there are agents and guides and salesmen around they must be paid, and you, as the ultimate passenger, will find the cost on your ticket some place. Freighter folk don't try to be ritzy, any time. Occasionally they may think they're putting on a very wee small bit of dog, but you'll never recognize the signs of what they call "snootiness" until you're an experienced Vagabond Voyager.

Wander down the pier until you find a landing ladder up the side of your ship. Some sailor will appear at the top of the stair. If it's a Jap boat, or one with a Malay crew aboard, the sailor will look at you so blankly that you'll begin to wonder if perhaps you haven't gotten to the wrong place.

Continue to pay no attention, with great gusto! Proceed up the ladder just as if you owned the place. This is a little difficult if you are unaccustomed to swaying gangplanks and rope railings, but go ahead, be nonchalant to the best of your ability.

Inquire the way to the Captain's quarters. Once there you'll start the inspection of the ship.

If you happen aboard ahead of time you'll likely find the Skipper in his shirt sleeves. Freighters are shirt-sleeve vessels. He may be short and fat and taking his ease in a big chair in his well-fitted-out suite of rooms, or he may be lean and lanky and busily engaged in checking papers with a representative of his agents. But when the Captain learns his visitors are aboard, he becomes a spruce, businesslike, genial host, and the ship is yours.

In port a freighter may seem small. Piers are huge affairs. Perhaps you've seen the *Europa* or the *Rex* lately? A 400-foot freighter like the *Venice Maru* looks dwarfed beside a 900-foot pier, but once you start walking around on her, you see the difference between the cargo vessel and a Staten Island ferry.

Swallow your feelings about size, don't let first impressions mislead. Stroll around and see just how many places there are for deck chairs. . . . Then remember that six or eight or perhaps ten will have all this space between them.

The Captain will show you the passengers' bath. Perhaps it will be a modern one, with hot and cold fresh water and hot and cold salt showers, or perhaps it will be a not so modern one with a huge iron pipe connected with an electric socket as a heater of bath water. Water gets just as hot when you heat it with one of these peculiar contraptions as it does when warmed in the most modern of hot-water tanks.

Look at the staterooms carefully. Some freighter beds are terribly hard. Ask about extra mattresses. Perhaps you'll come aboard when the ship is being overhauled with all the cabins stripped, the berths and beds out on deck and the mattresses piled up in the salon. If the cabin isn't in livable shape, ask questions and satisfy yourself before you decide to book. Look for space to hang your clothes. Some of our most modern freighters, equipped with short-wave wireless capable of communication across half the earth, with the most up-to-date automatic steering devices and mufflers on the motors, sometimes go to sea without any more space to hang a suit of clothes than you find in an upper berth on a pullman car.

Don't pay too much attention to cluttered decks. The big holds go far into the ships and cranes are required to hoist cargo from dock to deck. Cranes swinging all over the space between the bridge house and the forecastle are made shipshape, out of the way, when at sea; and swimming pools and golf games appear on the broad hatch-covers.

Don't pay too much attention to red sides, to chipped paint, to scarred walls. Freighters are constantly being repainted and the red sides are not rust, but special rust-proof paint put on before the final coat is added.

Freighters at sea have windswept decks; all gear is made fast. In port, lines coil around strange places, decks and woodwork are painted, and there's no strong ocean breeze fanned up by the motion of the ship to blow away the paint smell; no swift current of air to clear every speck of dirt and debris out from under foot.

Freighters in harbor are hot. Your sea-going home was not intended to rest alongside a giant warehouse, a floating log between the ship side and the pier. Cooling systems are found on the newest of ocean liners for use in port. But unless cargo requires chilling, your freighter will boast of no such apparatus. (And if there is refrigeration, it's not for the likes of you. "That's for meat," the C.O. will say.) Once at sea, you find blankets more than necessary at night; in port far from the sea breeze, it's a different story.

Don't be surprised to see the officers in their shirt sleeves. Don't be astonished if the steward comes along in his undershirt. After all, the freighter is his home. There's mighty little formality in port at best, and while the man who serves you coffee and cakes in the smoking room will wear a jacket, he'll likely be quick to peel it off once he's retired around the corner of the corridor.

Check up on your food before you book, but don't judge the meals by the fare furnished in port. Get-away day is a busy time in any enterprise that moves from point to point; a steward who has been busy checking last-minute stores isn't always able to take the time to make diced watermelon for a special luncheon the Captain may order on sailing day; especially if passengers arrive unexpectedly early.

Remember that as a shore visitor on a freighter you are in the same position as the chap who goes to see a family just about ready to move. You may delay your trip to Uncle John's at the beach until the last week-end of the season, but you make allowances for the fact that half the things are packed, ready for the shift back to town. Even when you give fair warning of the impending call, you are not surprised at a somewhat pick-up supper. Expect the same treatment on your freighter inspection. The Captain may have planned a most elaborate meal — and it will be served to perfection, even if the steward would have rather gone ashore to a movie. And again, the Captain may not have expected you at mealtime and the food set before you will be comparable to the Sunday-night suppers at home when the cook didn't stay to give you warm dishes, and Mother sort of poked around in the kitchen for a few minutes before piling things on the sideboard so everybody could help themselves.

Go down and inspect your freighter while she is in port; warn the skipper you're coming — then be ready to see a freighter at her very worst. If you have the true spirit of Vagabondia, if adventure calls you and you have the heart of an explorer, you'll see nothing but the sea-going home your freighter can be. But if you have just come from the Ritz, do not compare your half-caste steward with the waiters at "21" while visualizing the natty uniforms of the page boys on the Île de France — expect to find a freighter far short of the Edgewater Beach in Chicago in point of service or the Rice in Houston in excellence of fare.

A freighter is not a palace; it is not a giant hotel afloat; a freighter is a home, and in port is almost certain to be a bit upset, as all homes are at housecleaning time.

When you go ship-side visiting, you'll soon learn cargo carriers aren't particular where they tie up, or perhaps the way to say it is that they *are* particular. Passenger liners must dock at piers that can be easily reached by taxi-cabs and other forms of transportation. Freight vessels tie up where trucks, lighters and conveyor systems can economically bring cargo to fill the holds. If the cargo won't come to the carrier, you move over to the other side of the bay where things are ready to load.

Because of this factor and perhaps also because wharf space in the heart of a city rents at higher rates, passengers bound for a freighter voyage will find their ships at remote points rather than near-by downtown. In Manhattan, for example, you'll rarely find your vessel at the better-known Manhattan piers. Mitsui's *Azumasan Maru* will be at the Bush Terminal in Brooklyn, a short distance from the world-circling *Silvertean,* while the Booth boats are in Staten Island and the *Black Eagle* starts its trip to Europe from Weehawken. Several lines sail from Jersey, some even going as far as Port Newark to load.

Freighters stop at all the great harbors of the world — but usually in the lesser known corners of the waterfront, so even the experienced traveler coming to as well-known a haven as New York is likely to find himself seeing an entirely new vista as he looks at the skyline from the deck of the *Anita* in from South America.

New York, New Orleans, San Francisco and Los Angeles are the main points from which passengers embark on Vagabond Voyages. Boston, Baltimore, Halifax, Montreal, Savannah and other East Coast points are occasional ports of call, but most vessels also stop in New York as well. Twenty-odd routes are available from New Orleans as compared with one from Lake Charles, Louisiana. Some ports have only seasonal business, for example, Mobile Oceanic Line boats stop outbound at Tampa in the winter season, and at Panama City, Florida, on the return voyage from England.

In some places, such as Wilmington, Delaware, you'll find the lines rather inclined to discourage passengers embarking. The final load may not go into the hold until several other Eastern seaboard stops have been made, but if you argue and are inclined to put up with the discomforts of being around while cargo pours into the hatches night and day, almost any ship will take you at almost any port. Jacksonville shipping interests once got together and agreed not to take any freighter passengers from there, and perhaps one or two other Coast or Gulf towns are not ports of embarkation, but it's rather a safe bet that anywhere that there is cargo for a cargo boat you can also arrange for passage if there's a cabin still unsold.

Then check your health. Only a few freight boats carry physicians. You won't find a stewardess where there are only four passengers, so it's rather silly to expect the steamship company to have a doctor aboard for the convenience of half a dozen paying guests.

On the other hand, on the larger cargo boats you may find a medical man to care for the sailing. If your illness is contracted aboard ship there won't be any bill for services, but if you bring your sickness with you, the M.D. will charge according to the standard rates of the country from which your vessel hails. Many of the larger British freighters have doctors. If you are interested, check before you book.

Physicians will tell those who suffer from chronic diseases that voyaging of any kind is not advisable. No patient should wander too far from his own medico if he is likely to have a sudden seizure. Companies do not like to accept passengers who are likely to keel over with heart trouble in the heat of the tropical night, nor those who are prone to attacks from an appendix that should be left ashore before the trip is commenced.

On the other hand, if you are not subject to some disease that will strike you suddenly, there is little to fear in the way of health service when you go Vagabond Voyaging. The aged, those with chronic diseases, and those likely to have some recurrence of an old trouble should certainly stay off freighters, but the absence of a practicing M.D. need not worry normal folks. The Captain has his medicine chest from which he's been dosing sailors for years; he and the mate are both rough and ready surgeons of a sort.

The question of seasickness comes up in almost every conversation about freighter travel. The answer is usually the same. Practically every officer, freighter or passenger liner, can remember having been seasick, and they all report that after a few hours, or at best a day or two, the illness left and now it bothers them not a bit.

Ships loaded heavily with cargo are not as rough as those that ride higher in the water. People who get sick "the minute we leave the dock" on Atlantic liners go through a dozen freighter journeys without a trace of *mal-de-mer*.

At times, freighters are loaded light; particularly on

journeys seeking cargo from port to port in the United States before leaving for abroad; and if there's anything that bucks more than a light-loaded boat, it's got legs, and runs. But here a strange phenomenon is discovered. Instead of getting seasick and retiring to their cabins, passengers find it fun to get outdoors in the air, and rapidly learn to walk up and down pitching decks, developing a surprising dexterity at grabbing ropes stretched along to guide the passer-by from door to door.

Not every freighter travels light, not every freighter goes into territory where storms come up that call for "fiddles" (to hold dishes and tables) and ropes to hang onto, but some do, and when an empty freighter pitches — there's no kidding about it all, she pitches.

But don't worry about seasickness. The Captain knows what to do. The wife of a Philadelphia broadcast executive swears by the seasick remedies of Captain Nielson of the *Gertrude Maersk,* and a sailor on the same boat boasts of the Boy Scout knowledge displayed by the same radio man who devised a magnet from some iron and the ship's electric-light current. With this homemade device, a piece of steel filing was drawn from a sailor's eye when the ship was far, far out on the Pacific Ocean.

If some serious illness comes to you at sea and it is beyond the ability of the Captain to cope with the situation, a conference between the officers will quickly result. They've all studied the "family medical book" you'll find in the Captain's desk, and experience in meeting with the emergencies of the sea will possibly bring a solution for the problem. The conference failing to satisfy the passenger, there's always wireless. Physicians on passing ocean liners, hundreds of miles off below the horizon, are no farther away by radio than if they were in the next cabin. Even your own physician at home can be consulted in an emergency, code and local telephone circuits can be quickly hooked up to care for the one-chance-in-a-million trouble that might arise.

Passengers in rare cases are even transferred to passing vessels. Occasionally you put into ports to discharge an ailing customer, but as a rule, should sudden illness strike, you're better off aboard, than stranded in some tropical city. Rarely are you more than a few days' sail from your next stopping place. Worry about medical attention has no place in planning for a Vagabond Vacation. People who worry about their health too much are better off at home close to hospitals and near physicians who understand the treatment of hypochondriacs.

Put your worries away. If you're healthy, you'll be healthier for a visit in the sea air; if you're sick and know how to take care of yourself, there's no more danger in freighter travel than in any other form of sea voyaging.

In making your plans be sure your papers are right before you take a long voyage on a freighter — or on any other kind of ship for that matter.

Americans are in the habit of dashing off from Boston to California on half an hour's notice. They run over to Atlanta from New Orleans to see a football game, or fly from Los Angeles to San Francisco to collect a bill and then fly home for dinner. We think nothing of dash-

ing up to Montreal for a week end, international
borders mean very little to our travel lives.

There's many a guest registering at the Mount Royal
in Montreal who would have a great deal of difficulty in
proving his identity in Paris, and many others, including
automobile tourists, who visit Canada every year, are
greatly put out by the demands of the Immigration Department that they provide proper identification going
and returning.

Foreign governments have rigid rules and regulations
about immigration, about regulation of tourists, and
about the identification of visitors, much stricter than
those the average American traveler has met near home.

Carry sufficient identification at all times. Letters of
introduction are always useful, even if never presented.

The average around-the-world freighter voyager may
feel like a Lindbergh crossing the Atlantic, off to remote
lands and all that, on a new journey; but even as
America's Number One flyer spent a day before his departure on that famous first Atlantic flight getting letters
of introduction to people in Paris, every voyager should
be sure that he can establish his identity in India as
easily as in Indianapolis.

Get your passports in plenty of time. Get all the visas
you will need for your journey. It may save you a lot of
time and trouble if you settle all such details before you
sail. If you arrange your tour through a travel agent he
will tell you what to do and attend to most of the paper
work for you. If you handle the passport job yourself,
check with your steamship line; their advice will be
valuable.

Tuck your birth certificate away in your bag somewhere. If you belong to a fraternal order and your lodge has an identification for members, take that along too. The customs man at Algiers may have never heard of your organization but a really impressive-looking certificate always assists in the cashing of travelers' checks, no matter where you may be.

See your doctor before you sail. Check with the Line or the foreign consulates on the regulations as to inoculations. Some countries require one and some another set of antitoxin injections before passers-by can land. Get your medical papers in proper shape as well as your identification papers. If you can't prove that your doctor gave you the typhus shots before you left home, you'll have a tough job getting by some hard-boiled medical examiner at a port where they have just had a shake-up in the local public health service.

And be sure you have made plans for enough money to get you home. It's easy enough to have someone wire you some extra spending money if you make arrangements before you leave, but the guy who gets into the gambling house at Macao and hasn't someone back in Portland to cable, may find himself finishing up a journey around the world without carfare to go up to town in the most glamorous of ports.

The freighter traveler should take the same precautions about carrying money that are advisable for any other journeyer. Enough cash to cover small expenditures, plus a bank letter of credit if you plan spending any real coin, and certainly plus a few travelers' checks in small denominations for emergency cashing. If you are going all the way on one boat, of course, you won't need to worry about calling at a bank

There's No Harm in Testing the Beds

for cash, but if your trip calls for changing ships several times, or if you are not sure what vessel you will ride on your return, let your banker handle the arrangement of your funds — that's his business.

If you are going to a really far away land, it is also smart to arrange a cable code. Cable costs are coming down; telephone rates are lower today than cable charges were once, for that matter; but when you're paying by the word it's a lot easier to have a system all your own. Western Union has a cute little code book for travelers and there's a word for everything but "Will you marry me?" If you ask W.U. about this strange omission, they'll show you a page or two of symbols with no meanings written after them. "Pick your own phrases to suit these words," the clerk will tell you, and it's mighty good advice, too. Fix up your own communications scheme before you sail.

If you are voyaging on the popular Royal Netherlands boats out of New York, twenty or thirty days in the Spanish Main, you're taking only a short cruise and the need for complicated code systems is not so pressing. But if you're off for a world journey, figure a set of words to use in cables. Cut down the cost of your emergency messages.

Get your papers right — and if you plan any time ashore in any foreign country, study up on the regulations as regards visitors before you leave home. It's a lot easier than learning the law arguing with some official while your ship lies at anchor.

13 · Around the World

THE IDEAL freighter trip is the voyage around the world — it's also easiest to talk about. Get aboard the Blue Funnel *Prometheus* at New York, make the world tour, come home and join the Circumnavigators' Club. Cross the Equator and participate in King Neptune's barbershop ceremony as he initiates the neophytes; it's just as much fun on the *Tai Ping Yang* as on any Empress Liner.

Hoboken may be interesting but it's more fun to talk about Penang. There's no class distinction in the Circumnavigators' Clubs — unless it be that the folks who have earned their right to membership by an escorted tour hang around the tramp trippers at the monthly gatherings. The freighter passengers have usually seen a lot more.

Of course the nations of the world are just around the corner if you want to see them that way. There's Africa in Harlem and Berlin in Yorkville for the New Yorkers, yet Munich beer in Munich has a greater thrill than the same brew in Brauhaus in Philadelphia. The West Indies are as truly Oriental as Hindustan, the minaretted mosques are not all in Asia, but no traveler feels that he has completed his sight-seeing until his voyaging brings him back home as a member of that crew of globe-girdlers made famous by Magellan.

The Royal Netherlands steamships, in a twenty-one day voyage reach ten or fifteen ports, go into harbors

that are crowded with romance, past scenes of tropical
splendor unequaled anywhere. Now, twenty-one days
of a "world cruise" are often spent out of sight of land
in the run across the Pacific! There are lots of argu-
ments against taking the route all-around, but they matter not at all to the prospective traveler. Given the
time and the money, not one in a hundred thousand
would refuse the chance to board the Motor Vessel
Thurland Castle in New York on a cold winter morning, to set off on a five-month tour of the world.

There's real romance in the journey, the romance of
following in the footsteps of famous explorers, the romance of seeing natives and native lands, of seeing real
countries rather than their counterparts transplanted in
another hemisphere. The Zoo's a grand place to watch
sea lions at play, but who wouldn't rather visit the
Pribilof Islands?

The round-the-world freighter service that's best
known is probably the Prince-Silver Lines Combination.
Prince and Silver have a deal. Your tickets are inter-
changeable, you can buy a world passage with stop-
over arrangements, waiting in port to board the following vessel — if there's a space available for you.

Dodwell-Castle-Barber Line sends one of its famous
Castle vessels on the world voyage once a month —
there's a *Tai* sailing in between, and by changing ships
you can do a world cruise on them too. The *Tai* boats
have that word in their names; Castle boats have *Castle*
in their names: *Muncaster Castle, Greystoke Castle,* etc.

Blue Funnel starts a world cruise from New York
every month also, and several times a year Silver-Java
sends a ship, connecting with a sailing from the Gulf

that does the world cruise the other way around.
Maersk, N.Y.K., and several others have services where
you make the journey by changing ships; and O.S.K.
runs around the southern half of the world, Cape Town
to Buenos Aires being the Atlantic crossing.

World cruises offer the best opportunity to study
Vagabond Vacationing. Prince and Silver have been
carrying Americans in this service with more regularity
and for a longer period of time than most of the other
freighter companies now taking trippers off to prove
that the world is round.

When the *Javanese Prince* sailed from Brooklyn in
the summer of 1938, she began her thirty-second journey
around the world. Those who have followed the sun
on these ships are easier to find than people who have
made the circuit on other lines. "Ask the man who
owns one," is mighty sound advice. Comparing the
views and opinions of patrons of sister ships gives a
rather interesting series of pictures of freighter travel.
Every one is different, yet from the composite the
prospective voyager can get a fairly good idea of around-
the-world Vagabond Vacationing.

The boats of Prince and Silver are twin-screw motorships of 10,000 tons or more, The Prince boats are very
much alike, 442 feet long and 60 feet wide, with accommodations for eight passengers in four staterooms.
Their schedules call for completing the journey in about
130 days, but right here the similarity ceases. Each is as
different from the others as the officers and the passengers are different one from the other.

If Doumie is still the butler on the *Chinese Prince* it's
almost worth waiting several months to catch her to

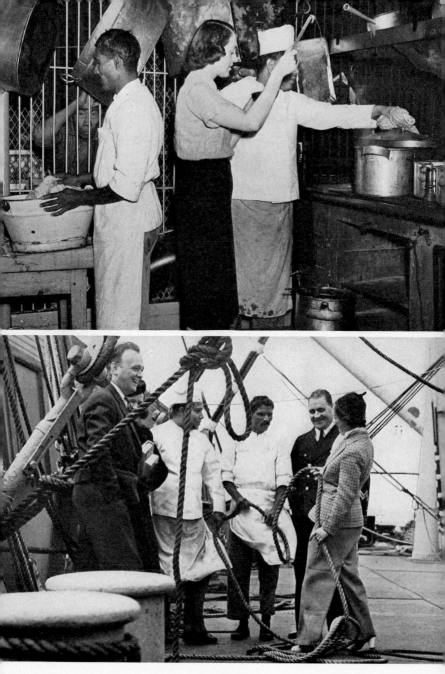

Visit the Cook in His Galley or Chat with Him on Deck

enjoy the perfect sandwiches he makes up every midnight. The *Siamese Prince* is the newest of the five, with
a flock of new gadgets in the engine room — perhaps
they've been put in all the other ships too, but they
were there first. The *Malayan Prince* and the *Javanese
Prince* are just names to most people, but to the few
who have been fortunate enough to journey in these
boats, one is known by her ex-passengers as the most
sturdy vessel in all history and the other is advertised
by loving friends as having the best long-range radio
set in the world, bringing in American stations at in-
credible distances.

Of course the sturdiness may have been gauged by
the fact that the freighter had an extra solid load on
the trip when passengers were interviewed, and certainly there's no guarantee that the radio set owned by
one of the officers will stay aboard any vessel indefinitely.
Officers get advanced and transferred, and even radio
sets get out of order, but be the facts as they may, several dozen favored ones are prepared to explain to their
friends, at great length, the superior advantages of the
Javanese as compared with all other ships afloat; or to
compare the *Malayan Prince* with all and sundry vessels
on the seas — to the discredit of the other boats, of
course.

The Silver boats, *Silverwalnut, Silverteak,* and so on,
alternate with the Prince Line in this service. Every
two weeks one of these vessels sails from New York on
this voyage; first one line and then the other provides
the ship. On the Silver boats, sister ships too, you find
only five passenger cabins in the regular deck plan.
Three cabins face forward, their portholes looking over

the bow towards the path of the vessel. The other two are on the deck above. Perched high on the midship house these quarters are far enough from the front of the ship to avoid all pitching discomfort, high enough to be cool, and close enough to the center of gravity to get away from the vibration which, incidentally, is much less on a motorship like the *Silvercypress* than on other, older, boats in general passenger service.

You are 160 feet from the bow and 315 feet from the stern in your bed on the *Silversandal* or any of her sister ships. The Captain's quarters occupy the top deck, the smoking room is on the deck with your cabin, and below that you find the dining salon and the state-rooms of the other officers. Promenades on three decks make it possible for each passenger to have a deck all to himself, if the notion strikes. There are electric lights and fans but no trick ventilation system. To get fresh air you just open the outside portholes and let the breeze pour in.

The food on these lines measures up to a high standard. The Silver boats are especially equipped for carrying fresh fruits and vegetables from Southern California to the Orient. They have been carrying passengers for several years; the commissary departments set stiff requirements; menus are exchanged between vessels, and regular checks are made on the efficiency of the passenger accommodations. Perhaps that's why space is often reserved several years ahead, and rarely is there an empty bed when the lights of San Pedro drop into the darkness as one of this fleet sets off on the trip across the Pacific.

Every freighter is different from every other freighter.

Sometimes a freighter differs from itself on one trip as compared with another. These are points you can't overemphasize in telling your friends about Vagabond Vacationing. To stress too strongly one point on one particular vessel oftentimes leads you astray. For example, a chap who made the journey on the *Silversandal* came home to tell his friends about it and after an hour or so of talking suddenly remembered that this boat had been recommended because one of the staff was said to have the best collection of sea stories afloat. He immediately phoned his adviser.

"Are you sure it was the *Silversandal?*" he queried. "I didn't hear any sea stories."

The two voyagers got together. The most recent returning booster admitted knowing the officer in question. Not only admitted knowing him, but proudly proclaimed having invented a brand new system of contract bridge with him as a partner. At cocktail time the first day on the *Sandal's* next visit, the officer was confronted by his two ex-passengers.

"I said you were the world's greatest salty sea-tale teller," the first visitor proclaimed.

"I say you are the best bridge-playing Chief in the Merchant Marine," the most recent voyager declaimed; "but what is this about sea stories?"

"How could I remember our *Silversandal* bridge system and still find time to tell about a sea serpent climbing over the bow?" countered the *Sandal* man.

There's the keynote of freighter travel. All things to all people. Vagabond Vacationing is exactly what you make it. The officers are glad of the chance to meet new people, to see new faces, to venture into new associations. The card player will find a partner; the whittler will come across an accomplished wielder of the knife, to teach him new methods of carving sailing ships inside of beer bottles; the adventurer with an ear for tales of the ancient mariner will be thrilled with stories of strange occurrences at sea, and the man or woman who wants to just *sit* will spend days and nights resting peacefully in a deck chair under the Southern moon. Go aboard looking for a fight, and possibly you'll bump into an Irishman who will be ready to accommodate you, but enter into the spirit of tramp tripping and you'll find memories to be treasured forever.

The *Silveryew* is the boat of preference for one set of returned passengers, certainly. Perhaps every other ship afloat boasts of as fine cooks; perhaps every other ship galley in the world is capable of turning out as fine food, but you'll never convince the *Yew*'s boosters. They recall a day far to the South, under the tropical sky, a blazing sun like July while the calendar said it was Christmas Eve. Wayfarers all, far from home and hearthside, it seemed unreal; perhaps a bit of sadness crept over the group as they lazed around the ship that afternoon.

Dinner was late. The Chief Steward came out on deck to explain, to apologize; but the passengers were not particularly interested. It was a lazy day, a day to watch the wake of the ship, a day to watch the drifting clouds as they formed patterns in the sky, a day for rest, for contemplation, perhaps for gin slings and lime drinks, but certainly not one for worry about food. When finally the three notes of the chimes announced that the table was spread, and reluctant feet took the idlers from the deck to their accustomed places in the dining room, a strange sight met their eyes.

The steward had found a Christmas tree. A tiny one, but brave in its glory, perched on the serving table against the front wall of the room.

"He kept it in the refrigerating compartment," one of the engineering officers explained. Its pine needles glistened with tinsel, tiny candles flickered in the dimmed lights. Holly wreaths hung at the portholes, and at each passenger's place was a little gift, a carving made by some of the men in the crew. How many midnight sandwiches had the steward given the men in exchange for these exquisite little replicas of the *Silveryew?*

The meal was not the conventional holiday dinner of old England, nor the Christmas dinner of a Southern plantation. A summer repast was served, chilled melon, and other light foods appropriate to the season; iced tea and cold beer replaced mulled ale; but at the conclusion, the crowning glory of the day was brought in.

Followed by his two assistants, while the lights were obligingly dimmed, the second steward proudly marched in with a giant English plum pudding perched in the center of a silver platter. Flames flickered from its top as the brandy sauce was burned in true traditional style.

Whether it came from a can, or was completely made in the galley, the passengers cared not. The English officers and the American passengers — even the Greek merchant who had Cabin C — all were loud in their praise. Some may proclaim that only in old Yorkshire is there to be found true British plum pudding. Some may think that only when the snow lies close on the ground, and the countryside around is covered with a white mantle that gives every familiar sight a strange look, when the holiday bells ring and the carolers sing outside — some believe that only then do you find the holiday dish of our English cousins at its best. But say not so to our voyagers of the *Silveryew*. They'll tell a different story — the story of the Equator, of hot nights and cooling drinks, and a touch of Old England brought in by a swarthy second steward from Portuguese East India, a typical British dish served by a man as much unlike the ruddy-faced butlers of English homes as daylight is from dark. Different, but Christmas just the same.

Tramp tripping is what you make it. Wherever you go you see strange sights, meet interesting people, and always you carry with you a breath of the old country, a bit of the home habits of the nation of which your ship is a part. "Your home away from home," one great hotel advertises. "A home around the world," Silver and Prince and all the others might well proclaim.

14 · Off around the World

PRINCE and Silver boats sail from Brooklyn. No fuss and feathers, no confetti or streamers. The Chief Officer glances around and says, "It looks like all our visitors have gone ashore."

The steward starts clearing up the salon, putting the sandwiches onto one plate, polishing the table where the last farewell party was held. The passengers go out on deck to see the pier gently drift away from the side of the vessel. The Captain is on the bridge with the pilot. The donkey begins its whine, reeling in the hawser.

One lone tug hauls away at a line aft somewhere. Sometimes four or five people gather on the stringer at the end of the pier. Occasionally, the only *bon voyage* visitor is a watchman who looks up to wave a friendly hand as your vessel slips into the stream.

The whistle gives a toot or two, the tug answers, and suddenly, sans ceremony, you're headed out to sea. No throngs at the end of a giant pier, no strings of flags or bunting, no band playing "Anchors Aweigh." Nothing unusual seems to have happened; you've simply gone to sea.

The officers and crew are occupied. The five passengers stand at the rail; you two a little apart from the others. There's a moment of sizing up, a moment when you begin to wonder if after all this will be fun, to wonder just how these strange people will wear. They look different here in the daylight. In the salon a moment ago they were old friends; now you wonder. That necktie! Does it indicate complete bad taste in color, or was the tie a present from the pretty blonde girl who clung so tight as they stood at the rail just before the gangplank was lifted clear of the dock?

You clasp her hand in an involuntary gesture, draw nearer to one another. No matter what strange sights are seen, no matter what odd people are met, you two have each other. A bond of comradeship is created anew, you're off adventuring together.

The setting sun strikes the towers of Manhattan, fast fading astern. The streets and trees of Brooklyn are passing by. There lies Staten Island. Liberty lifts her torch. Plugging steadily, nose down to the light seas of the harbor, your ship forges on. The wide ocean opens ahead, a gentle swell lifts the boat a bit, the vast Atlantic spreads before you — pathway to castles in Spain come true.

You linger on deck, even after the others go below, linger when the steward comes to report the time of dinner, linger as the land slips into the distance. The air is clear, there's a pure freshness not found in night clubs or city streets. Gulls circle overhead; already there is a little group of them following the wake of the ship. An officer passes by without stopping; he waves off into the distance where you see a light in the haze of the evening. Ambrose Lightship, you think. What matter if it be Ambrose or not? To you it is and that's enough. Already you've begun to identify the landmarks of the voyage, already you are voyagers, journeyers to strange lands, guided by lights ashore and by the stars above.

You stand side by side, hand in hand, as the setting sun dips into the ocean for its nightly immersion. Ships around are all far away. A trail of smoke marks the passage of another vessel; you wonder about those aboard her. They, too, perhaps, are bound on a voyage of discovery, on a romantic adventure.

The notes of the dinner chimes come faintly through the hush of the evening. It's quiet aboard ship, you glide through the water with simplicity, the throb of the motors seems muffled. Apparently without expenditure of energy you are pushing ahead, forging onward on your route.

You take one last breath, give one last glance to the faded shore line lights, then start inside together. Come what may, the journey's begun, the weeks of waiting are over, the time to live is here.

You turn to the dining salon. The Chief Officer is at the head of the table. The steward pulls out the lady's chair, you bow to your fellow passengers. They seem like nice people, in fact, they're friends of yours. You're glad to see them. The steward has an interesting face, he's smiling. Everybody's happy, not with riotous laughter or maudlin cheers, but pleasantly happy. They too, like you, are off adventuring. They too, like you, have castles in Spain, dreams that will now come true.

It is a pleasant company. The chap with the violent neckwear offers you a plate of rolls. That tie isn't so terrible, seen in the quieter light of the dining salon. He has a clear smile, a rather charming manner, likable enough at that. They're all delightful people, they're your companions, you're together, ship's company all. You butter a bun, the voyage has begun.

You're early up on your first morning at sea. The stilly quiet, emphasized by the throb of the motors, grips you as you lie abed. All sense of time is gone, there seems to be no need of hurry, yet try as you may you cannot remain beneath the covers.

Let lazy days at sea come when they will, today there seems to be much to do. Breakfast in your room; and then you're out on deck to start a tour of inspection.

THE FIRST LANDING

Hampton Roads is the first stop for Prince and Silver boats: Hampton Roads, that giant harbor on the Atlantic Coast within whose sheltering arms the navies of the world can come to rest, with plenty of room to spare. You pass Cape Charles and Cape Henry, sailing into the harbor that shelters Norfolk, Newport News, Old Point Comfort, Langley Flying Field, Virginia Beach — the countryside abounds with points of interest. But somehow your thoughts are not of sight-seeing trips to be taken during the two or three days in which the boat will be busy loading. You almost resent the stop *en route*.

The giant spread of the harbor extends before your eyes, mile after mile of pier after pier; ships from every port in the world here. The fog lifts and the panorama broadens; surely, this beggars description. The vastness of it all fairly takes away your breath. This you admit is wonderful; this leaves you, as did the Grand Canyon, ready to make feeble jokes about old razor blades to cover your awe. This is all that it has been called. But, at best, it's only another American port. You're restless for the seas again; before the motion of the ship ceases you are ready to push onward. The spirit of the Far East is upon you, the lure of ship life has you in its grip.

Of course you have things to do ashore. There are letters to mail, odds and ends to buy. An extra toothbrush, some film — who would have thought you would take six rolls of pictures in one afternoon? Film must be left for developing; the oldest cadet has promised to show you a place "right near the docks" where they'll get you prints overnight.

You haven't carbon paper, and there's a telegram or two to send to the folks who sent gifts. Shore day calls for many errands; and besides there's the chap who wore the funny necktie (thank the Lord, sweat shirts don't call for scarfs). Mr. Neckerchief was bragging about his golf last night; today he plans a match with the Chief Engineer and you've half promised the Chief to caddy for him.

Down over the side and ashore. In one hand the list of things you've promised to buy, the film in the other. The golf match is set for afternoon and you'll come back to the ship for lunch in an hour or so. But now, off for the errands!

Back aboard, there's mail to glance over. Some ninny has sent a seed catalogue. You start to throw it away and the Second Officer speaks up. "May I have that?"

You're a little startled to discover that sailors think about growing oats and geraniums. Being at sea gives a man a love of the soil, it seems.

Back from the golf match, there's the matter of arranging a dinner party at the Cavalier. The ladies will have a chance to wear their evening clothes.

Things happen in port; even in an American port. The boat stays-over an extra day: an opportunity to entertain the friends of friends who come visiting at the docks. A party aboard ship is nice. You get a thrill sitting at the head of the table, introducing the Captain to your guests. You proudly show off the fine points of the boat, as enthusiastic a freighter booster as any ticket agent.

And then out to sea again. Past Cape Hatteras on the way to the Canal . . .

At sea at last! No more American ports; Panama next. Savannah has been omitted from the route this trip. Panama — a foreign land where instead of the strange soft voices of vowel-slurring Southerners we'll hear Spanish, and perhaps a bit of native Indian languages of some kind or another . . .

At breakfast the Captain reports the next stop as Colón, Republic of Panama.

"We won't stop at Havana this trip," he announces.

"Havana?" the diners speak up. "The agent didn't say we were likely to see Morro Castle by moonlight."

"We sometimes get orders to stop there after leaving Norfolk," the head of the ship explains. "Occasionally it's Jacksonville or Charleston, big shipping points for resin and naval stores. Once we put into Kingston, Jamaica."

Jamaica, with the ancient city of Port Royal down at the bottom of the harbor — the wicked city of Port Royal, home base of the famous Sir Henry Morgan,

Lazy Days and Lazy Ways

greatest of all pirates, the city that God sent an earth-
quake to destroy when it seemed as if man could not do
the job . . .

It would have been interesting to see that sun-soaked
island, but why be bothered by near-by lands when
the whole world lies before one?

The swimming pool is set up on deck. The cargo is
stowed away; there will be no opening that hatch until
we reach Manila, according to the Chief Officer. The
swimming pool is a cloth bag — almost. Heavy canvas hung from four stout poles forms a square tank
about four or five feet deep, twelve or fourteen feet
square.

You think of the Lido deck of the *Rex,* of the tiled
pool far below decks on the *Empress of Britain.* You
are roughing it! The sea water is pouring into the tank;
there's no time to waste worrying about what might
have been. Here is your swimming pool, you might
better enjoy it than sit and think about the beautiful
one in the hotel at Virginia Beach, or the inland ocean
at Palisades Park.

Quickly donning bathing suits, in you go. It's surprising how big it seems once you're there. You can
actually swim a foot or two, and the salt water does feel
fine.

Now there are five of you in the water. The youngest
cadet suggests Puss-in-the-Corner. Someone's never
heard of this old game of childhood days. Even you
have to stop to think to get its application to the pool.
Explanations made, you're soon enjoying wild scrambles
for a corner, splashing about at a great rate. Soon
you're "It," out in the center of the tank, square in the

middle, jumping up and down, daring the others to venture from the safety of their corner refuges.

Deck chairs become beach chairs. The shadow of an awning spread by the steward keeps the glare from those who want to go slow about acquiring a tropical tan. The cadets are searching for the "nudists' house" used on the last voyage.

It's found and set up. There, in a little four-walled canvas tent without any top, you can lie and bake to your heart's content, on what amounts to your own private deck. Stewards bring tall Tom Collinses; a friendly voice is heard from the other "sun house" alongside. It's too comfortable to more than mumble an answer. You'll finish your bronzing perfectly this time.

Shipboard routine comes quickly to you. Coffee and fruit before breakfast; bouillon in the mid-morning if you care for it. Breakfast in bed most days, and cool drinks in the evening. You attach yourself to the Chief Officer, stand on the bridge at noonday when he participates in that strange ceremony known as shooting the sun, locating the position of your vessel by a sight at the sky. At night he shows you again how it is done, and explains the charts and maps and tables used in checking the ship's position by the stars.

Before you realize it, before you've even settled on the proper hour for the first afternoon drink, the Canal is announced.

EAST TO THE PACIFIC

Colón, Republic of Panama, first foreign port on a freighter world cruise, isn't actually on the list of stopping points in most schedules. Your vessel has a job of moving cargo fast and cheap. World circling ships rarely find a shipment waiting at Colón. Unless the tides, or traffic, or the Skipper's thirst, intervene, you're likely to go through the Canal without hesitating.

If you're lucky, there will be half a day ashore. Ordinarily ships do not make the Canal transverse at night, so arrival at four in the afternoon or so means a night lay-over.

Colón . . . the Tropical Bar . . . the cabaret girls who insist on telling you about when they were "at the Palace" . . . the aged Salvation Army lassie on the street corner . . . the tourists from cruise ships easily identifiable, even without tags indicating their sea homes . . . the numerous broughams . . . the low, long, touring-car taxi-cabs . . . the sudden rains (now it rains, now it doesn't) . . . sailors, American sailors finding an El Dorado in American travelers, glad to entertain a fellow citizen "so far from home" . . . Colón, with the New York newspapers down by air mail and priced very high . . . liquors cheaper, but the domestic brands not so highly recommended . . . the *Panama American* with one side of the paper in Spanish and the other side in English.

The pilot and the "coast crew" of West Indian darkies come aboard. This adds another race to the heterogeny of your ship: a British vessel, Scotch Engineer, Irish Radio Officer, Malay sailors, stewards from Portuguese East India, and an engine-room crew of Lascars; add to that the American tourists, and now the West Indian gang! Only half the people aboard can speak to the other half; no single individual can give orders that all will understand; yet the whole lot, passengers and crew, are under the domination of the iron will of the commander — the Skipper speaks and things happen.

Coming up to the locks, an item in the Panama paper takes on significance. Following behind is a wee white yacht; brave in her finery, polished bright-work gleaming in the sun.

"A crew of thirty-four." The Second Mate points out the celebrity owner in whites, reclining on deck sipping a drink.

"That's the life," says he.

Resting in your own deck chair you begin to wonder. Here on a "tramp" you have everything the millionaire can buy. Your drink is as tasty, and surely as cool, as any made aboard any yacht. Your chair is comfortable. Certainly, per passenger, there's more deck space. Your boat is big, five times the size of the pleasure craft.

The electric mules, motors on ratchets, three on a side, tighten the cables by which your ship is towed. In the lock ahead, high in the air, tower the masts of a ship that has preceded you — another freighter bound for the Far East. Crawling on their racked rails the mules pull the vessel into position in the huge deep basin of the first lock. The ponderous gates swing together behind the stern, the water boils up all around, and the side of the lock slips down until you have a clear view over the top again. Inch by inch, foot by foot, the water rises rapidly, then is still. Gates ahead open, the mules take up their towing, and presto the process is being repeated while the concrete and steel bath you have just left empties itself to prepare for the boat that follows.

High on the topmost part of the bridge you mount.

The view is better the higher you get. The yacht looks so tiny there behind you. The walls are impressively massive.

Five hours and you will be across the Isthmus. Five hours to cover the route Morgan traveled years ago, a journey the great pirate made in ten days, only by forced marches.

You ask for meals on deck; the panorama of Gatun Lake entrances you. Your vessel steams onward. The Canal is not what you expected. It's a lake. There are islands around you, islands on both sides. It's hard to realize this is a man-made sea, eighty-five feet above the level of the ocean you have just quitted.

The pilot on the bridge occasionally says a word to the wheelman. The Captain is by his side, officers not on duty join the passengers on deck. A screaming parakeet is heard in the distance of the jungle. You look at the great vines that come to the water's edge; you recline, with a cool drink at your side. . . . There's peace in the world.

The dead trunks of trees line the side of the lake, trees drowned when man turned the waters loose on the land, giant stalks that once were homes for birds and flowers. Crocodiles sun themselves on the banks, an occasional native hut is seen in a clearing. The ship follows the buoy-marked channel, whistling at the turnings as would the *Queen of Vicksburg* on the Mississippi.

The channel turns into a narrow stream. The jungle seems barely the width of Broadway on either side. The bird noises are louder, the play of children in a settlement by the side of the water seems oddly out of place.

The ship itself seems as a boat ashore. It's an *Alice in Wonderland* sort of existence.

Through the Cut, a giant man-made furrow in the backbone of the Americas, more locks down to sea level, and you are out into the Pacific, having come east (look at the map for yourself if you doubt it)!

Panama City and Balboa are the twin cities on this shore, the American settlement — American territory in the center of the Panama Republic — and the native city side by side. The Chief Officer starts to tell tales of the cabarets of Colón, of the entertainments of Panama. You listen half-heartedly, noting meanwhile the departure of the Canal crew. The pilot climbs overside and the ship prepares for sea again, the day consumed by the Canal transversal.

A jangle from the bridge and your vessel takes up the steady throb that marks the perfect operation of the motors. The lights of Panama fade into the background. Perhaps you stay on deck to watch them, or perhaps you find more interesting things to do inside. After all, a port is but a port, while a ship goes on forever. Land days are good days, but sea days are better; land food is a variation; land sights interesting, but the sea is the place, the ship your home.

All the familiar sounds of your vessel come back. There's the butler mixing another drink, your companions talking about a resumption of the rummy tournament, started two days ago. Even though you've been eliminated you want to form one of the gallery who watch the feverish play as Champion Chief Engineer battles against Champion Cadet. Youth and age in bitter conflict . . .

PLENTY OF ROOM FOR DECK SPORTS

Someday someone will speak of the Canal and Panama City. You may answer from the guidebooks, but the chances are you'll remember the light that shone on the cadet's face as he, a lad barely out of his teens, laid down the last cards that marked him Grand High 500 Rummy Champion of the Seventeenth World Tour.

SAN PEDRO — A LETTER

DEAR LARRY: —

We were playing hearts in the smoking room, just three of us, Kittie, the Chief Officer and I, an hour or so after dinner, dusk outside. Glancing through the porthole to see if land was in sight I noticed a lot of lights — like a flock of derricks strung with bulbs.

"San Diego," the Chief Officer volunteered.

We returned to the hearts game, to finish the round. At eight, the C.O. went on watch. I strolled out on deck for a bit of air and wound up on the bridge. There were two clusters of lights still visible in the distance.

"Two ships?" I asked the Fourth Officer.

"No, many warships," he replied.

I got the glasses and, sure enough, there in the distant haze were twelve ships in company front, as we soldiers would say — highballing it into port. I could have kicked myself overboard for having missed a closer view. Battlewagons are a weakness of mine. I looked and looked, drinking my fill, then turned to find Kittie to give her an eyeful.

I expressed a wish to see more warships at closer range and the C.O. told me he never passed San Diego without seeing them in practice.

We're back now in the so-called Temperate Zone. Somehow in the days down from Norfolk and the days up from Colón it was all too new, each hour was too full of things to see, there was no time to think of all I resolved to do on this trip. My typewriter's been neglected. The warm sun simply lured us outside. I couldn't drag myself off the decks except to sleep and eat. Not that it was at any time uncomfortably hot — ninety degrees was about the top, but it's cooler here and from now on there's not the same urge to loaf.

Tomorrow, San Pedro to take on fuel oil. We'll go dockside at dawn, resting at anchor outside the breakwater overnight. A few errands to do . . . Perhaps we'll try to dash up to Los Angeles, but the Chief Officer says it might not be a good idea, we're sure to leave right on the dot of three in the afternoon. It would be sort of silly to come this far and then miss the boat at the last American port.

The film, books, magazines, and other things we've ordered will be down by messenger from the ship's agent early tomorrow morning. The mail will be interesting, but somehow the ties that bind us to New York are not as strong as they were. Even at Panama — the air mail that came was welcomed, but not particularly awaited, and now even letters don't seem so important. The ship chandler will deliver the special food we ordered. The Coca Cola we've introduced to the officers will come aboard without any effort on our part. Perhaps it will be more fun to stay here all day while the pumps fill our oil tanks for the voyage across the Pacific.

I have a few letters to get off — tonight's the last chance for letter-writing. There's no floating mailbox in midocean where one can drop picture postal cards; no mail chutes outside bedroom doors. Either we write now — or the folks won't hear from us for seven weeks.

San Pedro and Wilmington — the harbor of Los Angeles. . . . The port of good resolutions for freighter voyagers; the port where you determine to finish that article promised an editor months ago. The port where you see strange friends out of your long-lost past.

Friends who have been buried in the slave shops of the motion picture industry come down to gibe at you — and secretly to express their envy of your leisurely attitude towards life. These high-pressure businessmen who only a few weeks ago seemed so familiar are now like figures from another world. What has a Vagabonder in common with them? What difference deadlines, or release dates, or huge rubber stamps reading RUSH?

(Later)

Kittie went up to town early in the morning. Something about shopping. A messenger boy brought down a ten-pound bag of glass beads — with a note: "Trade these to the natives for me." Vagabond Vacations inspire friends to cockeyed presents.

The mail man brought my dozen cigarette lighters. I'm buying them to give the ship's officers as presents — being a New Yorker, of course I ordered wholesale. Sent by air express, the total cost is ten cents each above the prices they're labeled in a Los Angeles shop window, if Kittie's story is to be believed.

Many drinks in the smoking room. Much back-patting and toasting from the old gang that sort of drifted off instead of staying on in New York. They're making money — lots of money — but I wonder who has the fun.

Today's the day to swap places — you can go your way — I'll go mine. You can have your good jobs — I'm away. Tomorrow I start a real adventure — twenty days across the Pacific to Manila.

FRED

Freighters calling at Los Angeles before crossing the Pacific may get out in a few hours or stay in port several days loading cargo.

Excursions to Hollywood, and to other points of in-

terest around Southern California, can be arranged
with local travel agencies. To see the inside of a motion
picture studio arrange for a pass before you leave home.
The manager of the Bijou Theater on Main Street might
wangle it for you. He'll do a better job of pass pro-
motion by mail than you can by knocking on studio
gates.

15 · Twenty Days to Manila

FROM America's West Coast, ships go to the Far East almost every day. Japanese speedsters from Los Angeles harbor, Dollar Liners from San Francisco, cargo boats from Seattle and Portland, and the great Empress Fleet from Vancouver — to Tahiti, to Honolulu, to Yokohama, to Shanghai, and Manila. To Australia and Asia, to Bali and Bata, ships of all nations, each on its selected route, plowing the Pacific. Huge passenger liners; giant N.Y.K. vessels; wee dirty tramps, badly in need of paint, the insignia on their smokestacks too faint for a landsman to make out. They all sail from our shores, ships of all conditions, bearing the commerce of the world.

Besides the San Pedro call, many freighters will visit San Francisco or some other town on the West Coast, "where cargo offers." Several passengers will join at the last American port; latecomers who could not spare time for the trip through the Canal. California is overnight by airplane from New York. Students hurrying from the close of school to catch the first boat off; tourists returning to their native lands preferring the exploration of America by land to seeing its coast towns, and voyagers who live in Western states are among the passengers you meet when America at last is left astern.

The pilot dropped, the engines running at full speed, the trailing birds fall in behind and the long trek commences.

Once at sea, the last farewell gifts are opened. The lady passenger with the packet of letters may save her billets-doux, one for each day as they are marked, but less romantic souls hasten to open envelopes, remove wrappings and cut string. The last gift must be quickly unpacked, the last telegram read, and the last goofy postal deciphered.

What is there about a freighter voyage that inspires friends to heights of so-called comedy? Weddings and freighter sailings have that in common. Some strange brand of lunacy — under the guise of so-called humor — inspires otherwise normal people to send policemen to arrest the departing bridegroom, or to handcuff mother-in-law to her new daughter (with the cuff keys lost). That blood taint seems to be present in many — but it only comes to light when friends journey afar or lives are joined at the altar.

Sea captains tell tales of departures. They remember the gift of a box of mice for a maiden lady of uncertain years. Also there's the story of the six midgets who were hired to visit a ship dolled out in children's clothes singing "Father, dear Father" in their high-pitched voices while a nervous young man, knowing it all a joke and too good a sport to interfere, wondered if the new lady passenger, just aboard, would understand too.

Then there's the traveler noted on the Dollar Line as the "man who got the mail." Postal cards, written so all might read; postals signed Sue and Bess and Ann; postals in unmistakable feminine script, with endearing messages, postals that singly would have seemed authentic, great showers of postals came from the mail sacks and were piled into his cabin. Some practical joker (or perhaps a troupe of them) had labored long to perfect this gibe.

The inane telegrams that Americans send! The long messages popularized by the late Florenz Ziegfeld and publicized, no end, by our telegraph companies' smart young men. Travelers always get telegrams; form telegrams out of the "suggestion book" reeking of the tone of *The Perfect Letter Writer* and other wires that indicate hours of lost sleep devoted to their composition.

The letters, some full of cheer and good advice, some overburdened with silly words — flowers, books and fruit, candy and cakes, cigars and cigarettes — gifts pour on voyagers in profusion.

Ship's officers are practical men. They are tolerant, but still they find it difficult to understand the excitement landlubbers make over a departure. The Chief Officer will gossip about strange gifts: a donkey sent down in a crate, carrier pigeons in cages, a tombstone in a box. He'll tell of other idiosyncrasies of travelers' friends; tell his stories with glee, but through it all he speaks as one recounting the inexplicable habits of a strange race.

So you come to the salon for dinner the first night out, resolved to say as little as possible about your farewell basket. Your silly pals are far behind — their gags *shall not* lower you in the estimation of those with whom you have thrown your lot.

How important the self-esteem of your fellow voyagers becomes at this point! Ship life magnifies the value of standing high in the eyes of those around you. The opinion of the Second Engineer is now pertinent; his comments on life and love are received with respect.

You are all together, everyone tries his hardest to shine.

The birds hang on astern. Sometimes only three or four; an hour later, nearly a dozen. Through the night and day they hover behind, ready to pounce down on the water with the daily emptying of the cooks' scraps. They follow your wake, searching the path of the ship in the hope that something will be churned up from the depths of the seas that will justify the long journey they have made. As you near land they will increase. Occasionally one will disappear for a day or so, then count reveals the number the same as before, either the wanderer has returned, or a brother come to take his place.

Travelers wonder at these birds. Do they have favorite ships to follow? Do they wait for a special vessel? Do they go halfway across the vast ocean and then turn back, or do they journey as do the ships: across, then a rest, then a return trip? Do they sleep while a-wing, or do they rest on the waves, then hurry at dawn to resume their places?

Books may answer these questions, but freighter officers have not too much truck with books about the "gulls." All birds at sea are "gulls," it seems. Let ornithologists name them as they will, "gulls" they remain except when the conversation grows quite technical; then, when pressed, some officer will show a surprising knowledge of the habits of the albatross, and identify its varying types by wing markings.

Watching the birds takes up most of a four-hour watch on deck. It is a duty few can escape; a sea occupation that looms greater in importance as time goes on. A pair of good binoculars is useful in this work; no good bird-watcher should venture topside without his lenses ready to train on a distant flashing wing.

Day by day of the voyage will pass. The radio grows dimmer and dimmer. Soon, only for a few hours at night can the most powerful American stations be heard. Then the mystery of short-wave is discussed by the Wireless Officer, who tries to show by diagram and chart just why one American short-wave station comes clearly into the receiver while another is only faintly heard.

The daily run of the ship is reported from the bridge and posted, just as is done on the largest of liners. Passenger pools on the ship's run are arranged and collected and paid off day by day, if the customers are of a mind to engage in petty gambling, but there's nobody begging you to play and no percentage taken out for anything.

On this run there's no question about the next port, so the talk in the smoking room and at the daily conferences on deck is devoted to weighing the possibility of a long or short stay in Manila. Arrival is set by the Captain as "sometime Tuesday." Then speculation runs rife as to the exact hour. Will we make the landfall by daylight, or at night? Will we get ashore the first day in, or will it be too late to dock? Most of the officers have been there before. They speak praisingly or disparagingly, according to their temperaments.

You make a list of what to see, places to go, things to buy. You resolve to look for the chap who was boss of the Philippine Legislative Building construction. You're a little skeptical of the story that workers using forty languages and dialects were employed during its erection, and that he was the only man in the Islands who could understand all the workers — a sort of modern tower of Babel, only the Philippine structure stands completed. A golf match is scheduled between the Chief Engineer and the man from Des Moines. Golf clubs and putting rugs are laid out on an upper deck, practice continues night and day. A deck tennis competition is attempted, but dies of sheer inertia on the part of the players. Shuffleboard, on the other hand, draws all passengers and officers, and regular tournament rules are drawn up, play-offs arranged and all the ceremony incidental to a championship match followed. The Australian passenger wins at shuffleboard after sixteen hotly contested games. The score is four all, then four and five, then five all, first the Aussie is ahead, one game, then the engineer officer. A cheer goes up from the gallery after the last shot. The winner stands treat to wine at dinner that night; the loser, proving himself no less a sport, spends a sizable portion of his month's salary for another magnum of the best from the steward's special stock.

The light beer by this time is about exhausted and the stock of Coca-Cola low. You're rationing yourself on the latter: three Cuba-libre highballs a day, no more. Unless a storm comes up you are set for two extra drinks to welcome the Islands. You speculate on the customs of nations, on how people carry their habits in food and drink with them. The Englishman with his Scotch-and-soda; the Southerner with Bourbon; the Dane, his cordials; the American with his catholic taste swinging first from one mad preference to another — you'll see them all "freighter class."

Ship life magnifies. You fuss and fluster over some-

Cooling Off during a Shuffleboard Battle

thing, perhaps knowing down deep in your heart that after all it does not matter; yet how important it seems! The Date Line, arrival hour; the possibility of a storm — all furnish topics of deck discussion, equaled only by the intensity with which world affairs are settled in the smoking room o' nights. The cracker barrel and the country store gang have gone to sea.

The conferences in the smoking room are stimulating. The Skipper expresses an opinion; everyone listens with consideration. After all, he is the supreme ruler of the boat, the master of us all. The Engineer pounds the table and talks about the dangers of inflation. How simple it all seems, what masterpieces of logic are spread each night!

Over friendly drinks, so ably mixed by the steward, many strange feats of memory are paraded. One recites from Shakespeare, another tells about the care of cattle on a Western range, while real mental marvels confound the group by reciting, in proper order, the names of barrooms in Hempstead or the subway stations on the new municipal underground in New York.

Afternoons are devoted to entertainment, to games, to showing off of individual achievements. Evenings are for heavier things, for deeper thinking.

Afternoons, the man with three steps of a tap dance must perform for every passenger and half the crew. The lady who can pronounce the name of the town in Wales with the longest name in the world — every day that lady parades her ability to mouth the Welsh syllables; someone always remembers to call on her! It is her one claim to fame, and famous aboard ship and through life she will be, to this company at least, and to their friends and their friends' friends. Old stories are brought out, polished up and presented anew. Card games take on new interest as new ways of ship competition are started, and the chap who took the voyage to read a lot and to study for his coming examinations finds so much to do, so much around him, that his books gather the dust of the oceans — an achievement in itself, since no cleaner place exists than the open sea with fair winds blowing.

The crossing may be good; or, perhaps, a storm will come to prove that God rules and man is puny after all. But fair weather or foul, the routine of the ship continues. The letters you planned doing the first day out are neglected until a flurry of writing descends upon everyone with port only twenty-four hours away.

Manila and the Philippines! The world voyager has the option of stopping for a time, or of continuing with the ship for a tour of Japanese ports before she comes back to Manila for her second visit. Plans are made and unmade, and the chap who once spent two weeks in the Philippines grows in popularity as his fellow travelers interview him and re-interview him on the proper places to go and the things to see once foot is set on shore again.

Twenty days to Manila . . . Each day a gem and each all too short. Let those who will take faster boats. Let those who have need for hurry take the silk ships from Los Angeles to Yokohama. Your twenty days pass like magic, not too long a time, not too short. Twenty days to Manila . . . Twenty days of the joys of ship life, twenty days of watching overside . . . Someone else may have been bored, but you are ready to go again. You feel as if you'll never be surfeit with sea and wave and sky.

Manila is Hot!

Manila is hot. Manila Harbor is hotter. Ship cabins in Manila Bay are hottest of all!

Perhaps some vacationers will find Manila charming, cool days and cooler nights. Perhaps they will find the sail past the breakwater to moorings or a dock a pleasant one; perhaps they will thrill with the American's sense of possession at the sight of Corregidor, heavily fortified island at the mouth of the bay. "The Gibraltar of America" it is called in the guidebooks. The aërated Manila Hotel, Government-owned and operated; the deft service of the entire staff; the pleasant persistence of the guides who insist on showing you the sights; the beauties of the old city and the strange interior; the vastness of Manila Bay, one hundred miles around; the piers; the bars that never close; these and more are praised by those who sing of the Islands, to all who will listen.

Be that as it may, one thing must be said — Manila is hot!

The heat rises in clouds, inside and outside your clothing, perspiration pours from every square inch of your body; fans running below decks churn the dead air around — you understand how a fish feels when out of water.

Every freighter spends a day or two there. You see boats of the seven seas at the sprawling docks: Dollar Liners, Blue Funnel vessels, great Empress boats — ships from all the world at Manila. Prince and Silver advertise two stops: first on arrival from America, then again after cruising to Hong Kong and Shanghai and perhaps one or two other places. Manila is the milepost that marks the start of the last half of the journey around the world.

Vacationers tell of weeks spent in the interior, of days and days viewing the wonders of the old city, of the progressiveness of the Filipino, of the war the Islanders face, the problem of having independence around the corner and not exactly knowing what to do about it when it comes.

By all means visit the Philippines; by all means spend some time in Manila — but remember you were warned: Manila is hot.

And be sure to ask about water buffalo.

Ah! the water buffalo! The draft animal of the farmer of the inland towns; the water buffalo, looking like an oversized gray cow, a peculiar animal with his rope harness pulling a primitive plow. . . . The carabao, native of the Islands for many years . . . yet his master knows that he must not be left un-cooled too long. The water buffalo's hide must be soaked with pails of water, he must be permitted to wallow in the muddy pools at frequent intervals — or his skin cracks, and he (or more often she) is unable to work.

Perhaps the story's untrue. Perhaps it's only an imaginative yarn spun for a credulous tourist — but ah! how the buffalo are envied. Manila, sir (in case you're slow on the uptake), is hot.

It's not the heat, it's the humidity; it's the wet, heavy heat. The thermometer seldom reaches much beyond

eighty-five degrees. The U. S. Department of Agriculture
obligingly furnishes the following record: —

MANILA, PHILIPPINE ISLANDS (16-year record)

(Jan. Feb. Mar. Apr. May June July Aug. Sept. Oct. Nov. Dec. Annual.)

Mean maximum temperature

86.5 88.0 91.2 93.7 93.2 91.4 88.2 88.0 87.6 88.2 87.3 86.4 89.1

Mean minimum temperature

68.0 67.8 69.1 72.0 74.3 74.7 74.3 74.5 74.1 73.0 71.1 69.6 71.9

Mean temperature

77.2 77.9 80.2 82.8 83.8 83.0 81.2 81.2 80.8 80.6 79.2 78.0 80.5

Highest temperature (49-year record)

93.0 96.0 98.0 100 101 100 97.0 95.0 96.0 95.0 94.0 92.0 101.0

Lowest temperature (49-year record)

58.0 60.0 61.0 63.0 68.0 70.0 69.0 69.0 69.0 67.0 62.0 60.0 58.0

(Jan. Feb. Mar. Apr. May June July Aug. Sept. Oct. Nov. Dec. Annual.)

SIGHT-SEEING IN THE PHILIPPINES

Maersk and many other lines from and to the Philippine Islands and the Far East offer a variation in the
trip after Manila is sighted. World-cruise lines do the
same. Practically no schedule is unchanged once this
crossroads of the far Pacific is reached. Barber Line
literature says: "Cruises in Chinese, Korean, Japanese
and Philippine waters for about a month." Maersk
announces: "Passengers may spend three to four weeks
ashore at Manila at their own expense while the ship
collects cargo in the smaller ports of the Island, or may
stay aboard at a per diem charge." (The rate varies
with the vessel.)

Dozens of returned travelers bring back romantic
tales of the wonders of the interior. Coastwise boats
carry passengers from island to island among the 7,000
that make up the Philippine archipelago. There's a

weekly sailing to the leper colony on Culion where an entirely new conception of lepers is gained. The ones shown to visitors are clean, live in houses or huts, have non-leper wives or husbands, rasing huge families of non-leper children.

Fortified by lots of good advice from those who have already visited Manila, you'll go ashore as soon as possible. Your first purchase will be *pina* — a fine cobwebby fabric, intricately worked into lacy patterns. Pina is made of pineapple fiber. Handkerchiefs, tablecloths and lingerie make wonderful gifts.

Warned against lone night travel in Intramuras (which is what everyone calls the old, walled city), you will set out immediately for that section in a *caramata* — that odd two-wheeled cart which everyone in Manila uses instead of streetcars or taxis. At rather reasonable rates, automobiles can be employed by the hour or the day.

Manila is the base of the East Asiatic Squadron of the Navy; young officers abound. There are dances at the clubs and other entertainment, and plenty of guides for those who want guiding.

Furnished rooms or apartments in the native quarter are not enthusiastically recommended, but every traveler who tries a few weeks living with the people writes marvelous tales of courtesies shown, of interesting insights into family life.

The Sultan of Sulu lives on one of the seven thousand islands. Other native rulers abound and the hunting at remote settlements or plantations is recommended most highly by those who have been fortunate enough to be invited inland for a visit.

Golf courses and country clubs are kindly disposed towards the visitor, but it's courtesy to get introductions in town before you go out to play. Everybody gives guest cards to his clubs. Freighter agents are almost always glad to help fix such things, even to the point of assigning a clerk to start you off sight-seeing.

Returning to ship for dinner, the average vacationer will unload bundles and start letters home describing the tiny horses that draw the *caramatas*, practice newly acquired Spanish words with emphasis on *Yea-a-llow*, the street peddlers' corruption of the Spanish word for ice.

The American Express travel department will make arrangements for almost anything, from the renting of a furnished apartment for a family of five to the securing of admission to a cockfight, or directing a visit to a native market with its attendant shouts and smells.

Shoregoing with a hard-drinking officer will usually wind up in the visitor's seeing more than could possibly be expected; and calling at country clubs with a natty, society-minded braid-wearer will bring about an introduction to Island society, made famous by many writers.

But don't miss the boat.

When You Miss Your Boat

Cebu, P.I.

Dear Larry: —

You said Manila was hot — you sure did underrate. It's the hottest town in the world, but I don't mean the climate.

I've just discovered what happens when you miss your

boat on a freighter cruise around the world. You just up and miss it, that's all. The Skipper blows his noise-maker a few times, and there's a little extra tooting or something, then away she goes and you can stay there until next trip for all the Captain seems to care. Commerce will not be delayed.

Of course I missed the boat deliberately. After years of making the 8:14 at Evanston, I certainly wouldn't be left standing on the dock by as leisurely a bit of transportation as a freighter. In fact, I sent a messenger boy to tell the Chief Officer that they could safely proceed without me. My host of the day, one of those dapper Navy commanders, sent a boy with a chit (don't I talk Far East swell?) and the guy who bought the last seven rounds of drinks got sort of excited about my not leaving the club when the siren *whoomed*, and he sent a special chauffeur, in one of these high-velocity Fords they have out here, the chauffeur being instructed to tell the Captain that Lieutenant Whoosis promised to deliver me ship-side at the next port of call.

But that's getting away from the story. You made me promise to tell you about traveling, not about the glories of shore-going, so this letter has no long paragraphs about the bartender in Bay View Hotel Bar, nor will it tell you about the habits of drinking as followed by sailors in the Islands. Any time you're curious just let me know and *I'll* write *you* a book!

Any-hoo, the good ship sailed away and I waved a glass with a pretty Miss from Kansas who has a brother out here on duty with the air corps. Gosh, she's been here four days and is engaged to two birds already, with two or three others giving her the grand rush in an effort to outdo their fellow officers. I'm heartily in favor of army aviation, but only on condition that no man be given his wings until he can produce the following: —

(a) One wife who knows how to drive home at night;

(b) One unmarried sister-in-law who can come out to spend a season.

(c) One native driver who had his training riding bucking broncos and who can make a Model T do all the tricks "Dynamite" uncorks at the Cheyenne Rodeo.

I've never been so entertained, wined and dined in my whole life. Manila for mine every time. Just as soon as this letter gets mailed so it's postmarked Cebu, I'm going to turn in and start thinking out ways and means of getting transferred out here, preferably without any work to do. Incidentally, I think I'll stop drinking right now to work up a proper thirst.

But getting back to missing the ship. The one thing to remember when you miss your freighter is to be sure that you know an aviator who either owns a plane or has the nerve to steal one, to take you flying to catch up with said freighter. Have that kind of ace in reserve, and you're positively all right all the time.

There might be something in the regulations about taking a civilian in one of Uncle Sam's ships, so perhaps you better change this around and say that I took a regular airplane of the Inter-Island Company out here — but I didn't. No sir, we hopped over the Islands and such from Manila to Cebu in one of the latest fighting ships, a plane every bit as good as the one I fly back home, a darned sight better than the ones used by the Aviation Reserve Group, in fact.

But say, maybe the commandant wasn't kidding when he said I was being sworn into active duty and all that. Do you suppose you can collect flying pay for me for the trip? Time 121 minutes, it goes down in my log. See what you can do about it. Drinks are cheap in Manila, yet I sure did make a dent in the old budget, and still, on the other hand, it seemed as if every time I turned around some waiter-boy was there saying something about Major So-and-so or Captain This-and-that having sent him on a mission of mercy to a parched stranger.

But I forgot, you want to print this in your book, and the book's supposed to sell far and wide, and lots of people, including your austere self, don't approve of aviators drinking, or of drinking aviators. Just to show you that I am a real worker I've just interviewed Mrs. Grundy — you remember she got on in San Francisco? Sure, I know that's not her real name, but I can't remember what's on her ticket and Grundy describes her perfectly.

Mrs. Grundy has spouted statistics and guidebook facts at me for thirty minutes. Cebu it seems is an island and a town both. Once the King of Cebu reigned here and some Spaniard named Magellan came along and tried to convert him to Christianity, and the King called his bluff and joined the church and got pally with the Spanish gent — then asked the visitors to do a little helping in the current private war.

The brave boys from the other side of the world pitched in and, I believe, won the war, but the boss died and there's a monument to Mr. Magellan here ashore.

Then there's some schools and convents and some towns with swimming pools, and a club where you can bowl or play tennis and another that has a golf course; and along the Bay of Cebu here somewhere or other, yesterday, they loaded on some coconut oil, and this is the center of the copra industry, whatever that may be (something about flies), and there's a big cross on the main street of the town that is supposed to have another inside of it, said first cross having been placed there by this Magellan. You may recognize the chap's name when I say that he sailed around Cape Horn and had some straits named for him.

We got up early in Manila this morning and went down

to the water in one of those jack-rabbit cars, and were rowed out to an open ship, where, seated on two spare chutes, my head was enough over the edge so I had an excellent view of the scenery.

The take-off at dawn was swell and we soared into as beautiful a pure blue sky as you ever want to see. The pilot waved at a flock of islands down below, but he got so darned high I'm afraid I didn't get enough view to properly appreciate them.

Mrs. Grundy is still raving in the next cabin — she hasn't missed me, thinks I'm there yet. She's talking about tiny coral reefs bordered with tall palms and phosphorescent fish that follow the ship and little groups of huts on stilts and bamboo thickets ashore and natives cooking over open fires. Does that give you a good enough picture of the Philippines?

Anyway, we flew over here in less than no time, flat, and came down on the Bay alongside with all the passengers and half the crew lining the rail. I'll bet this is the first time anyone ever took an airplane to catch up with a freighter.

One thing about Cebu. They tell me there's a street where the sidewalk has a red tile roof, where it's cool. I can see the roof from here. It seems the Spaniards built the roof a couple of hundred years back or so. And the second bar on this street is reported as having plenty of ice. I'm going over to investigate and to mail this letter. I'll write you from Davao.

Yours,
CHUCK

CRUISING THE ISLANDS

Cebu, capital of the Island of Cebu, oldest European settlement in the Philippines, is a stop for almost every world-cruising freighter. You reach there after a beautiful sail through the sleepy minor southern islands, a sail that is enjoyable in spite of the tropical heat, present with considerable emphasis. A variety of drives back into the mountains are available for tourists who want to see unspoiled natives living as they have for hundreds of years; or you can stay in port and study the townfolk.

The difference between the clothes-crazy, "dressed up" Filipino you meet in California and the native Filipino is one of the things you'll find to talk about. The simply dressed poorer natives in their *camisas* are a far cry from the flamboyant shirts and checked suits one sees in the States. The *camisa* is a shirt-like upper garment that is unlike an American's shirt principally in the fact that the shirttails, front and back, are worn outside and over the trousers, rather than tucked away out of sight.

The fact that the barrooms are for Americans rather than for natives will also come in for considerable comment. The Filipinos are of Mohammedan origin — they seldom drink. You almost never see a native under the influence of liquor in the Islands. You may see him strut, but it will be a strut based on pride of education rather than on the false pride given by alcohol.

Cebu is not the only loading place on the Bay of Cebu. Freighters make various stops along the shores to pick up coconut oil in one quantity or another. The tanks are occasionally used for other products, fuel oil, molasses, etc. This necessitates cleaning before loading the fruit of the copra refinery. The scouring is a tedious task, usually done in Shanghai, where labor is cheap.

Any effort to describe the travels of a world-cruise freighter from Manila to the Dutch East Indies must either talk in complete generalities, or cover one specific voyage of one particular line. The state of the markets of the world, the supply of oil available for shipment, the number of boats seeking loads — all these factors govern your journeyings.

One port is much like another in some respects, for the freighter voyager at least. There is always an agent, or a shipper, usually an American. He is more than likely a little excited over the job of getting his wares off to the world, but he's also mighty glad to see new faces from home, and, according to all reports, very anxious to see that the visitor enjoys himself.

Cruising the Islands, you see many tiny Moro fishing villages; little groups of houses on bamboo stilts, straw-roofed homes perched over the water, very close together; small half-naked children playing in the shallows under the houses; men and women in bright colors, working on the *vintas* moored to the back posts.

The *vintas* are boats of hollowed logs with bamboo outriggers pushed by large, vividly colored sails. They come out to cluster around any ship hesitating in the southern islands.

The Moros are interesting people. Zamboanga, capital city of the Island of Mindanao, is called their home. It is a spot worth visiting for weeks, but you can see a lot in the few hours stop made by the average freighter. You may hear the natives singing at night, accompanying themselves on native instruments. The droning of their music has a soothing effect on those who are already under the spell of the South Sea moon.

Zamboanga is the place to buy souvenirs: black coral said to be found nowhere else, coral worked up into beads and in strange forms.

Whole chapters could be written on the things to buy on a world cruise. Every traveler has a different hotel gift-shop, or Bombay store, or other firm to recommend as "the only place to buy, my dear." Check with the people on your ship, with the friends you make ashore, then do the best you can. The finest salesmen in the world are those in the shops of the Orient. Their ability has been developed to a high degree, and in those towns visited by cruise liners they have learned that Americans are fair game and once in a while pay the first price asked.

The black coral makes up into interesting pieces of jewelry, but the wood carvings of the Igorots in the mountain provinces furnish the bits that most people can't resist. The Igorots are said to be the finest native wood carvers in the world, and they have turned to with a will to make bookends and such claptrap for the tourists — and some real (and good) stuff for their own use.

The six-foot ceremonial spoons for the traditional dog feasts that hang over a few American mantels are always good for ten minutes' conversation in any party, no matter how dull the group. First one must explain that the Igorots have abandoned the dog as the *pièce de résistance* for a dog feast — they prefer pork now, it seems. The ceremonial spoons are still used, however, and occasionally they're found by freighter voyagers, purchased after some bargaining, and brought home with great ceremony, prized even more than they were valued by the Igorot householder to whom they originally belonged.

Several shore excursions at Zamboanga are worth while. A trip to the San Ramon penal colony is stressed by the guidebooks and even recommended by tramp trippers. The mountains rise to a height of over five thousand feet behind the little city, and a short drive takes you into the country where small bright blue birds flit about through the bamboo thickets along the shores.

Iloilo, at the mouth of the river of the same name, on the Island of Panay, presents a slightly different appearance. Concrete houses stand alongside nipa shacks; cathedrals are next to hovels. Ships stopping here give passengers a chance to visit the sugar mills on the Island of Negros, near by. The mills are little different from those on a Cuban plantation. Glass-bottomed boats are available for hire at most of the stopping places in this section of the Philippines; the marine life is tremendously interesting.

Golf, bowling, trapshooting and swimming pools attract visitors at most of the clubs, and you'll find an American club in every port. *Quinielas,* a variant of tennis, is a game well worth watching. Tournaments are run at various times of the year; your club sponsor will get the details.

Maersk and several other lines operate ships from the United States to the Philippines, spending three to five weeks cruising these outports. Returning vacationists bring back glowing reports of the variety of the scenery, and the entertainment on ship and ashore.

COPRA

Copra! "Something about flies," Chuck calls it in his letter. Statisticians may say the Philippines produce ten million dollars' worth of copra; other experts will announce that the oil obtained from copra goes into soap, margarine and candles; but every Island traveler will understand Chuck's rapid reference. Where there is copra — there are the copra flies, maddening little devils that make the mills and shipping platforms torment for any but the hardened Asiatics.

Natives on the thousand little Islands live off their nut palm trees. The nut milk makes a most heady wine to say nothing of being most refreshing as is. Copra is the dried kernel of coconuts; the money crop of the tree owner. Natives split the nuts on an iron railroad spike fixed in a block of wood. If your native hasn't a railroad spike he tries his *bolo,* a long knife carried for help in eating, fighting and housebuilding. Dried in the sun the nut becomes the copra of commerce.

American refining companies have pressing plants at strategic points in the Islands. Alongside these refineries you'll see little coastwise vessels, usually dirty and always infested with the famous flies. The coast cruisers gather up the dried nuts, unloading hundred-pound bags of them on piers. Workers take out the husks and shovel the copra onto modern conveyors that carry it to the boiling vats. After boiling, the copra is pressed and the oil extracted. The oil resulting is the coconut oil one reads so much about in the advertisements. A thousand coconuts will yield five hundred pounds of copra, which, in turn, will deliver twenty to thirty gallons of coconut oil. The nuts offend nostrils all along the journey; they distribute smells as they are transported, and an overpowering odor spreads around the rending plants — an oily, musty, sickening, penetrating odor. Perhaps that's why coconut oil is so pure, so clean; all the smells are left behind in the process of production.

Nearly every freighter that visits the copra country brings a return cargo of coconut oil. Vagabond Voyagers will have every opportunity to see the progress of the nuts, from the monkeys' throwing them down out of the trees to the final shipment of the oil to some soap company in America.

DAVAO

As you cruise the Islands to Davao, the gang in the smoking-room cabinet begins to consolidate its information.

The serious-minded chap wonders if something can't be done about the numerous quack doctors one meets in this country. This will bring about some conversation from the man who believes in signs. He will report the hundreds of boards offering "cure-alls" for leprosy. Another will tell about the peddler of magic medicine who stands outside a Botica Company's store in Manila, which will bring on laughter while someone explains that *Botica* is the name for drugstore. Continuing this theme, the linguist will say that *tienda* means just any kind of store, and *Calla M. H. Del Pilar* is "Street in honor of M. H. Del Pilar."

This will possibly bring up a discussion of the streets that have been visited thus far — the shopping sections of various cities. In Kobe the famous shopping street is the *Motomatsi,* talked about by tourists the world over. In Manila, it's an entirely different sort of street, but just as famous, given over to American stores and known as the *Escolta.* Call the stores in the *Escolta* "American" and you get a wave of objections from some of the officers. "His Master's Voice, Ltd." is certainly a British concern, and you'll have to admit seeing their shops all over the world; but it's the old Victor Talking Machine Company trade mark and the phonographs look mighty like those we used to have at home. This point conceded, the patriotic American must back-water further when the Captain explains that most of the stores, even those with American names, and staffed by American clerks — yes, in American Manila — most of these stores are owned by Japanese concerns. The Japs are progressive no end, and if American names and clerks can sell more goods, that's the kind of clerks you'll find behind the counters of homey-sounding firms.

When you come into Davao you find the Japs again present, this time in another guise. Here they dominate the hemp industry. Hemp producing is the main business of the country roundabout, and hemp shipping the main business of the port.

Of course when you start to tell the smoking room gang about hemp, there'll be someone around to explain it all to you. Hemp is *not* grown in the Philippines. Hemp is made from flax or something. Sisal is a fibrous substance made from the abacá plant, which *does* come from Davao. Sisal is every bit as good as hemp, and originally was called "Manila hemp," just as you might call rice "Japanese bread" because rice is, in fact, the bread of Nippon.

It starts from Davao as "sisal"; if it gets to be "hemp" en route to the States, that's another story; but certainly the cracker-box cabinet will never let you misname the silky stuff that goes in to fill part of the empty hold-space — great golden bales of it.

Davao is now a stop for almost every world-cruise freighter. Japanese producers there still find it profitable to ship in British and Dutch vessels. As more Japanese cargo carriers are added to those of the seas, this trade, following the trend, will settle with the boats carrying the flag of old Nippon. Then, however, American trippers will be able to visit the abacá plantations in modern, fast, perfectly fitted Japanese freighters, while the world-cruise boats will find new ports and new cargo.

Automobile-drivers who speak a few words of English are available on the docks for an inspection trip to the plantations and mills. Signs in Spanish and Japanese are reminiscent of Canada with its French and English signs.

The modern wharves of Davao are not used by all vessels. Most world cruisers anchor about a mile offshore, where you have a beautiful view of the charming harbor; cargo comes out on lighters.

Go shopping at the open-front stores. Japanese, Chinese and native stores are side by side in the tiny town. The souvenirs will certainly have the stamp of being bought at a real foreign port, not labeled with the mark of being made solely for tourists. There's a club in Davao (and not a bad one), but for a real taste of the Orient, spend a night at one of the Japanese or Chinese hotels. Of course there's no real reason for staying on land, or for even eating a meal there if you arrive freighter class. Returning to ship for meals is the accepted thing, in fact you'll develop the habit of coming aboard at mealtime to meet the guests there for lunch. Agents, and other town connections of your vessel, usually manage to be around at chow time. Doubtless, they find the steward's British roast beef a pleasant variation from the standard, and enjoy the change as much as you like the variety of native food.

If you haven't seen a cockfight by this time, make a special effort to look one up, unless you are one of those careful souls who not only considers the raising of game chickens a cruel proposition, but wants to stop all the rest of the world from inciting to riot even so small an animal. Guidebooks and travel writers devote space to cricket fights in Japan, but returning travelers seem always to have missed them. Cockfights are different. You can hardly go ashore in a Philippine town without seeing the details of a fight arranged. Hundreds of natives seem to have no other occupation than the tending and fighting of a single steel-spurred rooster. You'll see them everywhere, much more frequently than even in the smaller inland towns of Cuba, the second greatest rooster battling nation.

The tourist who steps from the beaten track in the Islands is also likely to get a shot at Jolo, capital of the Island on which the late Sultan of Sulu made his home. The Sultan ruled a thousand square miles in the Sulu Archipelago. Jolo is a pearl center; you'll see natives diving for shell and may be somewhat harassed by salesmen until taken in hand by a ship's officer or the agent.

It is in this section of the world that you bless the inclination that sent you vagabonding on a vessel that not only visits out-of-the-way places but is prepared to cope with their climates. Your stateroom portholes or windows facing the front will be wide open. The breeze created by the progress of the boat will be a pleasing addition to the stir caused by the electric fans. No inside stateroom would be tenable without a modern cooling plant. (Maersk has a freighter in service to the Philippines with an air-conditioned salon.)

Bathers going over the side of the boat in minor ports in the Philippines must expect to attract an audience of natives. Naked boys may be seen at all points, but a white woman in a modern one-piece bathing suit is still something rare, and bound to draw onlookers, who will have strange tales to tell for months to come. Red hair draws a crowd. Platinum blondes almost cause riots of the curious. The farther you wander from the beaten track the more you realize how you are being observed while you look yourself. To the resident of Macassar, you are as rare and interesting a sight as the Malay is to you. Your sweater attracts his eye as you are drawn to write home about the elaborately figured cloth used to make his sarong; your Paris hat is as unique to him as his oval velvet cap is to you.

16 · The Chinese Ports

WARS disrupt the commerce of nations, pulling freighters off regular routes to supply belligerent nations with fuel and other necessities, closing ports to visiting ships, diverting traffic and trade, paralyzing business of all kinds. When the war clouds hung over Europe, freighter operators made rapid plans to keep their vessels out of the seas where the winged death of the airplane or the sudden menace of the submarine might damage valuable ships or delay valuable cargos. American ship operators reduced their sailings to the Orient by fifty per cent. in the first six months of the undeclared war in China; crews demanded bonus pay; insurance rates jumped; less cargo was available for neutral bottoms.

This chapter tells the story of the three weeks between the first and the second call at Manila, as you journey around the world on a freighter; the story of a three weeks that may be completely eliminated now from world cruise routes. Shanghai's famous Bund is scarred by shell and bomb, scenes are different today than they were when this was written. It is included here for the record, as it were, with perhaps a bit of a prayer that not too much change will come when the dove of peace finally rests in the Orient, a prayer that colorful China will still be there for American tourists to view and marvel over.

Manila to Shanghai

Steaming out of Manila Bay you pass close to Corregidor, the fortified mountain that is called the hush-hush pride of the American forces. The Second Officer, ever the gossip, entrances the group on deck with long tales of the mysterious underground passages where food and ammunition for many months of siege are said to be stored. Miles and miles of passageways, to hear him tell it, far exceeding even England's famous Gibraltar. You strain your eyes for the trolley road that is said to run from the landing to the top of the mountain, interested because someone has told you that no fare is charged on this government-operated transportation system used by officers, men, and occasional visitors. You can't see the trolley lights and are ready to denounce the story altogether, when the conversation turns to the sunsets of Manila.

The sunsets of Manila! They're to other sunsets as orchids are to ordinary flowers. Every tourist is urged to join the procession that goes up the length of Dewey Boulevard along the Bay, past the Manila Hotel. Every evening American Manila drives in parade, admiring the display of cloud and color — brilliant oranges, reds, blues and blacks, pile on pile of brilliancy, sunsets that can be compared with nothing but themselves; tonight's more beautiful than last night's, and tomorrow's likely to be more beautiful, still.

It's just a few days from Manila to Shanghai. Just long enough to hear all the stories of shore excursions, to assure the lady passenger that the large roll she saw balanced on the head of a Filipino woman is an umbrella, the smaller roll (about a foot in length) a cigar. This brings the cigar question before the smoking-room gang, now on deck at night working over the problems of the world.

"American cigar interests conspired to ruin our sales to the United States," the passenger who got aboard at Manila will tell you.

"American cigar people worried about the superiority of our cigars," he explains. "They had tremendous investments in tobacco and plantations in other sections of the world and the Philippines represented a real threat to their prosperity.

"So they flooded the United States with millions and millions of cheap, terrible, Manila cigars, which they sold at low rates, and successfully accomplished their plan of making 'Philippine' a synonym for 'rotten' to the cigar smokers in the States."

The good Manila cigars are the best smokes in the world, according to experts, and even the average smoker will appreciate the fine flavor of the tobacco in a really high class Philippine cigar — "but every effort to market them to American customers has run against a stone wall of prejudice," he added.

You cluck your tongue in sympathy and wonder if there are any smokes left of the four boxes that came as sailing gifts from Manila friends. You resolve to have several hundred sent home when you get back, and carefully write down tobacconists' addresses in your little black book. Two years later you puzzle over them and say "I wish I could remember which was the blonde." But now it all sounds very important, and the discussion among the smoking room cabinet waxes furious, one

EIGHT WORDS OF ENGLISH ARE ENOUGH FOR CONVERSATION

group taking the view that "There should be a law" and the other proclaiming that "No deception has been practiced on the public, so why condemn the manufacturer for protecting his own investments in Puerto Rico and Cuba?"

You make your plans for shore-going in Shanghai — the greatest seaport of all China, which, strangely enough, isn't Chinese at all. Shanghai is land ceded to England and other foreign countries. The control of the city is vested in the Municipal Council. There is the famous Shanghai Mixed Court, with a Chinese judge sitting beside a foreign jurist; the mixed court where sailors are brought when they get a drop too much.

You'll also learn now that you're coming to the point where "whites" are uniform. Half a dozen suits of duck might be enough for one man in Montgomery, Alabama, but if you're going to do any shore-going in China, six will not suffice.

Shanghai is the town to buy new tropical clothes. The tailors come aboard ship. Give them an old suit; they haven't any tape measures. Don't pay too much attention to the old story of the tailor who got an order for a dozen suits "just like this one" and brought them all back with neat patches in the seat — but, it's a good bit of local color, true or not. They'll deliver suits in a few hours, just as tailors do in Kingston, Jamaica.

You drop anchor near the pilot cutter in the broad entrance to the Yangtze river. The pilot comes over the side and you wait for the morning tide. You've heard of pirates in these waters and unless you're unlucky enough to have the tide flowing so that you go right in, the pilot has a chance to spin a few yarns. Golden-haired women and fat Chinese Mandarin-type pirates are featured in his tales. Pitched battles between lone foreigners with many guns and scores of badly armed pirates with a cheap pistol to every third man; battles between pirates and native craft; robberies of silver shipments; tales of lighthouses overcome and lights doused so that brave ships come to grief on stormy shores.

You're ready for the mystery of the Orient when at last the anchor is lifted and you get under way, churning up the mud of the river, the muddy sea that spreads as far as the eye can reach.

From the Yangtze you turn up the Whangpoo river, rice fields on one side, ships on the other. American ships of the Asiatic fleet, British cruisers, and Japanese destroyers are anchored all along the middle of the channel — the Yangtze Patrol that kept the peace after the Boxer revolution. High-pooped junks of medieval design go back and forth across the river, ragged coolie sailors hauling at the ropes. Flat lighters (like our old-time canal barges with oars) carry freight out and return empty for another load, half-clad coolies swaying monotonously at the sweeps.

Your ship creeps alongside the dock, a line is tossed ashore and the engines stop. You are barely moored before a work crew comes aboard, coolies ready to labor for ten or eleven cents a day, ready to paint fore and aft, clean the tanks and do all the other dirty work that has been saved against the arrival at a port of cheap labor. Longshoremen bosses in whites, all spick-and-span, come to announce the readiness of men to unload cargo. The deck officer mounts to his bridge posi-

tion overseeing all — and the ship's shore work commences.

You'll hurry ashore to a hotel for the night, trying
to get away from the noise of Shanghai's harbor. Posted
as to prices and argument, armed with a supply of
Shanghai money and educated a bit as to the varying
kinds of coin and their values, you come upon the
Bund from the launch landing. There's a ricksha line.
Coolies fight for the right to carry your bag. You'll look
at their hands and decide to hold it yourself and battle
them away.

The Bund at Shanghai! It's merely another street, a
rather wide street, built down on the water, facing the
river; a street of imposing office fronts. There are traffic
lights; it's as American as Broadway and still as Oriental
as you've dreamed it would be.

The tall Sikh policeman raps the heads of coolies who
venture past the line when the lights change — your
man-horse will pant and puff as if the burden of your
bulk is greater than expected. Swear at the ricksha boy
in any language. He soon abandons the pretense, re-
alizing it will bring no larger tip. He swings with a
flourish; you're at the Cathay Hotel.

Returning in any foreign port is always an adventure.
Harbors are sometimes dark, dull places. Where labor
is cheap, great flaring lights shine and loading or unloading goes on through the night, gangs of laborers
replacing one another at frequent intervals while straw
bosses act the rôle of Mississippi River mates with clubs
and profanity urging the lagging workers to greater
effort. But whether you return to a deserted ship, or to

one feverish with activity, there's the same feeling. You are going home. There's much to tell those who were unable to go ashore, much to ask those who are wiser in the ways of this strange land. There are things to talk about, things to remember, and, perhaps, things you prefer to forget.

The noise and bustle of each stop is distinctive. The smells of the East differ, yet all ports are alike in the petty annoyances of shore-going, the harassment of strange customs and the depressing feeling caused by some strange sights. Returning to ship you are always cheered as you near your sea home. The smells may follow you aboard. The noises may filter into your cabin, but once there, in the smoking room rimmed with familiar faces, you realize that sight-seeing, adventuring and wandering are better when shared with those who are close to you.

And you are close to these men with whom you journey. You have braved the winter blasts of the North American coast; you've enjoyed the play of the dolphins in the summer sea off Lower California; you've stood against the fury of a tropical storm and now you stand against alien sounds and alien sights. The wailing cry of your ricksha boy who seems to think his tip should have been bigger, and the whining importuning of the troupe of filthy beggars who trailed you to the water's edge to shout Oriental obscenities when you gave them neither a look nor a coin — all these are left behind when once the voice of *your* steward is heard offering midnight sandwiches.

The romance of the almond-eyed girl who smiled at you from a passing limousine, the white Russian refugee who told the story of her life across the cocktail table, the thrills that come from shore-going, all these will be amplified when they're shared with your "family" at home, aboard ship. Homecoming's always grand — it's grandest in a foreign port, returning to your freighter — the great boat that for you is a private yacht.

THE FIRST FAREWELL DINNER

Shanghai is either a port you love to leave — or one you hate to see behind. Be that as it may, unless a stop-over has been arranged, the cargo is loaded out and in and you're off to Hong Kong, down the Whangpoo River, out the yellow muddy Yangtze, off to the broad China sea.

You discover you have not been the only souvenir buyer in Shanghai. One passenger has a thousand copper coins — "they're cheaper than poker chips," he explains. What fun it will be to introduce these as markers at the Saturday night stud sessions in South Orange, N.J. How many times will the game be delayed while some incident of the trip is told?

The lady who shipped at Los Angeles has three bird cages. "Singing birds," she explains. Shanghai is the center of the bird market of the East. Bird societies and clubs draw members from the poorest and the most wealthy. Her birds won't sing; perhaps she bought them at the wrong store, perhaps they cannot understand her language. The Second Engineer is helpful. He brings from below decks a shy brown chap, one of the engine crew who once was a bird man. He frowns and points and jabbers. The straw boss who also accompanies the officer interprets in what passes for English, barely understandable to you.

"The birds are afraid," the officer re-translates. "This one is moulting." He points to the middle cage.

"There's a lot to the care of these birds," he confides to the passengers who have gathered in the shade of the bridge.

Much conversation results in the covers being put on the cages. The birds go below with the brown chap. The passenger will take them ashore at Hong Kong. You'll never learn if they sing.

The night before Hong Kong is reached — the second day from Shanghai — a "farewell dinner" is given. The lady of the birds nears the end of her journey. She is the first of the company to depart. You feel a sadness as you sit down to eat. You haven't paid much attention to the lady — she's kept more or less to herself on ship. You hardly remember her name — and now she is being torn from your midst. The lady and her birds — how you will miss the birds, those dear little things that sing so bravely! Well they haven't sung yet, but they would.

The champagne flows freely. The Captain beams at his flock from the armchair at the head of the table. The Chief Officer goes on deck for his watch, but somehow the dinner isn't over. The butler brings more dishes, and fresh glasses. Ice cream for dessert; ice cream and hot ginger bread cake, with chocolate sauce to pour over it all. Ginger cake because that is her favorite dessert, ice cream for the climate. The coffee cups are set, the butler pours liquors, this *is* a dinner!

The Captain raps for silence. The author stops the long story he was telling the gentleman from Biloxi.

The Skipper starts a speech. The Second Officer whispers in your ear: "The old man loves to talk on his feet."

"Hands across the sea . . . and friends must part . . . our fairest flowers in oriental bowers. . . ." You blink your eyes to catch what the speaker is driving at. Severe concentration and you're able to get the drift. Heavens! She's on her way to be married, going out to China to marry an officer in the English Navy! There's the explanation of why she wouldn't look at the stars the first day out of San Pedro; why she sat mooning, alone so much.

Poor girl, you feel for her. A nice little American stenographer or bookkeeper from Des Moines — off to marry some swashbuckling English lieutenant. But she seems happy: she's a little embarrassed by the Captain's flowery language, yet she eats it up. Every word will be a memory for her.

"The Captain gave me a dinner," years from now she'll tell her guests at tea. Her grandchildren will hear: "All the passengers were so nice, they gave me presents when I left the boat." Now you understand the Why of the gifts for the departing guest. You're attending a shower for a bride! She's up to reply, poor girl, she is embarrassed, but happy. . . . "And you must all come and visit us in our new little home on May Road, The Peak." You fumble for a pencil to write the number down. You may never come to Hong Kong again, but then who can tell? Once a traveler, always one. At least you can send her postal cards, perhaps she'll answer. "My friend, Mrs. Blank, in China," you'll casually say at home one day.

The men adjourn to the smoking room, the women

help the bride-to-be to admire her loot. The butler has already set out the basket with the nightly bottle array. A wicker tray with three-inch sides, each bottle firmly and snugly set so no sudden lurch will send it toppling.

Your Scotch is in the left-hand corner. You wave a hand and the boy lifts it from its little nest, he pours the first after-dinner drink. Farewell parties *are* fun, this one is certainly grand, a swell guy the Skipper, too bad the little girl is leaving us. "Steward, give everybody a drink from *my* bottle."

HONG KONG

Hong Kong the third morning . . . The city built on the "Island of Fragrant Streams"; an island, incidentally, that must have been named either with tongue in cheek, or before the advent of the British who now occupy Hong Kong or the Chinese who manage to make the streams fragrant in a sense not usually associated with the word. It's easier to write about India and not mention the dirt and filth than to talk of Shanghai, Hong Kong or any other Chinese port without discussing the noise and smells.

Hong Kong harbor is a rendezvous. On either side will be seen other freighters, world-circling vessels. They've been met in other ports and will be met again. The Chief Officer points out one of the famous Castle boats a short distance away and recalls his last view of her a month ago; then identifies the N.Y.K. ship that was berthed near by two trips previously.

Twenty thousand Japanese, Americans and Europeans live in the "foreign city" — merchants, soldiers and sailors. Eight hundred thousand Chinese live in the smaller "native city." The 20,000 stamp their pattern on the mass. Another foreign city in a foreign land, Hong Kong is still British. The shops are London stores, even though they may be Japanese-owned.

Native workmen come aboard. Coolies working feverishly pile cargo on lighters on either side. The noise and bustle compel a shore visit and you set off towards dock-end trying to decide between the drive to Repulse Bay with its beautiful scenery, and a trip by cable car and sedan chair to Victoria Peak, eighteen hundred feet above the river.

You return that night full of your sight-seeing, overwhelmed by the vision of Hong Kong harbor from the top of the mountain. The loading goes on steadily. The Second Officer recommends a hotel, you decide his advice is sound and take yourself back ashore.

While the traffic of the mysterious Orient flows in a never-ending stream on the streets outside, you sit on the edge of a modern bed in a hotel room that reminds one of the Jefferson in St. Louis and check things over. The trip's half completed; you've seen the dives of Panama, the Filipino native with his shirttail hanging out, Shanghai, and now Hong Kong.

You balance your budget. You're spending more for souvenirs than you planned . . . but at that your living expenses have been less than at home . . . you've eaten strange food . . . met men of races far different from your own . . . you've traveled, yet, during all your journeys, your home has traveled with you. To date the discomforts have been minor . . . the costs low . . . and you have seen more than you expected . . . and you are barely halfway around.

You take out the list the Skipper penciled that morning and check off the ports to come. Three little places in the Philippines — a special stop at Messina in Italy in addition to Naples. And, tomorrow you will go across to Macao. The "City of Evil," the books call it. Macao, pioneer European settlement in the East, the city where the devil goes for his vacation! The gambling houses, fan tan and what have you; Organized Vice and the disorganized victims!

Freighter folk find a chance to slip into a town like Macao without the accompaniment of a brass band. When you stop from the steamer after your three-hour trip in sheltered waters, you know that Macao accepts you as an average run-of-the-mine visitor, one to be robbed perhaps, but also one who may be as strong and as fierce as any resident. When evil rears its head for *de luxe* liner cruisers, there's always the suspicion that the entertainment director has arranged this view of a den of iniquity for the sole purpose of providing a safe, synthetic Horror Hour for the lads from Sutton Place and the banker from Boston.

Take a day and see about this pioneer European settlement in the East — the round trip is only five Hong Kong dollars. Side excursions to Canton often tempt the traveler at Hong Kong, while many world tourists stop-over here or at Shanghai for a visit to Japan if their boat does not call at some Japanese ports.

———

The charm of Vagabonding often lies in the bypaths. Here's a letter that tells of a famous bypath, not as famous around the world as the Thames, but world-famous none the less: —

Shanghai.

DEAR LARRY: —

You haven't been vagabond voyaging until you go up the Yangtze river; until you take the Butterfield Blue Funnel boat as far as Ichang, and then transfer to a river launch. I have a swell photograph of the old chap who runs this launch, but I can't remember either his name or the name that was more or less painted on the ship itself.

He is a real character, stands on deck with a glass of whisky in one hand, and a length of pipe in the other. When we get into the gorges he beats on an iron pipe running down to the boiler room; his tattoo is a warning to the toilers below to pour on, as we are in the rapids and need every ounce of steam possible. The cliffs tower up two thousand feet on either side of you here; the current is the strongest I have ever breasted in a launch.

Boats going up must give way to boats coming downstream. The chaps going down are usually practically out of control, tossed about by the current.

At the end of the launch run you take a sedan chair over the mountains; on the trail you pass numerous prayer wheels. It's odd to see a heavily laden coolie squat down beside a prayer wheel, give it a turn, then rise and trot on his way with his burden.

Coming back down the river one of the missionaries from the Royal Society wanted to disembark. These missionaries ride down with the coolies, dress like them, live with them — they must be on the level with their religion. Anyway, the missionary wanted to go ashore at some unpronounceable village. A sampan came out to tie up to our boat to take the shore-goers off, and there was some confusion. Most of the Chinese are good sailors, but occasionally there's one who is all thumbs. Took us quite a while to make the transfer. We drifted well onto ten miles. The chap with me said the whole day would be consumed in poling that sampan against the current the ten miles back to the landing.

The river boats tie up at night — no channel lights. In the evening the natives get out their opium pipes and the air is filled with the sweet sickish odor of the smoke of the poppy. You have to keep the ports closed while the boat is under way, the rapids throw spray or something. The smell of the natives drives you out on deck, but the sights of the river are well worth watching.

Until you've been a deck passenger on the Yangtze, you haven't actually Vagabond Vacationed. Come try it some time.

Yours truly,

FRANK

17 · Crossing the Line

CROSSING the Equator is fun on a freighter — if your ship has a Chief Steward who takes his passenger entertainment seriously. If the Chief is one of those chaps who looks on you as an excuse to sit down and have another "spot" as soon as the sun comes over the mythical yardarm; or if he is a methodical Scot who spends his hours checking storeroom records to be sure that not one single bottle of "tonic" (sweet soda to you) has gone without a chit to replace it — well, of course you may pass over the line that marks the northern half of the world from the southern half and only celebrate the occasion with another drink. But if you have a Chief who has been trained in the Cunard service, or a Captain who thinks that the ancient traditions of the sea should be upheld — then you meet the King of the Seas, and attend a trial under His Majesty's rule.

The Equator is passed; all passengers who have never made the crossing before are mysteriously served with a "summons" calling for their attendance before the Court of King Neptune. Ship chandlers in Hong Kong keep these forms on hand, and some of the papers are weird indeed, while others are as legal-looking as Morris Plan documents.

Wise passengers immediately don their oldest clothes; or even take refuge in bathing suits and prepare for the trial.

The summoned prisoners gather on deck at the appointed hour. Up the side of the ship on a ladder that certainly wasn't there yesterday, comes elaborately costumed King Neptune, trident in hand. He is followed by the retinue that forms his court. The King oftentimes will be the Skipper himself. Old-time officers, who look on the traditional ceremony as one of the rights of all line crossers, take on the robes and go through the horseplay with great dignity. Occasionally, however, a Captain of the newer school will be found; then the Skipper, like a wise gent indeed, will turn the job of Neptuning over to one of the Mates.

Accompanying the King will be his wife, usually the rosy-cheeked youngest of the cadet boys. Bailiffs and other attendants accompany him, until the poor prisoners wonder if perhaps they shouldn't have stuck close to their cabins to avoid what begins to look like quite an ordeal. Jack Tar is a rough boy when he plays rough, and here the implements assembled begin to make it look as if this would be sailor play as is sailor play.

A whitewash brush, six inches wide, is used to apply the lather; the King unlimbers a wooden razor from two to four feet long (Chips has spent several hours in its manufacture). The first victim mounts to the "barber" chair, which is perched insecurely on a plank across the swimming tank. Flour and water, or whitewash, makes the best lather. Only in the rarest cases and where the closest friendship reigns between passenger and officers will there be a basket of feathers to add to the lather, to give the sea-going equivalent of tar and feathers, but the lather is there, feathers or no.

On goes the white stuff with a flourish. The King stands by importantly with his razor, his assistants wield

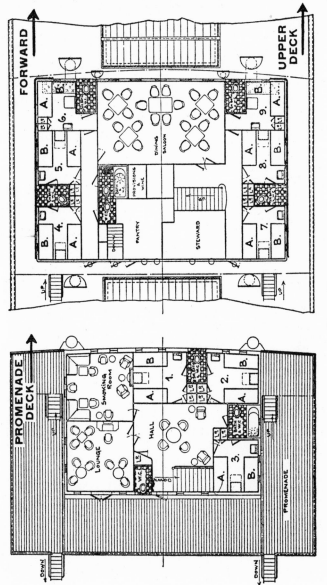

DECK PLANS

the whitewash regardless of yells. The King begins to scrape off the accumulation and the passenger settles down to enduring things, when suddenly the chair slips and into the tank goes the neophyte. Rescued and dried off, he joins the crowd while the next victim mounts to the slaughter.

The ceremonies will be as elaborate as the imagination of those handling the arrangements; but at the end tradition calls for the Ruler himself climbing up for his shave, winding up with a ducking in the pool.

Certificates, dated from Davy Jones's locker and attested to by the ship's officers, are then presented to those who have not been able to produce the papers to prove previous line crossings. At last someone suggests a drink. The crossing of the line has been properly recognized; you have another souvenir of your circumnavigation.

Not every freighter captain will stage such a party. Sometimes the Captain and the Chief Steward will consider this horseplay too rough for their passengers and the line will slip by without recognition, but where tradition holds forth at its best, there you will find King Neptune clambering over the side, watched by everyone who can escape from his duties of the moment.

THE DUTCH EAST INDIES

Prince, Silver, Blue Funnel and other freighters on the world circuit stop at Macassar, on the island of Celebes.

Here you'll have your first chance at the famous *reistaffel* or "rice table" of the Dutch East Indies —

that is, you'll have the chance at the Club provided there's four hours to devote to eating. The *reistaffel* is quite something. Parades of waiters bearing dishes in either hand come for hours, and the doughty diners wade in and do tremendous damage to the food supply, yet it never seems to diminish.

Shore visitors will bring back stories of their first look at a Dutch colony. As a rule they'll endorse heartily the policy that refuses to permit many missionaries to come to wean the natives from their ancient religions and modes of life. Bali, the unspoiled Island of the South Seas, claims much of its charm because of this strict policy. Without the Christianizing influence of the white man, according to Bali visitors, the natives also escape a great many of the demoralizing influences the white man brings in his wake.

Batiks are the buy here, but there's also much fine silver and delicately carved jade and even seashells done with designs that will always seem different no matter where you compare them.

Macassar is only three days from Davao. From Davao back to Cebu is only a couple of days, from Macassar on to Sourabaya only two more days. You're slipping from port to port, one after another, each presenting a different facet of the life of the East. Like a cruise in the Little West Indies on one of the Netherland Line boats you're seeing new waterfronts every few days, meeting new folks ashore, yet carrying with you the "goodly company of friends" who journey with your vessel.

There's not too much time between stops to engage in the occupation of watching the birds astern. With harbors near each other and distances between ports less, you count many more birds than followed your wake across the great Pacific. They fly out from islands just below the horizon, sail along behind for hours, suddenly pounding on some scrap stirred up by your propellers. They come from the sky, it seems, follow for a time, then as silently and rapidly slip over the edge of the world and are seen no more while others take up the watch.

There's much to see overside, too. Strange shapes in the waters in harbors, strange changing sights in the seas.

The daily after-leaving-port conferences come so frequently you find yourself talking about Davao when Sourabaya's the port just behind. There's much to discuss and you begin to realize what a store of memories you are piling up, the thousand little things in your journey that will come to mind when you return to the work-a-day world you left for this venture into Vagabondia.

Sourabaya is the chief city of Java: a harbor lined with metal godowns (warehouses to you), tanks of molasses and Javanese betel-nut-chewing natives. Individually the natives are not as huge as the godowns loaded with rubber, but black teeth and ugly red stains on lips, left by the betel nuts, so mark them that no description of the view from the ship's rail would be complete without mentioning the friendly Javanese. Two or more days in Sourabaya give the tramp tripper an opportunity to see the country around. You may have a little trouble getting your money changed to suit yourself, but it all works out and there's always the Captain and the local agent to help you, if you do need assistance.

This friendly co-operation in itself is another of the

charms of freighter voyaging. Bank representatives may come aboard to aid the passengers on the *Columbus;* the Gentleman from Cooks may meet every train and guide the wayfarer from point to point for the journey in Europe or Egypt; but in freighter travel you're expected to look out for yourself, and the customs officials seem to think you are capable of handling your own affairs. Ask for information and it will be given, ask for help and you'll find more than enough guides, or helpers, ready to steer you through the process of bargaining with a shopkeeper, or to settle on the proper method of packing souvenirs — but this aid is not forced. There is no MUST in freighter travel, nothing that simply *has* to be seen; that is, provided you're willing to make an exception of that cabaret in Curaçao the Chief Officer has been talking about for a month. The "things you must see" are the things that interest men who journey afar; you'll find them even more interesting than the Pyramids or the iceless slide your sled goes down at Madeira.

Sourabaya to Samarang is only another day. Samarang lies at the green foothills of a range of volcanic mountains. You anchor in the stream and your first visitors are the ever-present bumboats, these unlike any you've seen before. Bumboats around the world are of a pattern, yet all different. Bright-colored sails, or flour sacks spread on sticks to catch the air, black, brown or yellow owners, enterprising businessmen seeking trade, they are part of the nations you visit.

Every arrival of a freighter brings salesmen of the sea, who travel far to be the first to greet an incoming vessel. From the harbors of the East Indies to those of the

West Indies travelers will find merchants ready to come to them, if they are not inclined to venture ashore. Without leaving the deck of your sea-going home you can buy souvenirs, native foods and fruits, and enough variety of doodads and dingbats to stock a novelty store. Because sailors are good customers, jewelry merchants who carry their stock of trade in a single box come aboard at most Oriental ports. As a rule they are accompanied by a native helper who carries the case while the merchant stalks proudly ahead.

Sailors always buy; their love of home prompts them to bring back some taste of the far countries they visit. Stick on the decks of your own ship if you like; you still will bring home souvenirs.

Two days in Batavia are shown on the schedule of the Silver Lines, but don't plan the time there too carefully in advance. If the cargo is there to load, you may stay three days; and if you're running a little behind schedule, say a week, you may hustle through in little more than a day.

Freighters don't get very excited over dates apparently, yet when you add up the figures you find that in some fashion you're getting into each port practically on time, and when the long journey across the Atlantic ends, you hit Halifax on the nose, to use radio parlance for being exactly on time. As a matter of fact on the world circuit you usually land in Batavia a day late because of added stops at way ports, but the time's made up somewhere before long; the chief turns his engines over a little faster, and the shore crews work a little harder to get the old cargo off and new products in below decks for the journey back to America.

Telok Betong, on the southeast tip of Sumatra, is now a regular stop for Prince and Silver. Blue Funnel and Barber do not list it, but they often land when there's cargo of palm oil to be moved in a hurry. Turning from Batavia you sail to Telok through more tropical islands, dark low shadows. An overnight journey and you tie up at the docks of Pandjang, passing under the shadow of a vast volcanic mountain — Krakatoa.

A few hours ashore while the pumps fill tanks with coconut oil, and you return to your ship, having had a vision of another real community off the beaten track, of natives who live without regard for the rest of the world. The jungle comes down almost to the water's edge, it crawls into the outskirts of little settlements, right to the back door of Telok Betong itself.

Singapore is next. Singapore of the Raffles Hotel, Singapore of the native junks and sampans. Singapore, the crossroads of the Orient.

SINGAPORE HAS AN AIR — A LETTER

DEAR LARRY: —

It's true what they say about Singapore. It has an air. One you can really notice, miles out at sea. It's still a city of open sewers — except in the very few blocks around St. Andrew's Cathedral and the greens where Whites play rugby in the cool of the evening.

It also has another air — one that you don't smell. The air of a crossroads city where the freighter traveler, if he follows the usual round-the-world sequence, comes on his most varied assortment of his fellow beings. You see Chinamen, Malays, and the stranger, darker-faced folk who have come over from India, wearing their long hair piled up on their heads and held with ornate tortoise combs, and the white- (? — dirty white, anyway) robed white-whiskered patriarchs with the air of priests.

Singapore, in spite of the fact that it's the big city of the Malay peninsula, is really a Chinese city. It sticks in my memory that the population figures given me were 800,000 — of which 700,000 were Chinese, 50,000 were Tamils and East Indians, 25,000 were English, the rest 5,000 miscellaneous whites, Japs, etc., and 20,000 Malays, most of whom are employed as chauffeurs for the taxis that are auxiliaries for the rickshas, which are thickest in Singapore, carrying heavier loads than they do in China.

Your freightboat passenger misses a part of the spectacular entry to Singapore. You rarely anchor in the wide, interesting harbor where Chinese junks with great colored sails ride almost next to round-the-world liners and world-cruise floating palaces. The liner customers land right in the center of the city, climbing out on to cement walks into the most mixedup collection of business men, coolies, black, brown, yellow and whites to be found in any place in the world. Freighters go around to the back door.

My cargo boat today anchored miles away from the city center near the railroad yards; out where the cobbled streets are not much unlike those of the Embarcadero in San Francisco. Railroad yards here are like home, except that the freight cars are usually a coral pink, and somewhat reminiscent of the car graveyards of Kansas City because no one ever seems to be loading or unloading them, and they look so abandoned in their ancient coat of faded color.

But it doesn't make much difference where you anchor, you can always come downtown and look over the railings of one of the many bridges, and see the curving banks of the Singapore River lined with thousand after thousand of the houseboats and little river craft that are both homes and freight transports for a large percentage of the city's inhabitants.

The "white" part of Singapore is green, with hills in the background, and with really fine homes poking out here and there from a scenic vantage point. Many of the most European-looking homes are the residences of the rich Chinese, who have made their fortunes in the city.

Of course when you come out here you'll pay a visit to the famous Raffles hotel, but if you stay overnight off the ship, remember to get your passport stamped by the Chief of Police. The English are strict about keeping track of all residents, even though they be but one-day visitors. Be sure to report to the Chief's office when you leave. I don't know what would happen, but report there anyway. No hotel will dare give a room to a guest who has not left his passport with the room clerk, properly signed by the Singapore Chief — who is, I hear, a swell guy, entertaining visitors who come with proper letters of introduction.

The Raffles has an American jazz band playing dance concerts whenever there is an American ship in port. And always the wide, roofed, but not otherwise enclosed veranda is popular for groups who wish to sit around the small tables and drink their stengas. (Stenga is really a small whisky-soda, with a name that is corrupted from the Malay word stengah, which means half, and which is more generally called "stinger" than stengah, and almost never correctly pronounced.)

The Raffles faces right on the bay. The other leading hotel, and the one preferred by the English and more pompous visitors, is the Europa, which has no bathtubs, but has a better dining room, and gets a bigger play from the swankier patrons — like the carriage trade department stores at home. Then, too, there is another and newer hotel, the name of which I can't remember. Seems to me it's the Half Moon. Anyway, it's out of the city several miles, has an open swimming pool, and more of the country club manner.

Singapore is an important place for members of our crew, because Singapore and New York are the two places at which they are always certain to get mail, including letters from home, newspapers and occasionally Christmas boxes and birthday gifts that may miss by a couple of months the anniversaries they were intended to celebrate.

There are so many things to do in Singapore (usually a five-day freighter stop) that I haven't had time to just aimlessly prowl the more picturesque streets as much as I'd like. There are rubber plantations to be seen, but it's more interesting to lounge along the waterfront where the latex, looking like blankets, and folded like them, is sold by the Arabian, Indian or Chinese jobbers whose open-front stores line four or five blocks of one part of the waterfront.

Three of our passengers disembarked at Singapore, to travel inland by car to Kuala Lumpur, the capital (which has streets paved with rubber) and then on to Port Swettenham, which is the rubber-loading stop just beyond Singapore. There they'll join us again.

Singapore's zoo is well worth anybody's seeing. In the first place it has a really fine collection of birds and animals, including the rare Imperial pigeons, now almost extinct, and not to be killed (under severe penalty) in their native haunts in New Guinea. But the really interesting part of the zoo is the ramshackle old cages and sometimes the lack of any cages at all. Just two strands of barbed wire will enclose a couple of quiet tapirs, and anyone who wishes may climb over and pet the critters, provided they are inclined to stand still and permit it. I had a grand time with the camera, getting in and making close-ups.

Yours,

HAL

THE MALAY PENINSULA

Port Swettenham, Belawan-Deli, and Penang are the ports your world-cruise freighter seeks after a rest in Singapore, if you're aboard a Prince or Silver boat. Barber follows the same route, but the Blue Funnel ships cut across directly to Sumatra and then up to Penang.

Klang's the town that lies seven miles from Port Swettenham. A visit to Klang gives the traveler his first real introduction to the caste-marked children of India; smears on foreheads indicate family rankings.

Aboard ship you've noticed the caste system at work. The Portuguese Catholic native "Gawnee" who is the passengers' steward on your ship is assisted by a toilet-cleaner who undoubtedly has a name, but not one you can pronounce. The cleaner is of such a low caste that the Gawnee couldn't be induced to speak to him, not even to give a direct order.

It is funny to see the steward's look of pained contempt for a passenger who lowers himself by talking with the man who prepares the baths and cleans the bathrooms.

The old rhyme of Boston, with its "Lowells speak only to Cabots and the Cabots speak only to God" refers to a very minor caste system. In India there are hundreds of classifications, hundreds of divisions to set the people apart. Some groups may speak occasionally, but the greater the division between them, the more likely it is that even orders will be transmitted through a second or perhaps a third party.

At Port Swettenham you anchor in the stream. Strange

native boats with husky oarsmen come out to pick up casual shore-goers; the lighters come alongside to put aboard cargo. The Third Engineer takes a phonograph ashore with him — a box affair, winds with a crank. He bought it for five dollars from a secondhand dealer in Brooklyn. Out here it will bring considerably more if the Engineer is lucky enough to find someone able to pay him.

Radio's not much good in these waters. Programs, if any, are dull and badly cut up by static. Phonograph shops are everywhere though, the familiar plaster-of-Paris dog cocking an ear to a horn greets you from the center of every shopping district.

You walk along dark streets, through alleys that seem only as wide as a fat man and actually are no broader than the space required for the passage of a well-loaded pack mule. You look at forbidding exteriors, wondering what manner of people have their lives behind these doors. Strange weird music as from the pipes of Pan filters through to the street. You have visions of houris, slaves guarding the women of some fierce master, of dancing girls parading before their owners' guests. You hear weird sounds, wilder music — the native East!

And then you recall another afternoon, another early evening in another land. Jackson Heights and dusk. Open windows on great apartments; open windows on little homes; men hurrying by to the evening meal, returning from the day's labors.

Through the windows came sounds; through all the windows came similar sounds; there's music in the air — "Amos 'n' Andy," Boake Carter. The suburban quiet has been destroyed, radio has brought a furor of sound to shatter the peace of the home life of so many millions.

You speculate on the difference; compare the Orient with the Occident; and then remember the Third Engineer and his phonograph. You listen more attentively to the music, faint yet clear. You identify the tune. The Engineer had it on a record; he took it ashore to demonstrate; Ben Bernie and all the lads!

You walk a few steps and music is heard again — from another high, barred, dark door. Again and again the scratchy sounds greet your ears. His Master's Voice has made a new bedlam. You praise your lucky stars you have been able to start your circumnavigation tour before radio becomes as commonplace in Medan as it is in Oak Park.

Another overnight journey and your vessel hesitates at the lightship at the mouth of Belawan River. A pilot comes aboard and you sail directly toward the concrete riverbank. You wonder why the pilot; then shrug your shoulders as you remember the efficiency and inefficiency of pilots in general, the West Indian natives who act as harbor guides in the Indies, the romantic yarns spun by the men on the pilot's home-ship at Sandy Hook, New York harbor. You decide they are necessary, not so much for the guiding of your ship — you have complete confidence in the Skipper — but because they bring the first touch of a new country. They're the Greeters of the world. "The pilot is aboard" the cadet reports. Somehow that seems to give an assurance to timid passengers. You know that soon there will be a new set of sights unrolled before your eyes, new pictures for your entertainment and information. You stroll out on deck to get a glimpse of him. He is the first sample of the new land.

There's no tug to help you here at Belawan. With much shouting and hauling this way and that the vessel is moored to the concrete pier.

Here, with the steaming jungle a bare gunshot from the side of your ship, you get the full force of old Sol. The heat does not push against you as it did in the Philippines, but the glare of the sunlight gives every-thing an unrealness that reminds one of the brilliancy of klieg lights in a Quickie motion-picture studio.

Ice is rare in these ports. Sailors aboard ships like yours with its ever-working ice machine take scant time ashore. The cool drinks of the tropics may be available for travelers, but it's easiest to find them back on your sea home.

This touch of India prepares you for the stops to come, the turbaned merchants in their little open stalls being a pleasing variant from the rotund Chinamen and sleek Japs of other days.

Indian brass, enamelwork, and gold-decorated lacquer boxes are recommended for gifts for those at home, pro-vided there's any money left after your forays in Singapore.

There's a snake temple at Penang said to be worth seeing, and unless someone's dragged you to the Botanical Gardens at San Francisco and spoiled you for all artificial growing of strange plants, you'll enjoy every minute of a visit to Penang's famous home of strange and weird blooms and trees.

The tin pigs loaded at Penang, you're off for Colombo

and Port Said, the wickedest city of the world (if sailors are to be believed!).

PENANG — A LETTER

DEAR LARRY: —

Penang's the place that makes a freighter vessel into a merry-go-round.

Here in the open stream we've been anchored a day and a night, and every time the tide changes our vessel does a loop-the-loop around the anchors and we face the incoming stream. I asked the Skipper why we didn't drop anchors fore and aft, and let the darned current change whenever it pleased, but somehow there's something or other about what a position we'd be in if the anchor chains broke and we were adrift with our propellers to the current. It all sounds very goofy to me, but then you'd never expect a schoolteacher from Springfield to understand the niceties of navigation anyway.

Penang itself is an island — connected by a bridge to the mainland. The most important thing on the Island is the post office; the clearing house for most mail to and from the Orient. How that building does dominate the architectural layout of the town — reminds one of the ferry house at San Francisco or of the Leviathan with a dozen tugs around alongside. We got lots of mail here — and the postage stamps are so pretty we mailed cards to everyone we could remember.

The jungle comes down to the water-edge, reminds me of Panama, only if possible, it is denser and looks more forbidding. We're loading tin, shining pigs of it, about three hundred pounds' weight compressed into a twenty-inch bar.

We all went ashore, there's a very good hotel here, believe it or not, and the lobby is filled with big businessmen, rubber and tin operators.

. Half this town is Chinese, the other side is devoted to darker natives. The streets are very narrow, sometimes I wonder if the people who planned them had ever visioned Kate Smith — she'd certainly have trouble navigating some of the turns. The little open-front shops come one after another — watch out you don't spend too much.

The houses on the hill are lighted at night. The lights shine through the haze. It's pleasant to look at them from the peace of your ship.

Colombo next — then around Africa and home — my trip's more than half over. I wish it were just starting.

Regards,
ROSE

18 · The Indian Ocean

FOUR days across the Indian Ocean to Colombo. The Supercargo who joined us in China leaves the ship now. The rubber has been loaded; it was his job to see that everything went right with the stowing of the raw product scheduled to be made into auto tires. The Captain laughs and points out that some day, perhaps, this same rubber will make another trip on this vessel.

"We take raw rubber to the States," he said. "There it's made into tires, and whizzes around the concrete roads for a time; then the tires wear out, and are junked, and baled all up and shipped to Japan." Old rubber, old iron, old metal, make up cargoes for the Orient constantly, you'll discover. Ask someone what Japan can do with the junk of the world, and the Skipper's auto tire story answers your question in part anyway.

"Factories in Japan take the casings," the Captain explains, "flatten them out, push them through machines, add on straps, and — presto! we have a cargo of slippers with rubber-grilled soles all ready to carry back to the United States again."

The Supercargo decides to ride over to Colombo with us. He is being advanced by the Company or something. The farewell dinner's set for the last day out.

Every departing passenger or officer is missed by those left behind. The little life of a ship is a full one. Rudely yanking one of our companions from our midst leaves a gap. The smoking room cabinet will un-

doubtedly continue to gather nightly for discussion of
world problems, but somehow it won't seem quite the
same. This little chap with his accent and mannerisms
is a very important part of every argument. No matter
what the subject, he can produce food for thought. His
facts at times are slightly awry, often he lightly hurdles
the fence and jumps from one position on a subject to
the absolute opposite, but he always has an opinion, and
always expresses it.

Remembering bitter, lengthy disputes where he came
out on top, you feel a sense of relief that this master of
after-dinner debate will no longer be present to confound you with his unanswerable pronouncements;
yet you see him leave with a distinct feeling of regret,
too. What price victory, without an antagonist worthy
of the name?

Four days across the Indian Ocean. The map shows
Calcutta up in the far end of the sea; the Continent of
Asia is being left behind. Colombo is on an island, the
Island of Ceylon. You've made your last contact with
the Yellow Continent. Other freighters on other routes
will sail into Indian harbors; other passengers on other
vessels will see the ice towers of Calcutta, see the river
with its strange "Ghats" where the dead are cremated.
You give a sigh of regret for the sights missed, the
strange places yet unexplored. You can't see everything,
you decide, but then is born a resolution that this is
not the end of your voyaging. Another year there must
be another voyage and you will take a new route, one
that visits different ports. There's so much to see in the
world.

The smoking-room gang gets into hot debate over the

advantages of sight-seeing, discussing whether or not the true traveler is one who lives what he sees, or one who carries his own life with him. The Englishman who dresses for dinner in the heart of Africa and the Native Prince who carries his seventeen wives to London on his once-in-a-lifetime visit to the King are both discussed. A verdict is arrived at, a verdict that compromises. "Carry your own life along," the Supercargo explains, "take real English foods on a real English boat, just as we do here. But, with your floating home to rest in safely, go out and see the different lives of all the world."

A comparison of the habits of nations brings a strange summation from our sage: "The Taj Mahal, beautiful token of the love of a Rajah, is no different from the stately monuments built in American graveyards." The comparison is apt. It almost makes up for not visiting India this trip, for not being able to go inland to Delhi, not being able to see the Taj Mahal in the deserted city of Fatehpur Sikri.

The Monsoon, about which so much has been written, is found on the Arabian Sea. For six months in the year it comes down from the desert. The Monsoon is not just another name for a heavy wind. The Monsoon is the Monsoon. From October to April it blows across gently, not oppressive or depressing. The balance of the year it pours over you, heavy with moisture; hot blasts that make you wonder what joys at journey's end can compensate for the toil and struggle of the passage.

Into the roads at Colombo, and anchored to the designated buoy, the ship rapidly begins to load more cargo from lighters that come alongside. They're dif-

ferent, these harbor ferries: propelled by patchwork
sails instead of sweeps, lighters with strange faces and
figures aboard, the men black, bare to the waists, wearing gay turbans and brilliant sarongs. . . . A new colorful picture for your memories.

Merchants ashore here are hungry for business. What
a harvest they must reap when the *Reliance* makes her
annual visit! Watch that you are not torn limb from
limb by rival guides or runners for stores of one sort
or another. Fantastic fruits are brought back by returning shore-goers. The Skipper makes a long speech
on what a European should not eat in this country. You
listen, then promptly sample everything offered.

There's talk of an excursion to the tea plantations (I
wonder why they call them "gardens"?). A group may
take the six hour trip to Kandy with its famous
elephants.

Every tourist buys a carved teak wood or ivory
elephant (or gets gypped with some phoney imitation).
Officers on ships usually have commissions from friends
at home to buy more elephants. A mention of Colombo
without talking about the carved elephants would be
like describing Hollywood and neglecting the movies.

Fierce-looking merchants pouring priceless fortunes
in jewels and gems from torn and tattered rags that
look like oversized handkerchiefs; men wearing tortoise-
shell combs in their hair; snake-charmers on street-
corners circled by little crowds; curio shops and fortune-
tellers in profusion; bull carts, long lines of them,
creaking down the road bringing goods to the warehouses, or hauling them away; brightly clothed natives,
black faces shining above flamboyant colors; beggars

and bartenders — that is Colombo, port of the Island of Ceylon, according to the giant sign you see from your deck chair, the home of "Lipton's Tea, drunk in homes all over the world."

Fourteen Days to Suez

There comes a point in every journey when you feel as if perhaps it has been prolonged too much. On the *Chief* westward from Chicago to Albuquerque one always felt time drag, the hours moved too slowly. Many travelers have said that the airlines tried to fly over the trains in that territory as often as possible to inspire passengers when they were the most dissatisfied with the rails.

When you plan your world voyage the journey from Davao to New York seems easily half of the trip, but after you roll off Macassar, Sourabaya, Samarang, Batavia, Telok Betong, Singapore, Port Swettenham, Belawan, Penang, and Colombo, you feel that the last half is practically over. Only a little farther you say: Port Said, Naples, and then Halifax and home. But a check of the calendar reveals a different story. One month after your departure from Colombo you arrive in Boston. One fourth of your world journey from America is yet to be covered. Even on the map it hardly seems far, but when you're aboard ship it's quite a journey.

You're a bit dissatisfied with the world to begin with. The unending Monsoon's no encourager of good nature. The sand that comes sifting down from Arabia makes the Gulf of Aden no more pleasant than the Arabian Sea has been for five or six days past. It is only when you come through the Bab el Mandeb Straits from the Gulf of Aden into the Red Sea that you begin to enjoy this long stretch of ocean voyaging. If you're aboard a Blue Funnel vessel and make a stop at Cochin, India, you're lucky, not only for another strange port, but for a break in the routine. If you happen by in the season when the wind is from the right direction the monotony is not so pronounced, but unless you are completely able to enjoy yourself regardless of all discomforts, unless you have become so imbued with the thrill of Vagabond Voyaging that nothing matters, here you find the low of the circle tour.

A day, or two, perhaps only an hour, but only the most stouthearted can make the passage of the Indian Ocean and the Red Sea without being thrown into a speculative mood; without wondering if the cake is worth the candle; wondering if after all the wise ones are not those who stay at home; if perhaps explorers aren't silly folk.

The depression thrown off, you again enter into the spirit of ship life and start taking an interest in the communion with kindred souls that is the daily talkfest. One of the joys of freighter travel — in fact, one of the pleasures of all forms of travel — is not so much the seeing of things, as the telling of what you have seen. On a cargo vessel, with few organized distractions for passengers, this pleasure is magnified to its fullest. Oftentimes an afternoon's gab session on deck reaches the point where everyone is sitting on the edge of his deck chair, ready to jump into the conversation with a story just as soon as the other fellow gets through. But even with the competition keen, when you've finished your world voyage you'll discover that lots of things you have learned are things someone told you; some of your best stories are based on yarns spun on deck just behind the bridge house.

One passenger will tell about seeing a man go amok in British Malaysia. Like the story of the dead man in evening clothes in the New York subway, this one goes on forever. Possibly it has happened, but making sure is too much like looking for someone who has been bitten by a shark. Another will go into a serious discussion of the differences in food preference of the Asiatic races, while a third will entrance the whole crowd with an account of his visit to Tokyo when the ten thousand fireflies were turned loose at the fiesta in the Royal Gardens.

The fireflies are interesting conversation material. In many large Japanese cities you find stores devoted solely to the sale of the glowing little winged creatures.

There are six to a dozen of them in a standard wicker cage-lamp — they're used as illumination by many Japanese families, you'll learn — a cage will sell for thirty sen (ten cents), and they'll live a month or longer if they're properly fed and watered; but you can't bring them away from Nippon very easily. Fireflies don't bear up under a change of climate.

The passenger who tells the story of the Asiatic version of the lightning bugs of Mississippi will produce his cage-lamp to back up his yarn. You'll resolve to write a friend to send you one of the lamps, even if the flies can't stand the journey.

Once you pass Perim Island the mountains become visible on the eastern shore and the Chief Officer will tell you this is the region where the Children of Israel

ALWAYS SOMETHING NEW TO SEE

wandered for their famous forty years. Here the temperature begins to lessen, sailing's much more pleasant.

The peaks on the shores of the Red Sea! Right or not, the Chief Steward will name them all for you. The Islands you pass! The Twelve Apostles, Hell's Gates, and the Brothers and Sisters. A talkative officer will point out the exact spot where the water divided for the Children of Israel to escape, another will spin yarns of the pirates who once descended on ships and collected tribute.

The Canal guide comes aboard as you lie in the bay waiting your turn at the Suez passage. The carpenter brings up the giant searchlight that has been stored below decks, it's inspected by the pilot, and approved. Mounted on the poop it will search out the path between the sandy banks when nightfall finds you still on your way.

You are in the Suez Canal! No locks here: the water is at the same level on both ends. A narrow ditch; ships have to tie to the shore for others to pass, the desert on both sides seems almost underfoot when you look out from the upper deck.

Your ship glides slowly. Mounds of sand and little patches of cultivated land follow one another. It takes you twelve hours to make the eighty-mile passage. You watch the scenery and are bored until someone points out a native working a bucket on the end of a long pole. The pole rests on a forked stick, the bucket is a primitive elevator to raise the water to the level of the irrigation ditches along the shore.

The end of the Canal brings you to Port Said — "The cesspool of the East," to quote one group of travelers.

"The most interesting port town in the world," another will say.

Perhaps because some ships stay such a short time the merchants make a special effort for your trade. No matter what hour your vessel arrives, even if the anchor drops at 2 A.M. you'll find the largest stores in town all lighted up, and a full staff of clerks waiting to attend the passengers' needs.

Some companies maintain supply stocks here, which, of course, requires several extra hours of loading ship stores, but unless there's a reason out of the ordinary, your world-cruise vessel turns away from the port very quickly. Most world cruise freighters are pretty well loaded when Port Said is reached. The stop is usually only a few hours.

Your minutes ashore will either inspire another visit — or send you hurrying back to your cabin, glad to escape.

Avoiding Suez and the Red Sea, world-circling boats many times will make the journey around the Continent of Africa, sometimes stopping at Capetown or Dakkar for a few hours, sometimes passing Table Mountain in the distance, making the thirty-four-day run from the Indian Ocean to Halifax without a stop.

Passengers find a variety of amusements on long ocean stretches. Here's a letter from South of the Horn.

DEAR LARRY: —

Sparks is a curious chap. He lives for those funny instruments of his. His watch hours are set by law, but you soon find out that it isn't work for Sparks to sit with those phones on his ears — it's life to him.

There was never a ship had better news service than ours. All the way around the Horn, on the long haul from Ceylon to Halifax, past Capetown, Sparks kept us in close touch with current events through his copies of the wireless news of the world. When they came over in Dutch his translations might be rather difficult, but translate them he did, and we got to watch for the long typewritten sheets he handed around several times a day.

We were gathered behind the bridge house one afternoon, enjoying the sun and protected from the wind, when Sparks brought around his first report of the day.

"Who'll win the World Series?" the chief officer asked, looking up from reading the sheet.

"Gee, I'd like to see that game," the youngest lady passenger announced.

"I'd even like to *hear* it described," the gentleman who danced with her at every port chimed in.

"That might be possible," mildly spoke up our Sparks; and then the fun began.

First we had to figure out the time problem. "When it's nighttime in Italy it's Wednesday over here" might be O.K. for a song title, but more accurate figuring was required before we determined that four o'clock in St. Louis would be ten o'clock at night for us.

That little detail settled with the Skipper's assistance, we then began the business of running wires to bring a loud speaker out on deck. Sparks did it while talking learnedly about balanced circuits, which brought the Chief Steward over to give a complete explanation of how long-distance telephone lines were used by radio stations and why two waves were necessary for the conduct of a wireless phone conversation between ship and shore. Our "cracker box" sessions always ran on that way.

I'm afraid that I didn't take much interest, however,

because just as the steward got warmed up the speaker began giving out strange squawks, followed by silence.

"What's the matter, Sparks, can't you do it?" We climbed to the door of the tiny radio-room where the operator sat among his instruments.

"Of course I can — listen to this guy." He extended the ear phones.

"Dah dah, da da," the drones of a dot-and-dash transmitter came across.

"That fellow-lad is in Shanghai," Sparks proudly proclaimed.

"But it's code!"

"True, but it's a lot farther off than Schenectady or Cincinnati. We'll get them at sundown, just you wait."

It's cold down below when it's summer in America. The decks were nice in the afternoon, but the chill of evening usually drove us inside to sit long at dinner. This was one night when we hurried back from the evening meal; back to pester each other for more assurance, with much looking at watches and querying as to the possibilities of the game starting early.

Sparks made a brave effort to set up a horn in the salon, or at least to get something to work in the smoking room, but there was a terrible hum. The wires were short, and other difficulties arose.

As nine o'clock drew near we begged the wireless man to concentrate on service on deck. "Never mind the cabin, that can be done tomorrow," we assured him.

"O.K. if you like," he replied. "Let's see what is going on now."

Sparks retired to his room above; we clustered around the box as near as we could get. "Quiet now," the youngest lady begged.

"*Scarunch* . . ." the radio grumbled. There was a gibberish of code, a mixture of sound like far-off storms and the interferences caused by a passing trolley car (and the nearest a thousand miles away). Then through the static came a faint sound. A band was blaring. A voice, faint and tinny, came as the band faded away: "In a moment you will hear the umpire start the game. . . . Take it away, Graham!"

We clutched hands in amazement, Graham took it away, and the faint sound of a stentorian "Play Ball!" came through the ether.

Snow could have fallen on us unheeded. We were carried by this modern miracle right to that park in St. Louis, right to the stands where the vendors cried and the sun shone down so that the announcer apologized for asking someone to spell him while he got a cooling drink.

We clustered around. Sparks came down his little ladder. "All right?" he asked.

"Shush!" was the reply. "It's three and two with two men on!"

Yours,
NED

NAPLES — AND HOMEWARD BOUND

Two or three days in Naples, where you find civilization as we home folks understand it, and you are off on the last leg of your journey. Twelve days pushing across the Atlantic with every beat of the propellers saying "going-home, going-home, going-home."

Freighter routes change for cargo and for wars. When the Ethiopian conflict raged, many world-girdling vessels omitted the Mediterranean and the Suez Canal entirely, preferring the longer route around Africa, past Capetown. Naples was dropped by Prince and Silver, the run being made from Colombo to Halifax with only a five-hour fuel stop.

But, whatever your route, when you head across the Atlantic you are facing home; back on your way to the land of ice cream sodas and chocolate sundaes.

Halifax for a day, where you can buy American brand cigarettes, and are surprised at their flavor. The reason is carefully explained by the Congressmen-at-large in the smoking room. They bear the American brand, but inspection of the package shows they're made in Canada and the formula is different. Assured that your taste in smokes has not changed, you look forward to Boston with interest.

Arriving at the Hub City, the fumigation ceremony takes place. Passengers and crew are parked in small boats off where you can look at your ship. A great hue-and-cry goes up throughout the vessel in a dozen languages — noses are counted and the poison gas crew goes to work below decks. As you float about someone begins to talk about the possibility of a stowaway, which upsets the lady from Peoria no end. A little time, and it is over and you are back at home, given a clean bill of health, and ready for your first step on American soil again.

Occasionally, passengers will leave the ship here, but you'll stay on, not even particularly inspired by the possibilities of sight-seeing. You are not interested in Bunker Hill and its monument half as much as you are in the reaction of the youngest cadet to his first visit to the home of the cod and his report on Boston brown bread and baked beans.

"More like the Orient," he reports: "the darned streets turn corners and run away from you."

With Boston disposed of in that short sentence you set out to sea for the last outside run. Tomorrow it's New York, Brooklyn, and home to the grind again.

19 · Summing Up the World Cruises

THREE lines tour the world from the Atlantic Seaboard; they all go westward with the sun. From New York to Newport News or Savannah, with an occasional stop at some other American city, or a point in the West Indies. Then on through the Canal to Los Angeles for oil, and away to the Far East. Usually, it's the Philippines first; but occasionally they go direct to Yokohama, although the Japanese have corraled most of the trade there with their new eighteen-knot speedsters.

At the Philippines the routes operating around the world vary. Barber boats cruise for about a month, returning to Manila. Blue Funnel boats do the same, but the period differs according to freight demands. Silver and Prince visit two or three Japanese ports before the second Manila visit (once it was Shanghai and Hong Kong).

Once the Philippines are left behind the routes continue with only minor differences: Macassar, Sourabaya, Samarang, Batavia, Singapore, Port Swettenham, Belawan, Penang and Colombo. From Ceylon the routes again diverge, but as a rule you are pretty well loaded by the time the Indian Ocean is sighted; stops from there on are likely to be measured by hours, rather than days.

The Pacific-Java-Bengal Line boasts of the only regular world-cruise service that sets out to meet the sun, rather than to follow old Sol on his journey around the globe. Once a month their liners sail from New Orleans for Capetown. Before the departure from the "city that care forgot," stops are made at Galveston, Mobile, and other Gulf ports — "where cargo offers." Several times a year, Silver-Java has a sailing from New York or some other Atlantic harbor which either connects with the world-cruise service, or replaces it.

This eastward around-the-world service lists its fare at $700, the trip requiring 175 days as a rule. Passengers in a hurry can get ashore at San Francisco after four and a half months and save seventy-five dollars.

The vessels used are owned by the Nederland Line or the Rotterdam Lloyd, and fly the Dutch flag. They are motorships of about 10,000 deadweight tons with accommodations for from six to sixteen passengers. Some ships have enclosed promenade decks and pianos in the smoking room in addition to the ever-present radio and phonograph.

A typical cruise on this line would commence, say, on March 24th with the *Kota Baroe* setting sail from the wharves in New Orleans, dropping down the great mile-wide Mississippi River, through the narrower mouths, and out into the Gulf, with sixteen passengers in her eight double cabins. A month later, after traversing the South Pacific Ocean, her people gather on deck for the first sight of Capetown's famous Table Mountain. Due there April 23d, she remains until the 26th. Several passengers make up a party for a rail trip to the interior, visiting Johannesburg, Pretoria, the famous Victoria Falls and other points of interest in South Africa, but most of the company sticks with the boat, visiting Port Elizabeth, East London, and Durban. Three days are spent in Lourenço Marques, and stops are made at Beira, Colombo and Madras.

On June 4th, following her schedule, the ship arrives at Calcutta, where all the travelers troop ashore, most of them to spend a week at local hotels at their own expense. This runs the cost of the trip up by fifty dollars for those who demand superior quarters, but two college boys found it as cheap to live in Calcutta as anywhere else and spent most of their money on souvenirs and Kodak film.

One side trip is taken by almost all the tourists — to Darjeeling in the famous Himalayas.

The motor vessel *Bengalen* sails on June 8th with part of the party, stopping at Penang and Singapore, Manila and San Francisco, arriving July 17th; but most of the group wait for the *Kota Agoeng,* sister ship of the *Baroe,* sailing a few days later from Bombay. Railroad travel through India brings these passengers to the Bombay docks, where they board their new vessel. Stops are made at Colombo, Belawan-Deli (Sumatra), Penang, Singapore, Batavia (with time for a rail trip across the island of Java where the trains run only in daylight), Samarang, Sourabaya, Davao, and Manila, arriving at Los Angeles on August 4th, or four and a half months after leaving New Orleans.

San Francisco, the Panama Canal, and Mobile complete the circuit. Crossing the International Date Line from West to East, passengers live one day twice, on a voyage where every day is a day to be lived again and again in memories.

20 · Other Services

THE WORLD cruise, of course, is the ideal journey for the Vagabond Voyager, but not every vacationist can spend four to six months traveling, and not every passenger who has made the globe circuit is ready to say that this trip gives the maximum of enjoyment and entertainment.

Many lines operate regular service from the United States to the Far East, reaching as far as Penang, then returning the same way, while services to the Mediterranean from New York reach into small ports in true freighter fashion, ports that world cruisers pass by in lordly style, as, loaded to the Plimsoll mark, they scurry across the seas homeward bound.

There are river boats on the Mississippi and the Ohio right in our own United States where you can enjoy most of the pleasures of ship life, and always be able to step ashore and find a U.S. Post Office not far away. One of the most interesting freighter vacations ever reported was on a coastwise cargo vessel operating on the Eastern Coast southward to the shores of North Carolina and along the inland waters there.

Freighters on the Great Lakes are not as easy to do business with as are the boats on the oceans. This is probably because the owners of the lines are likely to decide suddenly that a vacation would be a good idea — and the owners' cabins must be kept ready for the bosses. Henry Ford is reported as being a frequent vacationer on his 600-foot Lakes freight carriers. If you have friends among the shipping companies, however, trips can be arranged on these Lake giants at prices that barely cover food costs. Most Captains have one or two empty cabins available.

Canal boats drifting down the sluggish streams of the inland waterways of the country have always entranced the traveler. Moving at two or three miles an hour, the speed of walking mules on the towpath, these floating homes have, to many, always represented the ultimate in leisurely languor.

Some of the canal barge trains, now pushed along by motor vessels, occasionally take a stray passenger; but here again it takes an acquaintance with the owner, or a trade with the chief of the paddle-wheel ship, in the rare cases when the Captain is in position to make such deals. The trip by air from New York to Buffalo takes two hours. By canal barge it runs three weeks to a month. Only one man is reported as having made the full journey, a year or so ago; he paid a dollar a day for his meals and bunked with the crew.

There are freighter services that operate in remote spots of the world: little launches that ply up rivers and small steamers running from outport island to outport island. These, too, offer an opportunity for the Vagabond Vacationer to see how the other nine tenths of the world live.

A Trip down the Amazon

And here is another letter, from a young lady who lacked the time to make a world trip.

August.

DEAR LARRY: —

It was with fear and trembling that I booked passage on this boat for a trip down the Amazon. I'm afraid that I had the same idea the other folks have — namely, that freighters are dirty, old boats with horrible little rooms that are hot holes. I've learned, thank heavens, and I've given up the swank of first class travel and can't wait until next summer when I'm going around the world.

But as usual I'm digressing. Let me tell you about my trip. I went aboard at the pier out in Staten Island. I found a large airy outside room with hot and cold running water waiting for me, and the bathroom right across the hall. I unpacked my things, hung up my clothes and cleaned up generally. A steward knocked on my door and told me that the Captain was awaiting my presence in the dining room. Imagine my delight!

Hurriedly I applied a last dash of powder to my ever-shining nose and darted in the direction of the salon. Believe it or not I sat at the Captain's right for the entire trip. I can't waste time telling you about the food except that it was delicious. And that first luncheon will always stand out in my memory as something to be remembered, even to the grand Martini with two olives.

At three o'clock that same afternoon we set out on our journey for Philadelphia, then on to Jacksonville for more passengers. By the time we got to Florida I learned that we traveled at fourteen knots per hour and that the other passengers were really quite nice. (I hadn't expected them to be, you remember?) Also that we needed two tugboats to get us out of dock.

Then the real trip began. We were on our way to Pará, which, in case you didn't know it, is 3,000 miles from New York. I was told that it took approximately sixteen days to get there and I was very much worried. You know my tummy isn't of the best: that is, it and the sea don't usually get along; but I am happy to report, sir, that neither I, nor anyone else aboard, suffered from *mal de mer* for a second. I became quite proficient at deck golf, to say nothing of the fact that I am the champion cross-word puzzler on shipboard and you thought I couldn't spell. All right, I accept your apology.

The best hotel in Pará is called the Grand. The food is "too, too divine" and the bills easy on the exchequer. There's a very impressive-looking cathedral and the most marvelous zoo I've ever visited. I still have a passion for giraffes.

Thence to Ceará, where the ships lie in the open roadstead. Everybody lands in a surf boat. I went swimming off Ceará's silvery beach in salt water that is neither too warm nor too cold. We stayed here an extra day because the Captain likes horseback riding, which was perfect for me because I too am a horse addict. By the way, the Captain improved my riding one hundred per cent. with some well-put comments. I learned that wax is imported from Ceará. It comes from the carnauba tree, the leaves of which are similar to those of a palm tree. This is the kind of wax that is used for ladies' facials, so the next time I have a mud pack I'll tell the know-it-all beauty operator of mine something she doesn't know.

Pernambuco and Bahia were the next ports of call. Bahia has 365 churches and honestly Larry I think 200 of them are in use. Cabedello is the only whaling station in South America. One of the whalers reported catching a sixty-five-ton whale early one morning and by nightfall the wireless man said they had also snared her mate, who was considerably smaller. Always when the female whale is caught first, the male is sure to be the next victim, because he hovers around until evening and then it's just too bad for him. Even male whales are gallant, you see.

STRANGE NAMES IN YOUR AUTOGRAPH BOOK

Natal is where the Trans-South Atlantic aviators landed. Then back to Ceará and Maranham, the seat of the last of slave traffic in the Western Hemisphere. Then on to Pará and Manaos! This is absolutely virgin forest and I have the assurance of the First Mate (and I know he's truthful) that no white man has ever set foot here. About 15 miles from Manaos, the yellow water of the Amazon changes to a deep coffee color, and the Rio Negro begins. A few miles from there is an island called Marapeta, which has an interesting tradition. As you pass by you cast away all good resolutions made ashore and pick them up when you pass on the return voyage down the Amazon. Larry, it's true. Ask the Captain.

Manaos is quite a town. Twenty-five years ago they built the finest opera house south of the equator. They also had streetcars before Liverpool did. These folks are progressive. They made their money in rubber beans and they know how to spend it.

It's amazing how friendly one becomes with one's fellow passengers. John (who owns a plantation in Manaos) invited us out for a day's wild duck shooting. It was the most exciting hunt. We brought a horde of wild ducks back and the chef prepared a super-special dinner party for us. Was it good? The chef at the Waldorf had better look to his laurels.

I'm bringing back a new pet to add to my collection. It is a bird called a Curo Peon. However, I've christened him Fernando after one of the boys on the boat. Fernando (the bird I mean) sings extraordinarily well and his plumage is black and gold. Mac, our radio operator, assures me that Fernando will survive in New York if I indulge him just a bit. Really, Larry, he's a thing of beauty and I'm sure he'll be a joy forever.

My Captain is a darling. He's English, of course, and was a destroyer officer during the World War. His mother's family was composed chiefly of sailors since the time of Lord Nelson and he has a handsome son who is an officer in this same company, but doggone it not on this boat. The old gentleman tells the grandest tales and makes cocktails without measuring any of the ingredients — the best I've ever tasted. Also he's my idea of a perfect and gracious host. Next time he gets to New York, I'm going to show him the town. The Rainbow Room isn't good enough for him — he's a Prince among men.

We've just landed in Pará again and I think I should post this letter to you, because our next stop is Madeira and I know you don't want to wait that long to read my raves about freighter travel. I haven't decided whether I should bring you a dead *kapavara* — that's a wild pig — they make swell pigskin gloves with their hides — or a ton of Brazil nuts. And are those nuts succulent — yum! yum. I've devoured about ten pounds in the last three weeks. I wouldn't advise that quantity for you however, since they're fattening. Or maybe you'd rather have some wax. I tried to pluck the statue of Lord Nelson out of the Square in Barbados but I wasn't quick enough so you'll have to be satisfied with something that isn't quite so hard to carry.

I'll write again from Lisbon, if I find time. Honestly Larry, there are so many interesting things to do on shipboard that I have very little time to pound my typewriter. Anyhow I can't write any more now because I have a date with the First Mate to beat him at honeymoon bridge. Until *mañana* — I am your devoted slave or words to that effect; *you* taught me about freighter travel.

BETTY

CUBA

Havana, August 15.

DEAR LARRY: —

Your request for information about freight boats carrying passengers in inter-island service around Cuba was awaiting my return from Santiago de Cuba (the de Cuba is necessary for some mysterious reason I haven't quite figured out yet). Santiago d.C. is around on the other side of the Island from Havana. I made the journey in a small freight boat called the *Camagüey*.

The Cuban Steamship Line is the only one that I've found so far that carries passengers except on local runs. The company sign reads *Empresa Naviera de Cuba S.A.* (The S.A. means "Incorporated.") The local office is at San Pedro 6 — that is Number Six San Pedro Street — and the head traffic boss is a nice chap named Collado. All of this I mention in case you want some local color to sprinkle in your chapter.

This outfit has a large fleet operating throughout the North Coast of Cuba. I'm told here that even the freight service to the South Coast has been discontinued. They have, I believe, five boats that carry passengers: the *Cuba,* the *Habana,* the *Julian Alonso,* the *Las Villas* and the *Camagüey.* The last-named, "my" boat, carries a maximum of four passengers.

The biggest of these is the *Cuba,* probably around 2,000 registered tons. The *Cuba* operates a "cruise," if you please: Baracoa, Guantánamo, and Santiago, then she goes over to two places in Santo Domingo and then to Puerto Rico. After that she returns to Santo Domingo and then goes directly back to Havana, not stopping elsewhere in Cuba. The round trip takes sixteen days from Havana, and compared to the other fares charged the rate is enormous. Round trip is $138 including no maintenance in Puerto Rico (and you can't live on the ship). After my trip on the *Camagüey,* Mister, I announce the boat isn't worth any $138 for sixteen days.

Of course when you look at it one way, the *Cuba's* not a bad craft. It's the only one in the lot, I believe, that has any public rooms to speak of. On the others the public rooms are all the same room, lounge, dining salon, cocktail bar, depending on the hour of the day. On the *Cuba* it's different, there's a room for each of the occupations, loafing, eating, and drinking, and they're not badly fitted out either. The public rooms are small perhaps, but they're there.

The decks are rather nice. I doubt if they have deck chairs — although they might. It's usually a question of luck whether or not there's a chair for rent. The cabins are okay for freight boat cabins — no rugs on the floor, of course, but that's true of the finest home in Cuba. It's a custom. And the beds, too, are all right. I sat on one to see if it was softer than a concrete walk. It gave a bit, so I endorse the springs. The *Cuba,* incidentally, *looks* like a passenger boat. It isn't just a lot of cabins bunched on a tall superstructure in the center of the ship, but a long promenade deck running the normal length of the vessel, with all the cabins on that. It looks good and if the pictures I made come out okay, you'll have a snap in the next mail.

The other boats of the line are unquestionably freighters, even if the *Cuba* isn't. They may take ten or fifteen passengers, but they're still freighters. Tiny, around fourteen hundred tons, they are freight from the ground up — or do you say from the water up? Anyway, on the *Habana,* for example, the rooms are on one deck and open inside to the one and only public room. A long table is stretched down the center of this room and everybody eats there, except the crew (passengers and officers I mean). That's the boat — but she has big decks. I'd just as leave traveled on her. The *Julian* is pretty much the same, as is the *Las Villas.* All are very low to the water, the promenade deck being only fifteen or twenty feet high.

The *Camagüey* is different. She looks more like a ship than any of the rest except the *Cuba.* She is a pretty little thing, built normally, with the cabins located on either side of the Captain's quarters at the front of the Promenade under the bridge. The dining room is aft, on the same deck. The dining table has a built-in seat running around three sides — like the old speak-easy cozy-corners. Passengers and officers (not counting quartermasters) all eat here. There's unusually good deck space — the deck I was on is wide, and the upper deck, aft of the bridge for a little way, also wide.

The itinerary of the ships runs like this. There are two sailings a week for Santiago de Cuba — Tuesday and Saturday. The Tuesday boats are locals and make frequent calls down the Island, taking six to seven days to reach Santiago. (I left that de Cuba off once — do you mind?) The fare is forty-one dollars. Sailing is around 5 A.M. on Tuesday (according to the Line's office — I didn't get up that early to see) and you reach the first port of call, Nuevitas, Thursday morning, early. From there on God and the cargo determines the schedule. The one good Tuesday boat is the *Camagüey* which I happened to take on a Saturday, sort of like the old Tuesday, Thursday train between San Francisco and Seattle that used to run every Monday, Wednesday and Friday also. (Honest it did, ask the old time railroad men.)

The Saturday boats are the so-called "express" vessels, making only three stops on the Island. But I'll be specific about my trip — after all, freighter travel is something you have to be specific about, generalizations get confusing when you start reciting the exceptions.

We were due to sail Saturday at eleven (in a Tuesday boat, now mind you). We shook off from the dock at one. All Saturday we followed the shore. Sunday we could barely see the Island at intervals. Monday it was more of the same until about three in the afternoon when we picked up land again and kept it in sight until arrival at Baracoa at eight that night. It is very pretty down the coast into Baracoa, which port is set in a wild and unapproachable neighborhood, the only contact being water or by air.

Baracoa was the first town built in Cuba, according to the United Fruit man there. The U.F. man was one of two Americans living in the city. Christopher Columbus is said to have made a landing here on his first trip across the Atlantic. I felt like a second Columbus walking through the narrow streets. The Main Hotel is the only place I could find to eat — the Cabaret is strictly a native place and the theater is in the hotel. There wasn't time to see a movie.

It's quite a stunt to bring a boat to its moorings in this harbor. Your berth is between two other ships, and you gain in respect for the Cuban navigators when you see how the skipper brings her up to a point, then lets the tide swing her around until you're safely in position, facing the current with other vessels on either side. Anvil Mountain is a flat-topped affair that sort of overshadows the city. If you can understand Cuban Spanish you'll get plenty of native legends, mostly ghostly.

On special occasions you can persuade the United Fruit boats to take a passenger or two direct to the States, but it's not easy. In fact it's darned hard to get passage from Cuba — except on Cuban-owned boats or one of the regular passenger liners. We were in Baracoa until four or five the next afternoon — they don't load or unload cargo at night there.

Overnight to Guantánamo where we arrived early in the morning. It's a grand sight when the Fleet's in the Bay, they tell me — but when there're no sailors, the towns here sort of droop.

It's an hour's ride up Guantánamo Bay, past the Naval Station. You sort of let your voice fall at Guantánamo Bay — it stinks, figuratively and literally and every other way. The boat docked at Point Desire (a warehouse to you,

Mister) and by walking a railroad track you come in Caimanera. Honest Larry, I don't mind filth. I like Port au Prince, and some other places — but Caimanera made me ill. It's the recreation grounds for the sailors — and a horrible dump. They tell me the town of Guantánamo isn't much better, although that's an hour away by train, and we didn't have time to make it.

About noon the boat moved over to Boqueron, the same kind of place — only residential rather than business. We were there about two hours. Then we went away along for about six hours to Santiago where we arrived at about 8 P.M. There's no need to describe Santiago de Cuba, except to say that its harbor is the prettiest I've seen in the West Indies, and the boat enters at dusk — it's light until you pass all there is to see.

Now about the life on the ship.

It was my first freighter trip and so I have nothing to compare things with — but I had a swell time. I got two good breaks — one that my roommate was a traveling guy who had been to Europe five times, and so naturally wasn't a thug. Somehow I had expected to find either a song plugger or a retired bank safe opener, so he was a pleasant surprise. The other good break I got was that the third passenger got ashore at Baracoa, and we had the ship to ourselves. She was a mulatto girl — one of the evils of freighter travel here — and somehow she just didn't seem to belong.

Naturally the passengers had the run of the ship. We could go on the bridge whenever we wanted to and the officers were politeness itself — all the time. Of course none of them spoke any English and my Spanish leaves something to be desired — but we got along.

The only real trouble was the complete absence of deck chairs. The Supercargo had one he let us use, but there were otherwise no chairs to sit in on deck, except one or two goatskin, typical Cuban chairs on the after bridge. But there was always the deck — and it was clean, so somehow I didn't mind.

Meal hours were a little unusual for a guy from New York. There was nothing for breakfast except fruit, bread and butter and *caf' con leche* (coffee with milk). I hear you can get eggs for breakfast but I got mixed on the right Spanish word and gave up the idea. Breakfast comes at 7:30 to 8 A.M. Lunch piles right in early, just like in San Quentin Prison (no you dope, I only visited there). You get the noon meal at eleven, and dinner comes at five P.M.

The food is good, if you don't look at it or its preparation. Fish, for example, is served with heads, tails and everything else — but when you don't look, it's good fish. *Arroz* (rice), the native dish here, is served in large quantities; cooked with chicken or with black beans, or with anything else the cook happens to think about. There usually were four or five courses, the same as the regular Cuban lunch or dinner. It was quite all right.

For its size the *Camagüey* is quite a boat, a good little sea boat. The water between Havana and Santiago is *always* a little rough, and always the current is towards Havana. On the trip out you have the current to buck as far as Guantánamo — from there on the current is with you. The cabins have cold running water (I don't think there is any running hot water here in the tropics on boats). The shower has hot and cold fresh water. The boat was surprisingly clean, as I understand are all the ships of this line. My bed was hard as a brick, but it's better than a featherbed in the tropics, and you get used to things like that in time.

I can only sum things up by saying that when that darned little skiff got out in Havana Harbor and I began to get a bit green around the gills from the motion, I wouldn't have given a plugged nickel for my chances of finishing the trip, and certainly would have wagered against my ever doing it again. But now that I've made the journey, I'm all sold on it, and intend to make it again some day. You may quote me on that, Sir.

Yours,

ROY

THE CUBAN TOURIST COMMISSION REPORTS ON FREIGHTER SERVICE FROM CUBA

Foreign governments have discovered the American tourist, establishing special bureaus to ladle out information. The Cuban National Tourist Commission is representative of the more intelligently operated government travel-boosting organizations. The following submitted by them is representative of the information that will likely be forthcoming when you make investigations as to the possibility of freighter travel from some foreign shore.

STEAMER SERVICE IN AND FROM CUBAN PORTS

There are only two lines of steamers doing the coast-wise service in Cuba; the names are *Empresa Naviera de Cuba* and *Compañia Naviera de Cuba*.

Empresa Naviera de Cuba owns the following steamers —

S.S. *Camagüey*	(freight)
S.S. *Cuba*	(freight and passengers)
S.S. *Las Villas*	(freight)
S.S. *Julian Alonso*	(freight)

Compañia Naviera de Cuba, S.A., owns the following steamers: —

S.S. *Tropical*	(freight)
S.S. *Oriente*	(freight)

The tonnage of the above mentioned boats runs from 400 to 2,000 tons.

THE FRENCH LINE

      S.S. *Mexique*   (freight)   12,220 tons

HOLLAND AMERICA LINE

      S.S. *Leerdam*   (freight)   5,307 tons
      S.S. *Burgerdyk*   (freight)   4,229 tons

Ports of Call: Vera Cruz, Tampico, London, Antwerp, Rotterdam.

Of the Steamship Lines in the States, we do not give you detailed information as we presume that you do not require these from us; however, the lines with regular sailings between American Ports and Cuba, carrying passengers and freight, are the following: —

    United Fruit Co.
    New York Cuba Mail S.S. Co. (WARD LINE)
    Panama Pacific Line
    Munson Line
    P. & O. S.S. Company
    Standard Fruit Company

SPANISH TRANSATLANTIC CO. (passenger and freight)

    S.S. *Marques de Comillas*
    S.S. *Juan Sebastian Elcano*
    S.S. *Magallanes*
    S.S. *Cuba*
    S.S. *Cristobal Colon*

These steamers ply between Havana and Mexican ports, and Spanish ports in the North and Mediterranean.

LYKES BROS. S.S. COMPANY, INC. (freight only)

    S.S. *Margaret Lykes*   3,537 tons
    S.S. *Ruth Lykes*   2,612 tons

Ports of call: Cristobal, Panama, Cartagena, Puerto Colombia, Ciudad, Trujillo, ports in Texas.

NORWEGIAN LINE (freight)

S.S. *Gottemburg* (plying between Havana and Scandinavian ports)

S.S. *Oslo*

PACIFIC STEAM NAVIGATION COMPANY (freight and passenger)

S.S. *Orbita*	15,445 tons
S.S. *Orduña*	15,506 tons
S.S. *Reina del Pacifico*	17,770 tons

Plying between Europe and Cuban and South American ports.

NORTH GERMAN LLOYD (passenger and freight)

S.S. *Memel*	3,200 tons
S.S. *Faal*	3,200 tons

Ports of call: Antwerp, Bremen, Hamburg.

S.S. *Minden*	4,650 tons
S.S. *Borkum*	3,800 tons

Ports of call: Vera Cruz, Tampico, Galveston, Houston, Antwerp, Bremen, Hamburg.

FREIGHTER FOLK ARE FRANK

The operators of freighter lines are honest with passengers. There have been complaints about freighters, but never one of misrepresentation. If the only recreational equipment on a freighter is a ping pong table owned by the Second Engineer, the freighter line won't tell prospective passengers they can play deck tennis all the way around South Africa.

A fair sample of the exactitude with which freighter lines describe the accommodations is shown in the following bulletins from a Steamship Company to its agents. The bulletins are reproduced exactly: —

February 13th, 1936.

To: Boston	Los Angeles	Kobe
Philadelphia	San Francisco	Shanghai
Baltimore	Cristobal	Hong Kong
Norfolk	Yokohama	**Manila**
Savannah		

PASSENGER SERVICE. MEMORANDUM.

Norwegian m.s. "Bronxville."

Built 1929.
Deadweight: 8423 tons.
Gross Register: 4663 tons.
Net Register: 2793 tons.
Speed: about 10½/11 knots.

For your guidance in the solicitation of passengers for this vessel we quote below from a letter just received from the Master:

"Regarding passenger accommodation on this ship, this is same as on the 'Bonneville,' which I understand has been on charter to you. There is one stateroom on the starboard side of the salon for *two passengers,* and the bathroom and W.C. is close to same. Then there is a *single* room next to my cabin on the lower bridge. In all there is place for three passengers. The rooms are heated by steam. There is plenty of deck space; but only the Salon, no smoking room, etc. As regards food, there is a refrigeration plant on the ship so we always have fresh food and fruit."

The "C"-rates will apply for passage on this vessel. There will be no extra charge for the single room.

ISBRANDTSEN-MOLLER COMPANY, INC.

Mac
c.c. Copenhagen
    A. L. Thomson, Esq.

February 15th, 1936.

To: Boston	Los Angeles	Kobe
Philadelphia	San Francisco	Shanghai
Baltimore	Cristobal	Hong Kong
Norfolk	Yokohama	Manila
Savannah		

PASSENGER SERVICE.   MEMORANDUM.

Norwegian m.s. "Soloy."

Built 1929.
Deadweight: 8300 tons.
Gross Register: 4402 tons.
Net Register: 2624 tons.
Speed: about 11/11½ knots.

For your guidance in the solicitation of passengers for this vessel we give below description of the accommodation as received from the Master on the occasion of the vessel's previous voyage on the Maersk Line:

"Lower Bridge Deck.
One large comfortable passenger cabin, equipt with one bed, sofa, writingdesk, easychair. A clotheslocker, washstand, three portholes. All in Mahogany finish.
Bathroom and W.C. separated, across the passage.
On this deck is the Captain's cabin and office-dayroom.
"Shelterdeck, bridge house.
A large saloon (18' × 14'). Two tables, sofa, and the usual equipment. Very nicely finished.
A cabin starboard side, large, one bunk, sofa, table,

clotheslocker, washstand, all in Mahogany. Entrance from the saloon passage, one porthole in front, two at the side. In this cabin is the ship's library with English and Norwegian books.

A cabin on port side, a little smaller than the above-mentioned, same equipment, one porthole in front and one at the side. Entrance from the saloon.

"A cabin in the after end of the bridge house. Entrance from deck. Two bunks, clotheslocker, washstand, table (no sofa). All oak finish. This serves as the ship's Hospital, but can be used for passengers. On this deck in the saloon passage there is a W.C.; for bath they must go up on the lower bridge deck.

". . . there is no 'recreational equipment.' We can, however, make a few arrangements, as there is a good deck-space on the lower bridge. There is a refrigeration room and cooling storage for fresh provisions. As you will understand, this ship is very comfortable for three passengers, and only fairly so for two more. There is a large gramophone in the saloon and a plug for a loudspeaker from the ship's main radio receiver. All electric fans belong to the officers and crew private."

The "C"-rates will apply for passage on this vessel. Cabins are numbered 1, 2, 3, and 4 in the order given above. No. 1 will be sold as a double; Nos. 2 and 3 as singles at no extra charge; No. 4 is not recommended for passengers but will be sold as a double if desired.

ISBRANDTSEN-MOLLER COMPANY, INC.

CL:Mac

New York, March 3rd, 1936.

To All Agents:

PASSENGER SERVICE.   MEMORANDUM.

Danish m.s. "Astoria."
Built 1926.
Deadweight: 8370 tons.
Gross Register: 4454 tons.
Net Register: 2694 tons.
Speed: about 11 knots.

For your guidance in the solicitation of passengers for this vessel we quote below from a letter just received from K. Jensen, the Master:

"Number of passengers comfortably carried is five. One double and one single cabin are located in the saloonhouse, and two single cabins in the captain's house. All are furnished with bunks, settees, wardrobes, washstands, etc. All can be steamheated when required and are ventilated by ordinary ventilators.

"There is one bathroom available for passengers on same deck as saloonhouse.

"Refrigeration space of sufficient proportions to enable the ship to carry an ample supply of fresh provisions.

"Public rooms: the saloon.

"Recreational equipment: none but what can be made on board. Deckspace ample for the number of passengers."

For convenience sake the cabins will be numbered as follows:

Cabin No. 1, Single.   (Captain's House, Amidships, Aft.)
Cabin No. 2, Single.   (Captain's House, Starboard, Aft.)
Cabin No. 3, Double.   (Saloonhouse, Port, Forward.)
Cabin No. 4, Single.   (Saloonhouse, Starboard, Aft.)

The "C"-rates will apply for passage on this vessel. There will be no extra charge for the single rooms.

ISBRANDTSEN-MOLLER COMPANY, INC.

CL: Mac
c.c. Copenhagen
A. L. Thomson, Esq.

New York, November 30th, 1936.

To All Agents:

PASSENGER SERVICE. MEMORANDUM.

German m.s. "Anneliese Essberger."

Built 1935.
Deadweight: 9153 tons.
Gross Register: 5173 tons.
Net Register: 3052 tons.
Speed: about 13 knots.

For your guidance in the solicitation of passengers for this vessel we quote below from a letter received from Messrs. Robert C. Herd & Co., Inc., Baltimore:

"With reference to passenger accommodations, Captain tells us he can take two passengers in the Owner's room, which is a nice large room with a bed (not a bunk) and this room has a combination lounge and bed, full size, also a combined writing and dressing table, and large mirror, and a nice center table with three comfortable chairs. Adjoining this room is a bath containing shower and tub, wash-stand and toilet. Across the passageway, there is the hospital room, which has two beds for two passengers and a wash-stand, with running hot and cold water and two lockers. The Owner's room also has a locker. This room has a door opening on to the passageway, which is directly opposite to a door leading into the bathroom, previously mentioned. In both of these rooms, both hot and cold sea and fresh water is available.

"In addition, farther down the passageway, and opposite the Captain's room, there is a reserve room with a full bed and also a short-size sofa. This room also has a wash-stand, but no running water, which must be carried from the bathroom adjoining the Owner's room, which bathroom must serve all three of the rooms mentioned. The Captain's room is also located adjoining these rooms, but, of course, he reserves same for himself.

"These rooms are thoroughly clean, and have good ventilation — all being directly on the same deck with the Captain's quarters. They all have electric heat and vessel has electric refrigeration for food. Each room has radio connection excepting the reserve room.

"There is a large dining room, which represents the only public room. There is ample deck space for recreation, and Captain says the passengers can play shuffle-board and other games.

"We consider these accommodations good for a freighter."

Captain Schmidt is in command of this vessel.

The "C"-rates will apply for passage.

ISBRANDTSEN-MOLLER COMPANY, INC.

CL:Mac
c.c. Copenhagen
A. L. Thomson, Esq.

New York, March 19th, 1938.

To All Agents:

PASSENGER SERVICE.   LIST OF VACANT BERTHS.

---

m.s. "Bonneville." From L.A. Mar. 24:
    Cabin No. 2, Single.   (No extra charge)

m.s. "Marchen Maersk." From L.A. Mar. 31:
    Cabin No. 4, Single.
    *Cabin No. 5, Berth "B," Lady.
    *Cabin No. 6, Berths "A" & "B."
    Cabin No. 7, Berth "B," Gent.
    Cabin No. 8, Berths "A" & "B."

m.s. "Thalatta." From N.Y. Mar. 28, L.A. Apr. 18:
    Cabin "A,"   Berths Nos. 1 & 2. (Special Suite,
               10% extra)
    Cabin "D,"   Berths Nos. 1 & 2.
    Cabin "E,"   Berths Nos. 1 & 2.

m.s. "Anna Maersk." From N.Y. Apr. 9, L.A. Apr. 30:
   Cabin No. 1, Single.
   Cabin No. 2, Single.
   *Cabin No. 3, Single.
   *Cabin No. 4, Berths "A" & "B."
   *Cabin No. 5, Berths "A" & "B."
   Cabin No. 6, Single.   (RT)
   *Cabin No. 8, Berth "B," Gent.
   Cabin No. 9, Single.   (RT)

m.s. "Hopepeak." From N.Y. Apr. 27, L.A. May 20:
  No passenger accommodation.

m.s. "Niel Maersk." From N.Y. May 11, L.A. June 2:
   Cabin No. 1, Berths* "A" & "B." ("B," Lady,
      RT)
   *Cabin No. 2, Berths "A" & "B."
   Cabin No. 3, Berths "A" & "B."
   Cabin No. 4, Berths "A" & "B."

m.s. "Motorship." From N.Y. May 25, L.A. June 17:
  Accommodation later.

m.s. "Peter Maersk." From N.Y. June 11, L.A. July 2:
   *Cabin No. 3, Single.
   *Cabin No. 6, Single.   (RT)
   *Cabin No. 8, Single.

m.s. "Gertrude Maersk." From N.Y. June 25, L.A. July 17:
   Cabin No. 1, Berths "A" & "B."   (RT)
   Cabin No. 2, Berths* "A" & "B."
   Cabin No. 3, Berths "A" & "B."

m.s. "Grete Maersk." From N.Y. July 10, L.A. July 31:
   *Cabin No. 3, Single.   (RT)
   Cabin No. 4, Single.   (RT)
   *Cabin No. 6, Berths "A" & "B."   (RT)

*Cabins or berths under offer but not definitely booked.
 RT indicates roundtrip accommodations; all other space
 available outward bound only.

Agents Who Specialize in Freighter Travel

NOTE: These agents will give you information about freighters; about cargo boats, carrying fifteen to one hundred and twenty-five passengers, and all the larger passenger liners as well. Many agents include liners in lists of freighter voyages to avoid endless correspondence with prospective travelers who haven't the necessary time to travel *à la* freighter, yet who are allured by advertising, etc.

American Express Company, 65 Broadway, New York, N.Y.
Freight Boat Travel Bureau, Los Angeles, California.
General Steamship Company, San Francisco, California.
Tramp Trips, Stone Street, New York, N.Y.
Viking Voyages, Inc., 245 Broadway, New York, N.Y.

These five organizations have been most helpful in assisting in gathering data for this volume. Knowing that publication will doubtless inspire a great many new freighter travelers who may possibly book direct so that the commissions are lost to these agents, they have nevertheless been most helpful, endeavoring to aid the traveler rather than merely striving for their own personal gain.

A great many other travel agents have compiled information on freighter travel and are making bookings every month. Omission of these agents from this list is no slight; it merely indicates that the assistance they have given the author covers only one or two lines. The agents listed here have furnished information on ten to a hundred lines each; and more important, they'll answer *your* letters, too.

THE following classification of points to which freighters run from American ports covers tours listed in detail in Chapter 24.

AROUND THE WORLD

Barber
Blue Funnel
Dollar
Java-New York
Maersk
O.S.K.

Port
Prince-Silver
Silver-Java-Bengal
Silver-Java-Pacific
Wilhelmsen

TRANSPACIFIC

Barber
Blue Funnel
East Asiatic
Klaveness
Kokasai
Matson

Maersk
Mitsui
O.S.K.
Salen
Silver-Java
States S.S. Co.

FAR EAST FROM GULF PORTS

Kokasai
Lykes Brothers (American
    Gulf Orient)

Mitsui
Silver-Java
Wilhelmsen

FAR EAST FROM ATLANTIC PORTS

Barber
Blue Funnel
Java-China-Japan
Java-New York
Kokasai

Maersk
Mitsui
Kerr-Silver
Wilhelmsen

INDIA

American Pioneer	Silver-Java

AFRICA

American-South Africa	O.S.K.
Blue Funnel	Robin
Elder Dempster	Silver-Java
Java-New York	Kerr-Silver

MEDITERRANEAN

American Export	U.S. Navigation
Dixie-Mediterranean	

SOUTH AMERICA FROM ATLANTIC COAST

Booth Lines	Panama
Essco-Brodin	Royal Netherlands
Furness	Standard Fruit
Grace	United Fruit
Lamport and Holt	Wilhelmsen
McCormick	

SOUTH AMERICA FROM GULF

Aluminum	Standard Fruit
Delta	United Fruit
Humphrey and MacGregor	Weinberger
Lykes Brothers	

CENTRAL AND SOUTH AMERICA FROM PACIFIC PORTS

Goloria	McCormick
Grace	Westfal-Larsen
Johnson	

ALASKA

Alaska	Northland Transportation
Canadian National	Union of B.C.
Canadian Pacific	

NORTH ATLANTIC

Clarke
Furness
Gypsum Packet

Hudson's Bay Co.
Newfoundland Canada
Newfoundland R.R.

COASTWISE DOMESTIC

Clyde Mallory
Dollar
Eastern S.S. Lines
Luckenbach
McCormick

Morgan
Pan-Atlantic
Savannah
Shepard

TRANSATLANTIC

American Merchant
American Scantic
Baltimore Mail
Belgian
Bernstein
Black Diamond
Bristol City
Cairn-Thomson
Canadian Travel League
Capo Line

Elder Dempster
Fjell
Head
Holland America
Johnson-Warren
Joseph Constantine
Manchester
Royal Netherlands
U.S. Navigation

TRANSATLANTIC FROM GULF

Dixie-Mediterranean
Dixie U.K.
French
Hamburg American
Holland America

Mobile Oceanic
Silver-Java
Southern States
Wilhelmsen

TRANSATLANTIC FROM COAST

Blue Star
Donaldson
East Asiatic
Fred Olson
French
Fruit Express
Furness
Hamburg American

Holland America
Interocean
Italian
Johnson
Knutsen
North German Lloyd
Silver-Java

WEST INDIES

Baltimore Insular	N.Y. Cuba Mail
Canadian National	N.Y. & P.R.
Ena S.S.	Panama
Furness	Porto Rico
Grace	Royal Netherlands
Monarch	Standard Fruit
Munson	United Fruit

WEST INDIES FROM GULF

Aluminum	Mobile-Miami & Gulf
Humphrey and MacGregor	Standard Fruit
Lykes Brothers	United Fruit

AUSTRALIA

American Pioneer	Port
Canadian Travel League	Transatlantic S.S. Co.
Matson	Union S.S. of N.Z.

22 · *How Much Time Have You?*

IF YOU CAN VACATION ONLY ONE WEEK

Coastwise
Bermuda
Nassau
Havana
North Atlantic
Alaska from Pacific Coast

IF YOU CAN VACATION TWO WEEKS

Coastwise
Alaska
North Atlantic
West Indies-Caribbean — Cargo and de luxe boats, few
   ports only.

IF YOU CAN VACATION THREE WEEKS

Coastwise
North Atlantic
Alaska
West Indies-Caribbean
Central America

IF YOU CAN VACATION FOUR WEEKS

Coastwise
Alaska
North Atlantic

West Indies-Caribbean
Central America
Transatlantic

IF YOU CAN VACATION SIX WEEKS

Coastwise
Alaska — Vagabond Tours
North Atlantic — Vagabond Tours
West Indies-Caribbean
Central-South America
Transatlantic
Scandanavian Ports
Mediterranean

IF YOU CAN VACATION TWO MONTHS

Coastwise
South America
Transatlantic from Gulf — Vagabond Tours

IF YOU CAN VACATION THREE MONTHS

Far East via Africa, or via Los Angeles
Arctic Circle

IF YOU CAN VACATION FOUR MONTHS

Around the world
Dutch East Indies via Africa
Around South America
Around Africa
Australia
Transatlantic from West Coast

IF YOU CAN VACATION LONGER THAN FOUR MONTHS

Around the world — either direction
Far East either direction
Australia

UNDER $100

Coastwise (if space is available)
North Atlantic (Canada some trips)
Alaska (from West Coast)
West Indies (a few trips only)

IF YOU WILL SPEND UP TO $200

Coastwise
North Atlantic
Alaska (from West Coast)
Transatlantic
Caribbean
Central-South America

IF YOU WILL SPEND UP TO $300

Coastwise
North Atlantic
Caribbean-West Indies
South-Central America
Transatlantic

IF YOU WILL SPEND UP TO $400

Europe from California
Caribbean-West Indies
South-Central America
Transatlantic

Transpacific
South America
Australia

If You Will Spend up to $500

Far East
Africa-Dutch East Indies
South America
Mediterranean
India
Australia

If You Will Spend up to $600

Around the world
Far East
Africa-Dutch East Indies
South America
Australia

If You Will Spend More than $600

Around the world — either direction
Far East — either direction
Arctic Circle

24 · A List of Freighter Trips

THE list of freighter trips that follows was compiled several months before publication. Some of the tours undoubtedly will not be operating within six months, but many others will continue for many seasons. Some of the services listed here have been operating for ten or fifteen years. Many of them have government mail contracts or other subsidies that insure their continuation.

New York City addresses are given for the lines wherever possible. Many of the concerns, as will be noted, operate more than one service. As new routes are added the chances are in favor of this being under the management of these companies.

It is not advocated that this list be considered the beginning and end of all freighter voyages, but it gives a fairly representative picture of what is available. Naturally all routes and fares will change with the fluctuation of exchange, and routes may even change after voyages have commenced.

COMPANIES OPERATING SHIPS — ROUTES COVERED, FARES, ETC.

This list includes all known freighter services as far as information could be secured. It also lists many of the cargo-boat services that are now so popular with Vagabond Vacationers.

The information is given for what it is worth and naturally is not guaranteed. In most cases, however, the information is based on statements from the operators of the lines.

ABERDEEN & COMMONWEALTH LINE, 2 Australia House, Strand, London, W. C. 2. Cunard Line, agents, 25 Broadway, New York, N.Y.

This company operates one-class (tourist) vessels from London to Australia. 11 sailings per year. Southampton to Brisbane, about 45 days. Fare 60 pounds minimum for 90-day round trip. These ships travel via the Suez Canal, Port Said, Aden, Colombo, and Australia. These boats are not freighters. Round-trip fares not returning on same vessel run from 67 pounds to 128 pounds depending on accommodations and ship.

ALASKA PACKERS ASSN., 111 California Street, San Francisco, Calif.

Under new laws the ships of this Company are permitted to carry passengers but the Company advises: "However we do not take advantage of that right, nor do we solicit passenger trade."

ALASKA STEAMSHIP COMPANY, Pier 2, Seattle, Wash.; 604 Fifth Ave., New York, N.Y.

Seattle to Prince of Wales Island.
Trip 10–12 days. Fare $76 ($95 with bath). There are 14 sailings per year; 12 passengers.
S.S. Dellwood, S.S. Lakina.
Ports may include: Craig, Waterfall, Klawock, Steamboat Bay, Hydaburg, on west coast of Prince of Wales Island; Port Conclusion, Port Walter, Port Armstrong, and Washington Bay in Chatham Strait; Skowl Arm, Hidden Inlet, and Union Bay and other points in Ketchikan district.

Seattle to Alaska (trips of varying lengths).
From Seattle to Seward (year-round service), 12-day round trip; fare $130; 25–40 per cent. extra for room with bath.

Steerage for men only. Fare is $41 one way. Steerage passengers must furnish blankets and their own meals. Sailings weekly.

CARGO VESSELS: *Baranof, Alaska, Yukon, Mt. McKinley, Aleutian, Columbia, Denali.*

Ports: Ketchikan, Wrangell, Petersburg, Juneau, Cordova, Valdez, Seward.

Occasional calls: Haines Chilkoot Barracks, Skagway, Yakutat, Latouche.

Summer season only: Weekly sailings beyond Seward, to Nome and St. Michael.

From Seattle (summer only) to Bering Sea Ports.

Round trip 20–30 days. Monthly sailings. Fare $160 up. Dutch Harbor (Unalaska), Nome, St. Michael, Golovin, Teller, East Cape (Siberia), Pribilof Islands, Juneau, Ketchikan, Taku Glacier.

Connections: Juneau — *M.S. Estebeth* for Sitka and Chatham Strait Ports. Skagway — White Pass and Yukon route. Cordova — Copper River and Northwestern Railway. Seward — Alaska Railway weekly train to Fairbanks.

The United States mail steamer *Starr* is 525 registered net tons, 141 feet in length. Other ships 6,000–9,000 tons.

From Seward, Alaska.

S.S. Starr, sails monthly, on arrival of ship from Seattle, for Portlock, Seldovia, Ouzinkie, Kodiak, Shearwater Bay, Port Hobron, McCord, Old Harbor, Uyak, Carmel, Alitak, Kanatak, Chignik, Perryville, Sand Point, Squaw Harbor, Unga, Belkofski, King Cove, False Pass, Sanak, Scotch Cap, Sarichef, Dutch Harbor (Unalaska), Makushin, Kashega, Chernofski, Umnak.

On October trip also calls at Naknek, Nushagak, Kanakanak, and Dillingham on Bristol Bay.

Annual Arctic Vagabond Cruise, from Seattle.

Trip 25–35 days. Fare $260 and up. Route varies, but includes Pribilof Islands, Aleutian Islands, Siberia.

ALUMINUM LINE, American Bank Building, New Orleans, La.

Caribbean Cruise.

Trip 37–40 days. Fare $220. Sailings every other Saturday. Tonnage 5,000; 12 passengers.

New Orleans via Mobile and Tampa to Kingston, Pointe-à-Pître, Fort de France, Bridgetown, Port of Spain, Georgetown, Paramaribo, Port of Spain, Kingston, New Orleans. (Occasional calls at Moengo.)

Gulf Ports to South America.

Trip 34 days. Fare $200. Sailings every other Tuesday. Tonnage 5,000; 12 passengers.

New Orleans via Mobile, Port au Prince, Trujillo City, Willemstad, La Guaira, Paramaribo, and return via Trinidad, to New Orleans. (Occasional calls at Moengo.)

AMERICAN EXPORT LINES, 25 Broadway, New York, N.Y.

Mediterranean.

Approximately 45 days. Fare $395 minimum. Shore excursions $200 extra. Cabin de luxe $545. Sailings every other Tuesday.

Gross tons, 9,000. First class; 130 passengers.

Gibraltar, Marseilles, Naples, Alexandria, Jaffa, Tel Aviv, Beirut, Haifa, Alexandria, Piræus, Naples, Leghorn, Genoa, Marseilles, Boston, New York.

Formerly operated a freighter service reaching smaller ports but passengers were not carried on their freighters after the spring of 1938.

AMERICA FRANCE LINE. Transatlantic passenger service has been discontinued.

AMERICAN–GULF–ORIENT LINE. (Gulf to Orient.) (See Lykes Bros.-Ripley S.S. Co.)

AMERICAN HAMPTON ROADS LINE, 110 State St., Boston, Mass.

Transatlantic (to East Coast United Kingdom).

S.S. *Capulin* may carry passengers on some crossings. Fare $60 to first British port. Other ships of this line do not carry passengers.

Not all offices of this company will agree that passengers are carried, which is indication of small capacity available.

AMERICAN MERCHANT LINES, 45 Broadway, New York, N.Y.

Transatlantic to England.

Trip 10 days. Minimum fare $105, room with bath $25 additional. Rates are slightly higher in season. Weekly sailings.

About 8,000 gross tons. Ships are 448 feet long, 58 foot beam. Carry about 85 passengers.

New York to London or Liverpool.

AMERICAN PIONEER LINE, 1 Broadway, New York, N.Y.

New York to India.

Takes 48 days to Calcutta. Fare is $500 round trip. Sailing monthly.

New York to Port Said, Suez, Bombay, Colombo, Madras, and Calcutta and return.

New York to Australia.

Takes 50 days to Australia one way. Fare is $300. Round trip 3½ to 4 months. Fare is $450. Sailings ten times per year.

Carries 12 passengers or less on each ship.

New York, Panama, Brisbane, Sydney, Melbourne, Adelaide, Freemantle (Auckland, Wellington via Sydney).

Occasional service to Honolulu, Manila, and Shanghai.

AMERICAN SCANTIC LINE, 5 Broadway, New York, N.Y.

Transatlantic — New York to Scandinavian ports.

Trip 48–50 days. Fare $225–$325. Summer only. Carries 5 passengers. Two sailings monthly. No one-way service on freighters.

First class.

40-day cruise including shore excursions, $225 winter, $375 summer. New York to Helsingfors about 18 days. Winter rates, minimum fare is $118; between seasons, $159; during season, $175. About twenty sailings per year.

First-class ships, a little over 5,000 tons each, carry about 85 passengers. Freighters carry 5. First-class ships have air-conditioned dining salon.

New York to Gothenburg, Copenhagen, Gdynia, Stockholm, Helsingfors. A week loading at ports in Baltic Sea, and return. One first-class summer sailing usually includes Leningrad.

AMERICAN SOUTH AFRICAN LINE, 26 Beaver Street, New York, N.Y.

South Africa.

Trip 105 days, approximately; $558 minimum round trip. Sailings first of each month from New York, every month from New Orleans.

Trip 95 days, all expenses, including 27-day sight-seeing in South and East Africa and Rhodesia (on first-class *M.V. City of New York* only) $1150.

Rates are the same from New York or New Orleans.

Motor Vessel *City of New York* (15,000 displacement tonnage) makes the trip every three months.

Freighters, 12,000–14,000 tons, make other sailings carrying 12 passengers only. Ships: *Henry S. Grove, Charles Cramp, Chincha, West Cawthorn, Challenger, West Isleta.*

Cabins with private bath on *M.V. City of New York* at higher rates. All double cabins on freighters with the exception of two single rooms on the *Henry S. Grove*. Charge of 25 per cent. extra for these single rooms.

Capetown, Port Elizabeth, East London, Durban. Lourenço Marques, Beira, Dar-es-Salaam, Zanzibar, Tanga, and Mombasa. Return via the same route, stopping at Trinidad on return.

Vessels from New Orleans stop at Trinidad outbound also.

AMERICAN–WEST AFRICAN LINE.
No longer carries passengers on freighters.

ANGLO–NEWFOUNDLAND DEVELOPMENT CO., Grand Falls, Newfoundland.

This company has asked that they be listed as *not* offering passenger service. Their ships operate in the transatlantic trade from Newfoundland ports. One ship occasionally has carried passengers, but most passenger accommodations are utilized for members of their own staff, and, according to statements by company officials, no passengers will be booked from outside of Newfoundland under any consideration.

AUSTRALIAN ORIENTAL LINE, 6 Bridge Street, Sydney, Australia.

Lord Howe Islands Cruise.

Trip 10 days. Fare 10–14 pounds. Sailings twice monthly. Room with bath, 17/17.

SHIPS: *S.S. Changte, S.S. Taiping.*

Sydney, Lord Howe Islands, Melbourne, Sydney.

These ships are first class only.

BALTIMORE MAIL LINE, 313 N. Charles Street, Baltimore, Md.

Transatlantic.

Trip 10–13 days. Baltimore to London, $110. Weekly. One-class vessels carrying about 80 passengers.

Baltimore and Norfolk to London, Havre, and Hamburg. Return from Bremen or Southampton.

BARBER LINE, 17 Battery Place, New York, N.Y.

Round-the-world.
Around the world, New York to New York, about 135 days, $550.
Around the world, Los Angeles to New York, $475.
Ten per cent. less on *Raby Castle.*
Sailings approximately monthly.
SHIPS: *Tai Yin, Tai Ping, Tai Ping Yang, Tricolor, Thurland Castle, Greystoke Castle, Toulouse, Triton, Raby Castle,* etc.

Freighters have about 7,000 gross tons; Castle boats about 15,000 tons displacement; *Tai* boats about 10,000 tons displacement.

Carry from 8 to 12 passengers.

To Far East and return.
Trip 120–135 days from New York. $600.
Los Angeles to Far East and return to New York, $500.
Sailings about twelve times per year.

Tai vessels operate to Manila and Shanghai, from New York via Norfolk, Panama Canal, Los Angeles, cruising minor islands of Philippines and calling at Japanese ports (Hong Kong, Shanghai, Kobe, Yokohama, if cargo offers) returning via San Pedro, Panama Canal to New York.

Castle vessels operate over the same route to Philippines, continuing to Hong Kong, Shanghai (second call), Kobe, Nagoya, Yokohama, Macassar, Sourabaya, Samarang, Batavia, Singapore, Port Swettenham, Penang, Belawan-Deli, Colombo, then occasionally to Calcutta. Returning either via Suez Canal and Port Said, with occasional stops at Naples and other south European ports, or running from Colombo around South Africa, Cape of Good Hope, Dakar and such other stops as may be called for by available cargo.

Castle boats usually make New York the first port of call on the Atlantic, but if cargo offers may land first at Halifax, Boston or even Hampton Roads.

During war in Far East this line, like other world cruise vessels, omitted many Far East stops. During Ethiopian-Spanish war these vessels avoided the war zone completely, circling Cape Horn in some cases without stop.

Barber Steamship Company acts as agents for Wilhelmsen Line, Blue Funnel, Booth Line and other operators of freighters.

Tai boats have "owners' suites," consisting of day room, bedroom and bathroom, in addition to 4 or 5 other double cabins. For "owners' suites," when available, add 25 per cent. to fares.

Some of the *Castle* boats have two cabins with private bath. Charge of 15 per cent. over regular fare for these accommodations.

Outdoor swimming pools on many ships.

BARRINGTON TRANSPORTATION CO., care Canadian Pacific Railway, Montreal, Canada.

This company operates a regular weekly service by Diesel-propelled river boats from May to October, running from Wrangell, Alaska, to Telegraph Creek, B.C., via the Stikine River, a distance of 185 miles.

Carry 15 to 50 passengers. Three days one way. Round trip fare, including meals and berth, $45.

BELGIAN LINE, 10 Pearl Street, New York, N.Y.

Transatlantic.

New York to Antwerp (occasionally sail from Albany, N.Y.).

Trip 10 days. Fare $85, one way (with bath $100). Fare $155 round trip, with bath $175. Sailings every ten days.

One class only.

This line also has cargo-boat service from Antwerp to Belgian Congo.

ARNOLD BERNSTEIN LINE, 17 Battery Place, New York, N.Y.

Transatlantic.
Tourist-class vessels.
Trip 11–12 days. In the off season fare is $100 one way, $189 round trip. During season fare is $110 one way. Outside single rooms are $10 additional each way. Inside single rooms are $2.50 additional. No other higher rates.

BALTIMORE–INSULAR LINE, Pratt Street, Baltimore, Md.

Baltimore to San Juan, Puerto Rico; San Juan to Philadelphia.
Fare $60 one way; $108 round trip. Room with bath $10 to $15 additional. Sailings every three weeks.
S.S. *Barbara,* carrying 50 passengers.

San Juan, St. Thomas, Christiansted, St. Thomas, San Juan.
Round trip to St. Croix.
Fare is $27 round trip. Twice weekly.
American mail steamer, *Catherine.* Carries 50 passengers.

This company also operates about 20 vessels to the Dominican Republic and in other coastwise service. Passengers are not carried on these vessels, which range from 2,000 to 8,000 tons.

BLACK DIAMOND LINE, 39 Broadway, New York, N.Y.

Transatlantic.
Trip 10 days; $75–$80 one way; 4–8 sailings per month; 8,000 tons (deadweight); 2–12 passengers.
New York, Rotterdam, Antwerp.
SHIPS: *Black Condor, Black Gull, Black Falcon, Black Heron, Black Osprey, Black Eagle, Black Hawk,* etc.

Women must be accompanied by adult male relative of immediate family.

BLUE FUNNEL LINE, 17 Battery Place, New York, N.Y.

Around-the-world from New York.
Trip 4½ months. Fare $520. Sailings on the 25th of each month. Carry 10–12 passengers. 12,000–14,000 tons displacement.

New York to Norfolk, Savannah, (Kingston), Cristobal, Los Angeles, many ports in Philippine Islands, Singapore, Dutch East Indies, Batavia, Malabar Coast, Penang, Colombo and Boston.

Women must be accompanied by male relatives.

New York to Orient.
Fare, one way $290. Sailings monthly.
Carrying 6–10 passengers.
New York, Trinidad, British West Indies, Panama Canal, Batavia, Straits Settlements.

Pacific Northwest to Orient.
Trip 41 days, fare is $155 one way. Sailings monthly.
Seattle and Vancouver to Yokohama, Kobe, Miike, Shanghai (Dairen), Hong Kong, return via same ports with a stop at Nagoya also.

New York to Straits, China, Japan, via Africa.
One way $290 to Straits. To Japan, $350.
Sailings monthly; 6–10 passengers.
New York and/or other Atlantic ports, Trinidad, various ports in Africa, Singapore and other ports, Batavia.

Fare (via Panama Canal), New York to Japan or Straits, or Java, $300 one way.

It is possible to arrange around-the-world bookings by using Blue Funnel east bound to Orient, Maersk, or other lines from Manila east bound through the Panama Canal to New York.

London to Far East.

Freighters carrying 8–12 passengers. London to Belawan-Deli, £97 4/, round voyage. At least one ship a week from London to Far East, but some sailings are A-class ships, 120 passengers, fare to Belawan £75 as compared with £55 on freighters and £59 on B-class vessels carrying 22 passengers.

BLUE STAR LINE, Vancouver, B.C.

West Coast to Europe.

Trip 46 days en route. Summer fares, $185; winter fares, $210. Sailings monthly in summer months; two or three sailings a month from September to June.

These are 10,000-ton vessels. Six passengers on most boats, a few carry more.

New Westminster, B.C., Vancouver, Seattle, Portland, San Francisco, Los Angeles to Liverpool, Glasgow, London, Rotterdam and Newcastle.

England to Australia and New Zealand.

This company operates a variety of routes from London and Channel ports to Australia and to New Zealand. Weekly sailings — about 100 days. Fare £96 round voyage.

Route to Australia is normally around the Cape of Good Hope with several stops in Africa, and a variety of stops in Australia and return. Fare is £96 round voyage and up, depending on route and ship.

Ships to New Zealand usually proceed via the Panama Canal with stops in the West Indies, but also may operate around South America. Fare is £96 and up, round voyage, depending on route and ship. These fares are for freighters carrying 8 to 12 passengers. Many new vessels are in service, including several with private bath with every room. Tonnage runs from 5,000 to 15,000.

Also operates London to New Zealand via Suez and Far East via Suez.

Blue Star services also operate to South America from London.

The *Arandora Star*, carrying 400 passengers, is operated by this company, usually in special cruises from London.

BOOTH LINE, 17 Battery Place, New York, N.Y.

New York to Brazil.

Trip 60–80 days; fare $325–$360 round trip. Sailings bimonthly.

These are 10,000–11,000-ton vessels; 10–14 passengers.

New York to Barbados, Pará, Maranham, Tutoya, Ceará, Natal, Cabedello, Pernambuco, Maceió, Manaos, Iquitos, Bahia and return.

Doctor on ships.

England to Brazil.

Liverpool, Portugal, Madeira, North Brazil ports, Amazon River as far inland as Manaos. Ships of 11,000 tons displacement; 100 passengers. Round voyage seven weeks. First class fare from $360. Company also operates 12 passenger freighters of about same size in this same service from Liverpool to Amazon River ports. Connections at Pará or other Brazil ports for New York from London can be arranged from time to time. Once in a while freighters change runs so that same ship will make complete voyage, New York to Liverpool via Brazil.

BRISTOL CITY LINE OF STEAMERS (DOMINION LINE), 1 Broadway, New York, N.Y.

Transatlantic.

Trip 14 days, fare is $67 per person. Sailings about every two months.

S.S. Toronto City is the only ship of this line carrying passengers. 12-passenger capacity.

Atlantic ports to Bristol Channel ports, usually first stop is Cardiff, Wales.

This company will not make bookings for advanced dates because of possible change in departure port.

West-bound passage must be booked at Bristol, England, offices.

BRITISH INDIAN STEAM NAVIGATION CO., 122 Leadenhall St., London. Care Cunard Line, 25 Broadway, New York, N.Y.

This company operates a variety of cargo-passenger services: —

Calcutta to Rangoon, Singapore, China, Japan.

Rangoon to Madras; to Mergui, to Penang.

Madras to Madras Coast Ports.

Singapore to Bangkok.

Bombay to Karachi, to Persian Gulf (24–35 days) to East and South Africa.

Other services to East Africa Coast; to India, Burma, Java, Australia, New Zealand and Mauritius.

Sample Service. *M.V. Dumra,* Mombasa-Mikindani £15, about 5 days.

Sailings twice monthly. Ports: Mombasa, Tanga, Zanzibar, Dar-es-Salaam, Kilwa, Lindi, Mikindani, Ibo. Returning via: Lindi, Ruvu Bay, Dar-es-Salaam, Zanzibar, Tanga, Lamu and Mombasa.

London to Beira. One-class ships. Every four weeks. About 28 days. Fare £48 one way.

Some ships of this service are freighters with limited accommodations, but vessels on London run, and on many other services, are exceptionally well fitted, carrying only one class of passengers as a rule, but giving them exceptional quarters at rather reasonable rates.

BURNS PHILP CO., 815 Spring Arcade, Los Angeles, Calif.

Local cruises from Australia (Sydney).

Three-week cruise, fare is £28. Sailings every six weeks.
CARGO-PASSENGER SHIPS.

From Sydney to Lord Howe, Norfolk Islands, Vila, Bush-
mans Bay, Malo, Tangoa, Segond, Aoba, Norfolk Islands,
Lord Howe, Sydney.

Local cruise from Sydney.

Five-week cruise; fare is £46 (round trip). Sailings every
six weeks.

CARGO-PASSENGER SHIP: *S.S. Malaita.*

From Sydney via Brisbane to Tulagi, Makambo, Gavutu,
Su-U Domma, Mamara, Aruligo, Lavoro, Yandina, Banika,
Ufa, Faiami, Younger, Pepesala, Kaylan, Meringe, West Bay,
Somata, Gizo, Faisi, Kieta, Arigua, Teopasino, Numa,
Rabaul, Soraken, Keta, Faisi, Gizo, Tetipari, Russell
Group, Gavutu, Tulagi, Brisbane, Sydney.

Other cruises at similar rates. Monthly sailings.

CAIRN–THOMSON LINE (c/o FURNESS), 34 White-
    hall Street, New York, N.Y. St. Sacrament St., Mon-
    treal, Canada.

Transatlantic.

Trip 11 days, $80 one way, $150 round trip. Sailing every
two weeks; 8–12 passengers.

Montreal, West St. John, Halifax and Newcastle. Return
from Leith. Sail from Halifax in winter.

CANADIAN NATIONAL STEAMSHIP CO., 675 Fifth
    Ave., New York, N.Y.

West Indies.

Trip 30–32 days, fare is $225 round trip and up. Sailing
twice monthly.

This company operates the famous Lady boats, 8,000 tons,
120 passengers.

Halifax, Boston, Bermuda, St. Kitts, Nevis, Antigua,

Montserrat, Dominica, St. Lucia, Barbados, St. Vincent, Grenada, Trinidad, British Guiana and return, same ports, and to St. John, N.B.

Stopovers are available on Lady boat sailings, although space is in great demand at certain seasons.

Bermuda, Nassau, Jamaica.

Trip 25 days. Fare is $190 and up. Cheaper at certain seasons. Sailings from Montreal about every three weeks in summer.

Lady boats, around 8,000 tons, and carrying about 120 passengers.

Montreal to Bermuda, Nassau, Kingston, and return.

This line operates from Halifax and Boston over the same route the rest of the year, twice monthly, $180 and up.

Freighter Service to West Indies.

Trip 30–38 days. Round trip voyage $170–$195, depending on the season of the year. Sailings about every six weeks.

FREIGHTERS: S.S. Colborne and S.S. Chomedy, about 6,500 tons; 12 passengers.

Sails from Montreal summer months, other months from Halifax to Puerto Rico, Barbados, Trinidad, British Guiana and return. Other ports (as cargo offers): St. Kitts, Antigua, Guadeloupe, St. Vincent, Martinique.

There are no stopovers.

Jamaica to Belize, British Honduras.

Trip 4 days; $40 one way, $75 round trip. Twice monthly.

SHIP: R.M.S. Connector; 1,787 tons; 18 passengers.

Alaska Service.

Trip 5 days $45; 9 days $95; 11 days $115. Weekly sailings.

SHIPS: S.S. Prince Rupert and S.S. Prince George, about 4,000 tons.

Vancouver, B.C., Powell River, Alert Bay, Ocean Falls, Prince Rupert, Ketchikan, Taku Glacier, Juneau, Skagway, Wrangell, Anyox, Stewart and return.

Charlotte Islands Service.

Trip 5–6 days; one way — Vancouver to Massett; $26 one way. Sailings fortnightly.

SHIP: *S.S. Prince John,* 905 tons.

Vancouver, Alert Bay, Rose Harbor, Jedway, Lockeporte, Atli Inlet, Lagoon Bay, Cumshewa, Sandspit, Queen Charlotte City, Massett, Port Clements, Buckley Bay, Prince Rupert and return.

Other ports as cargo or passengers offer.

CANADIAN PACIFIC S.S. CO., 344 Madison Ave., New York, N.Y.

Alaska Service

Trip 9 days; fare round trip $95. Sailings about every ten days. Summer sailings more frequent.

SHIPS: *Princess Norah,* 3,000 tons; *Princess Mary,* 3,000 tons; *Princess Louise,* 5,000 tons; *Princess Charlotte,* 5,000 tons.

Vancouver, Alert Bay, Prince Rupert, Ketchikan, Wrangell, Taku Glacier, Juneau, Skagway and return. West Taku Arm, Whitehorse, Dawson, on some sailings.

Vancouver to Powell River.

Two-day trip, sailing 11:45 P.M. Tuesday, Thursday and Saturday. Returning Thursday, Saturday and Monday. Buy berths and meals aboard ship.

Vancouver, Powell River, Blubber Bay, Hornby Island, Denman Island, Union Bay, Comox, Blubber Bay, Powell River and Vancouver.

Triangle Service.

This company also operates a triangle service between Seattle, Vancouver and Victoria during the summer months.

This company operates the famous Empress, Duchess and other vessels in transatlantic and transpacific service. They usually operate one world cruise each season also. These de luxe conference services are not listed here.

West Coast-Vancouver Island.

Princess Norah leaves Victoria, B.C., three times a month for: — Port Renfrew, Carmanah, Clo-oose, Bamfield, Sarita Bay, McCallum Bay, Kildonan, Green Cove, Nahmint, Franklin River, Underwood Cove, Port Alberni, Ecoole, Sechart, Lucky Creek, Ucluelt, Port Albion, Tofino, Clayoquot, Kakawis, Ahousat, Matilda Creek, Refuge Cove, Hesquiat, Nootka Cannery, Danzig Mines, Ceepeecee, McBride Bay, Hecate, Zeballos, Tahsis, Espinosa, Markdale, Chamiss Bay, Caledonia, Kyuquot Village, Winter Harbor, Quatsino Village, Jeune Landing, Spry Camp, Port Alice, and return.

Seven days round trip. Not all ports on both voyages.

Fare $1950 one way.

Vancouver-Ocean Falls-Prince Rupert

SHIP: *Princess Adelaide.* Weekly sailing. Fare $36–$42; 4–5 days.

To: Campbell River, Englewood, Alert Bay, Port Hardy (Namu), Ocean Falls (Walker Lake Cannery), Butedale (Bishop Bay every other trip), Prince Rupert and return.

CANADIAN TRAVEL LEAGUE, 410 St. Nicholas Street, Montreal, Que., Canada.

This concern acts as general agent for a variety of freighter services. They are also agents for many lines.

Also see Addenda.

CAPO LINE, Coristine Bldg., Montreal, Canada.

Transatlantic.

Trip 17–19 days. One way $100–$120. Round trip $175–$210.

Carrying 8–12 passengers. Twice monthly.

Montreal (summer months), St. John, Marseilles, Genoa. Naples on return trip.

CLARKE STEAMSHIP CO. LTD., 655 Fifth Ave., New York, N.Y. Dominion Square Bldg., Montreal, Canada.

Cruises of 11–12 days on Gulf of St. Lawrence.
About 12 days at fares from about $65. Sailings twice monthly, May to November.
SHIP: *M.V. Père Arnaud;* 10 passengers.
Quebec, Rimouski, Natashquan, Harrington, Blanc Sablon, Natashquan, Quebec.

Trip 12–13 days, minimum $74. Sailings twice monthly, May to November.
SHIP: *S.S. Sable I;* 28 passengers.
Same ports as above but also stops at Baie Comeau, Clarke City, Havre St. Pierre, Mutton Bay, going and coming. Sails from Montreal.

Trip 13 days, $90. ($72 for early and late season cruises.) Sailings from May to November.
SHIP: *S.S. Gaspesia;* 43 passengers.
To Newfoundland and North Shore points.

Gaspe Coast Cruise. Magdalen Islands Cruise.
Trip 5½ days for $50 on Gaspe Coast cruise; 6½ days for $60 on Magdalen Islands cruise. (Fare 20 per cent. cheaper on early and late sailings.) From May to November, Gaspe Coast one week, Magdalen Islands alternate week.
S.S. North Gaspe; 24 passengers.
From Montreal and Quebec.

De luxe cruises from Montreal.
Trip 12 days at $135 and up. Four sailings during July and August only.
SHIP: *S.S. North Star,* carrying 330 passengers.
Montreal, Quebec, Gaspe, Charlottetown, Pictou, Corner Brook, Loch Lomond, St. Anthony, Forteau, Havre St. Pierre, Saguenay River, Murray Bay, Quebec, Montreal.

De luxe cruises on *S.S. Northland.* (170 passengers.)
Varying cruises during the summer from Montreal, fares ranging from $10 and up, per day.

CLYDE MALLORY LINE, Pier 34, North River, New York, N.Y.

Coastwise Service.

Trip 60 days; $60 or $50.

Fares range at slightly above general cargo rates and under de luxe liner rates. Four weekly sailings in season.

New York to Galveston, Miami, Jacksonville, Charleston.

COLOMBIAN LINE, 17 Battery Place, New York, N.Y.

Haitian outports.

Trip 23 days; fare $135.

S.S. *Martinique* carries twelve passengers.

New York to Cape Haitian, Port de Paix, Gonaïves, St. Marc, Port au Prince, Petit Goave, Miragoane, Jeremie, Aux Cayes, Jacmel, Petit Goave, St. Marc, Gonaïves, Port de Paix, Cape Haitian and New York.

Outdoor swimming pool.

This service suspended summer of 1938.

JOSEPH CONSTANTINE STEAMSHIP LINE LTD., 309 Board of Trade Bldg., Montreal, Canada.

Transatlantic.

Trip 12–15 days; one way $80–$95, round trip $155–$185. About 5 ships monthly.

Carrying 12 passengers.

Montreal to London, Hull, Newcastle, Liverpool, Manchester or Avonmouth. (Port of first arrival overseas varies, announced only a few days prior to sailing.) Return from Port Talbot, Wales, or Swansea.

Lady passengers must be accompanied by near relative unless other ladies are booked for the same voyage.

This company also operates occasional sailings from the United Kingdom to South Africa, Mauritius, Australia and South America. For particulars address: Constantine Line, Baltic Exchange Chambers, 24 St. Mary Axe, London E.C. 3.

DAVIS TRANSPORTATION CO., Juneau, Alaska.

Juneau to Sitka, Alaska.
Trip 4 days, $16.50. Meals 50 cents each extra. *M.V. Estebeth;* 64.6 in length; leaves Juneau each Wednesday at 6 P.M. 16 passengers. 4 individual staterooms. 12 berths.
Ports: Juneau, Point Retreat, Funter Bay, Hawk Inlet, Tenakee, Hoonah, Excursion Inlet, Point Gustavus, Lemesurier Island, Dundas Bay, Inian Island, Cape Spencer, Port Althorp, Soapstone Point, Apex, El Nido, Pinta Bay, Hogan Island, Hirst Cove, Chichagof, Sitka (Chatham, Baranof, Killisnoo).

DELTA LINE, New Orleans, La.

South Atlantic.
Trip 20–30 days each way. New Orleans to Rio de Janeiro, $175; to Buenos Aires, $225 ($393.75, round trip). Time ashore at passenger's expense. Sailings twice monthly. About 10 weeks round trip.
CARGO VESSELS, carrying 35 to 42 passengers.
New Orleans to Rio de Janeiro, Santos, Montevideo, Buenos Aires. Return via Buenos Aires, Santos and Rio de Janeiro, Victoria to New Orleans.
Ships carry physician, stewardess, laundry.
Swimming pools.

DIXIE MEDITERRANEAN LINE, Whitney Building, New Orleans, La. (LYKES BROS.–RIPLEY S.S. CO., 17 Battery Place, New York, N.Y.)

Gulf ports to Mediterranean.
Trip 21 days; $100 one way, $200 round trip. Two to four sailings monthly.
SHIPS: 8,000–10,000 tons, carrying 2–8 passengers.
New Orleans, Houston, Galveston to Barcelona and/or Genoa.
Return trip from Venice or Spanish port.

Ships sometimes proceed to Trieste, Fiume, Patros, Piræus.

No unaccompanied women.

DIXIE U.K. LINE, Whitney Building, New Orleans, La. (LYKES BROS.–RIPLEY STEAMSHIP CO., 17 Battery Place, New York, N.Y.)

Gulf ports to Europe.

Trip 21 days, $100 one way, $200 round trip. Two to eight monthly.

SHIPS: 8,000–10,000 tons. Average ship carries 2 passengers.

New Orleans, Houston, Galveston to Liverpool, London. Return trip from Rotterdam.

Sailings monthly to Glasgow.

No unaccompanied women.

DOLLAR LINE, 29 Broadway, New York, N.Y.

Around-the-world.

About 3½ months. Minimum tourist rate around the world, $658; minimum cabin rate around the world, $854. Sailings every two weeks. Tickets permit stopover.

Cabin and tourist class.

Normal route: New York, Havana, Cristobal, Balboa, Los Angeles, San Francisco, Honolulu, Kobe, Shanghai, Hong Kong, Manila, Singapore, Penang, Colombo, Bombay, Suez, Alexandria, Naples, Genoa, Marseilles, New York, Boston.

Chinese and Mediterranean ports may be omitted as occasion requires.

DONALDSON LINE, 351 California St., San Francisco, Calif.

Transatlantic from Pacific Coast.

Trip 42 days, Europe to San Francisco. $165 one way; $306 round trip; 18 sailings per year.

Carrying 3–6 passengers.

North Pacific Coast ports, San Francisco, Los Angeles to London, Glasgow. Return from Liverpool.

Women not booked unaccompanied.

EAGLE PACKET CO., St. Louis, Missouri.

This company is the last of the riverboat operators on the Mississippi.

For 1938 they offered a variety of short cruises at around $7 a day for meals and berth.

1939 will likely show about the same service with perhaps a slight increase in rates.

Greene Line, Cincinnati, operates on the Ohio and other rivers.

EAST ASIATIC LINE, 433 California St., San Francisco, Calif. Alaska Bldg., Seattle, Wash.

Transatlantic from Pacific Coast.

Trip 36–60 days. Fare $352, room with bath additional. Sailings twice monthly.

CARGO VESSELS: 17,000 displacement tonnage; 53–73 passengers.

Vancouver, San Francisco to Cristobal, Kingston, St. Thomas, London, Southampton, Rotterdam, Hamburg, Copenhagen, Malmoe, Gothenburg, Oslo.

M.V. Canada, Erria, Europa, Amerika.

Bangkok from Europe.

Trip 45 days one way. 55 pounds. Round trip $96 up. 18 sailings per year.

VESSELS: 11–15,000 tons displacement; 28–75 passengers.

Antwerp, Southampton, Marseilles, Port Said, Colombo, Penang, Port Swettenham, Malacca, Singapore, Bangkok.

Doctor and stewardess.

Transpacific — West Coast to Orient.

Fare $120 one way to first port of call. Sailings as cargo offers.

Portland, Seattle or Vancouver to Yokohama, Kobe, Shanghai.

Europe-Japan.

Trip 50–60 days each way; £70 each way; £122/10 round voyage.

Sailings monthly.

SHIPS: 10–14,000 tons; 4–12 passengers.

Hamburg, Genoa, Port Said, Singapore, Manila, Hong Kong, Shanghai, Dairen, Yokohama, Kobe, Singapore, Port Said, Tel Aviv, Jaffa, Haifa, Rotterdam.

EASTERN STEAMSHIP LINES, Boston, Mass.

Coastwise.

This company operates a variety of passenger services on luxurious coastwise vessels at rather reasonable rates. These ships are not freighters, however, nor can they be classed as cargo boats.

Fares will run ten dollars and under, per day, for minimum accommodations.

ELDER–DEMPSTER LINES, Board of Trade Building, Montreal, Canada. Daniel Bacon, Inc., agents, 26 Beaver Street, New York, N.Y.

Montreal-South Africa.

Trip 35 days one way; $225. Sailings monthly.

Carrying 10–12 passengers.

Montreal (summer only), St. John, Freetown, Walvis Bay, Capetown, Port Elizabeth, East London, Durban, Beira.

London-West Africa.

Mail steamers sail every two weeks, carry first, second and third class passengers. Trip 20–25 days. Minimum rate £45; round voyage £72.

This company operates a large fleet of Intermediate Cargo vessels, all one class, sailing every two weeks or oftener.

London to Dakar, £26; to Victoria, or Fernando Po, £41/10.

Ports: Liverpool (London, Antwerp, Hamburg, Rotterdam, Dover), Madeira, Las Palmas, Bathurst, Bissao, Conakry, Freetown, Sherbro, Sulima, Manoh, Cape Mount, Monrovia, Grand Bassa, Sinoe, Cape Palmas, Blieron, Lahou, Grand Bassam, Assinee, Half Assinee, Takoradi, Cape Coast, Saltpond, Winneba, Accra, Ada, Keta, Lome, Whydah, Cotonou, Lagos, Apapa, Forcados, Benin, Warri, Koko, Sapele, Bonny, Port Harcourt, Opobo, Obonema, Calabar, Rio del Ray, Victoria, Duala, Kribi, Fernando Po. No vessel makes all ports, calling as inducement offers.

M.V. Calabar connects with mail service ships at Lagos for Forcados, Warri, Port Harcourt and other ports.

Female servants, not more than one to a family, when traveling with their employers two thirds of first-class fare. Male servants full fare.

Wives en route to Africa to join their husbands, or wives accompanied by their husbands, get 25 per cent. reduction on one-way voyage.

London to Canary Islands.

Round voyage cargo ships, £15. First-class ships, £17. Frequent sailings.

New York to Africa.

Freighters sail about 12 times a year to three different groups of African ports. Passengers are not carried on this route.

ELLERMAN & BUCKNALL S.S. CO., Ltd., 104 Leadenhall St., London, E.C. 3. Norton Lilly & Co., 26 Beaver St., New York, N.Y.

London to South Africa.

Trip 33–36 days one way; £50–£60 one way; £90–£108 round trip.

Sailings every four weeks. First-class vessels.

City and Hall Lines of this company operate first-class

vessels, Liverpool to Bombay and Karachi, India, via Suez; 9,000–11,000 ton vessels; 40–45 days round voyage, £65 round trip; 15 sailings per year.

City and Hall Lines also operate to Colombo, Madras and Calcutta, via Suez, about 10 sailings per year. About 30 days each way; £45 one way; £79 round voyage.

Ellerman and Papayanni Lines, operate London to Beirut, to Istanbul and Constanta, 7 to 9 weeks, round voyage fare £50, to Sicily and Italian ports.
Trip 6 to 8 weeks, round voyage £40.

Ellerman's Wilson Line to Mediterranean, 9 weeks round voyage.

Ellerman, Westcott & Laurance Line, London to Alexandria and Istanbul; 9 weeks round voyage; £45.
Some cargo ships on this service, round voyage to Alexandria, first class £45, cargo ships £40.

EMPRESA NAVIERA DE CUBA, Havana, Cuba.

Cuba-West Indies.
First-class and second-class passengers.
(This company also operates freighters in around Cuba service from time to time.)

Havana-Santiago, about 7 days.
Santiago, Trujillo City, San Juan, Trujillo City, Havana; about 9 days.
San Juan to Havana — 5 days — $55 first class.

ENA STEAMSHIP LINE, Nassau, N.P., Bahamas. Saunders & Mader, Terminal Dock, Miami, Fla.

Miami to Nassau.
Trip 20 hours one way; $17 round voyage including taxes.
SHIP: *M.V. Ena K*. Six–seven sailings monthly; 12 passengers.

ESSCO–BRODIN LINE, Eskert & Stockard, Inc., 17 Battery
   Place, New York, N.Y.

New York to Brazil — River Plate.
Trip 22–27 days one way; $315 round trip, $175 south
bound, one way. Sailings monthly.
Carrying 12 passengers.
SHIPS: *M.S. Anita, M.S. Astri.*
New York, Rio de Janeiro, Santos, Montevideo, Buenos
Aires.

FABRE LINE, 17 State St., New York, N.Y.
Passenger services "temporarily" discontinued.

FALKLAND ISLANDS S.S. CO., Montevideo, Uruguay.

Montevideo to Stanley, Falkland Islands.
Sailings about 12 times a year.
SHIP: *S.S. Lafonia* (768 tons).
One way ₱ 250; round trip ₱ 450.

FJELL LINE, 75 East Wacker Drive, Chicago, Ill. J. Brock
   Shipping Co., Coristine Bldg., Montreal, Canada.

Transatlantic.
Montreal to Europe.
Ships of this line occasionally sail from various North
Atlantic ports.
Carry 3–9 passengers. Fares, when space is available and
travel agents can book, will be in line with other services.
This line at one time carried passengers from Chicago to
England and European ports at a fare of $100 for the
journey of three and a half weeks. Line officials say this
service is not now available, all bookings being Montreal
to first port of call in Europe.
The Chicago office of this company writes: "Over an
entire season we can carry only a maximum of about 150
passengers. Our inquiries and requests for bookings amount
to well over two thousand during the course of the season.
It is evident that listing the Fjell Line is superfluous."

FRENCH LINE, 610 Fifth Ave., New York, N.Y.

Pacific Coast to Europe.
About five weeks, $310 one way. Monthly sailings.
Cabin-class ships, 12 passengers.

Vancouver to French Ports.
Vancouver to Havre.
Trip 36 days, $205. Sailings irregular.
SHIPS: *S.S. San Diego, S.S. San Jose, S.S. Antonio, S.S. San Francisco,* and others, which are about 6,000 tons each, carrying 12 passengers.
Vancouver (occasionally Portland and/or Seattle), San Francisco, Los Angeles, San Jose de Guatemala, La Libertad (Champerico and Aculta occasionally), (Corinto, La Union, Puntarenas subject to call), Cristobal (stop at Balboa if weather permits), Havre, Bordeaux. (Occasional stops at Puerto Colombia, Colombia.)

Europe to West Indies, Central and South America.
About three weeks each way, $230 one way. Sailings about twice monthly.
SHIPS: 10,000–11,000 tons. First, intermediate and third class.
French ports to French West Indies, Trinidad, Colombia, Panama Canal.

Fort de France to Haiti.
About 20 days. Sailing monthly. Francs 1150.
SHIP: *S.S. Domingue;* 40 passengers.
Fort de France, Pointe-à-Pître, Trujillo City, Jacmel, Aux Cayes, Santiago, Port au Prince and return.

Fort de France to Cayenne.
About 18 days, monthly sailings. Francs 1250.
SHIP: *Duc d'Aumale;* 40 passengers.
Fort de France, St. Lucia, Trinidad, Demerara, Surinam, St. Laurent, Cayenne and return.

Cuba-Mexico Service.

About 14 days each way. First-class fare is $240 one way.

SHIP: *S.S. Flandre,* about 13,000 tons; carrying first, tourist, intermediate and third-class passengers.

St. Nazaire, Santander, Gijon, La Corogne, Vigo, Havana, Vera Cruz, Port au Prince, Trujillo City, San Juan, and French ports.

France to Gulf Ports.

About 30 days en route, fare is $105–$115 one way. Sailings two or three times a month.

This is a freighter service.

French Channel ports to Havana and Tampico. Usually Galveston or Houston is the final Gulf port of call.

About once a year a cabin-class French liner calls at New Orleans carrying much larger numbers of passengers at cabin-class conference rates.

French Channel Ports to South America.

About 40 days; fare is $150–$170 one way. Europe to Chile. (Cargo types of steamers fare is $100.) Sailing irregular. Space very limited.

Havre, Cristobal, Callao, Valparaiso (other ports as cargo offers).

This company operates cabin-class de luxe liners transatlantic, and is American representative of various other French services reaching Moroc, Africa, and Australia.

FRUIT EXPRESS LINE, B. W. Greer & Son, Vancouver, B.C. Reidar Gjolme, Douglas Bldg., Seattle, Wash.

Pacific Coast to Europe.

Trip 21–35 days. Victoria-European ports, one way $220 up. Round trip 10 per cent. less. 16–25 sailings per year; 12 passengers.

September to March, ports: Vancouver/Victoria/New Westminster, B.C., via Seattle, Portland, San Francisco/Los

Angeles, via Panama Canal to Havre, Rotterdam, London, Liverpool, Glasgow. Summer months sailings only from Los Angeles, omitting northern Pacific Coast ports. Passengers booked to first port of call in Europe and returning from last port.

FURNESS LINE, 34 Whitehall Street, New York, N.Y.

Pacific Coast to Europe.

Four weeks from California, $242–$274 one way; six weeks from Pacific Northwest, $267–$299. Sailings fortnightly.

Ships 6,000–7,000 tons; 12 passengers.

SHIPS: *Pacific Shipper, Pacific President,* and others.

Vancouver, Seattle, Portland, San Francisco, Los Angeles, Panama Canal to London, Liverpool, Manchester and Glasgow.

New York to West Indies.

Trip 21 days, fare from $175. Sailings fortnightly (monthly in summer).

SHIPS 6,000–7,000 tons; 150 passengers. *S.S. Nerissa, Fort Townsend.*

New York, St. Thomas, St. Croix, St. Martin, St. Kitts, Antigua, Montserrat, Guadeloupe, Dominica, Martinique, St. Lucia, Barbados, Trinidad, Demerara. Return via Grenada, St. Vincent and same ports.

New York to Bermuda.

Room with bath, $60–65–70 up round trip, according to season. De luxe ships.

New York to South America.

SHIPS: *Western Prince* and so on, first-class liners; 6,000–7,000 tons; 100 passengers.

Stewardess and swimming pool on European-bound ships.

New York to St. Pierre. Furness Red Cross Line.

Trip 12 days; $135 round voyage; 100 passengers. Sailings weekly.

New York, Halifax, St. Pierre, St. Johns, Halifax, New York.

This company also represents: —
Prince Line, *England to Mediterranean.*
Johnson Warren, *transatlantic.*
Prince-Silver, *around the world.*
Manchester, *transatlantic.*
(For listings see these companies.)

FYFFES LINE, Elders & Fyffes, Ltd., 31 Bow Street, London, W.C. 2. United Fruit Co., 632 Fifth Ave., New York, N.Y.

England to Caribbean.
Trip 31–35–45 days. £32–£50 round voyage, depending on route.
SHIPS: 5,500 tons; 12 passengers. Sailings weekly, though irregular.
Sailing from Liverpool, or Swansea, returning to these ports or Southampton.
To Jamaica and/or South America. Touching, on one voyage or another, Port Limón, Montego Bay, Oracabessa, Port Antonio, Kingston, Port Royal, Salt River, Bowden, Santa Marta, Tela, Puerto Cortez, Puerto Barrios.
VESSELS: *S.S. Aracataca, Chagres, Samala, Mopan, Tucurinca,* etc.
15 vessels in this service.

This company also operates first-class vessels with barbershop, swimming pool, etc., carrying 100 first-class passengers, sailing weekly for Bermuda and Kingston, from Bristol, England. Round voyage £50, about 4 weeks including three days in Jamaica. Only one sailing a month touches Bermuda.

GLORIA S.S. CO., 1001 4th Street, San Francisco, Calif.

San Francisco to Aramuelles, Republic of Panama.
Trip 19 days; $200. Weekly.

SHIPS: 5,000–6,000 tons. 12 passengers.
Each room with bath; 6 double cabins each ship.

GRACE LINE, 10 Hanover Square, New York, N.Y.

New York to Dutch West Indies and Venezuela.
Trip 12–14 days one way, fare is $95–$110. Weekly
sailings.
Carry 8–12 passengers.
SHIPS: *S.S. Mara, Falcon, Tachira.*
New York, La Guaira, Puerto Cabello, Curaçao, Aruba,
Maracaibo.
The passenger department of the company advises they
are only booking one way passengers on these ships to enable
them to take care of local business between ports served
by these vessels.

Pacific Coast to Chile-Peru.
About 40 days, San Francisco to Chañaral, Chile. Fare is
$250 one way, $280 from Portland. 12–15 sailings per year.
Carrying 12 passengers.
Seattle, Tacoma (other Pacific Northwest ports as cargo
offers), San Francisco, Los Angeles, (Manzanillo), San
Jose de Guatemala, Acajutla, La Libertad, La Union,
Amapala, (Corinto, San Juan del Sur), Puntarenas, Guaya-
quil, Talara, Lobitos, (Paita, Eten, Pacasmayo, Salaverry,
Chimbote, Supe, Huacho), Callao, (Tambo de Moro,
Pisco), Mollendo, Arica, Tocopilla, Antofagasta, Chañaral.

Caribbean Service from New York, 17 days for $285.
Also first class service to West Coast of South America.

Cristobal to Central America.
S.S. Mayan sails every 28 days. Trip 22 days, approxi-
mately $122.
Balboa, Cristobal, Puntarenas, San Juan del Sur, Corinto,
Amapala, La Union, La Libertad, Acajutla, San Jose,
Champerico, and return.

California to Central America.
Trip 20 days one way; $100 one way; $200 round trip.
Carrying 12 passengers. Sailings every three weeks.
San Francisco, Los Angeles, Mazatlan, Manzanillo, Champerico, San Jose de Guatemala, Acajutla, La Libertad, Amapala, La Union, Corinto, San Juan del Sur, Puntarenas. Return with stop at San Jose del Cabo just before Los Angeles in addition to other ports.
S.S. Curaca and *Chipana.*

Also operates de luxe passenger service to West Coast of South America. Two ships in this service now carry only 12 passengers, but still charge minimum $330 one way which is minimum cabin-class rate.

GREENE LINE STEAMERS, Foot of Main Street, Cincinnati, Ohio.

Riverboats from Pittsburgh and Cincinnati.
STEAMER *Gordon C. Greene* operates on Ohio and Tennessee rivers. This company has several cruises of ten days for summer at $60 round trip.

Also likely to operate special cruise from Cincinnati to New Orleans for Mardi Gras in spring.
Fares will be in this neighborhood.

GYPSUM PACKET CO., LTD., 361 Richmond Terrace, St. George, Staten Island, N.Y.

To Nova Scotia.
Carries 4–16 passengers.
Takes 5½ days round trip.
Boston to Windsor, $15 one way; $28 round trip. New Brighton to Windsor, $30 one way; $55 round trip. Philadelphia to Windsor, $35 one way; $65 round trip.

HAMBURG AMERICAN LINE – NORTH GERMAN LLOYD, 57 Broadway, New York, N.Y.

Gulf ports to Europe.
Trip 17–24 days; $100 one way.

Irregular sailings.
Male passengers only.

West Coast to Europe.

Trip 30–45 days; $245–$310, varying with ship.
Three sailings monthly.
SHIPS: 8,000 tons. North German Lloyd ships cabin passengers only, Hamburg-American ships cabin and third class.
Pacific Coast to Europe via San Salvador.

Mexico-Cuba-Germany.

Trip 24 days to Tampico; $275 first class, $175 tourist.
Trip 50 days round voyage.
Sailings monthly.
Channel ports (Vigo, Lisbon), Havana, Vera Cruz, Tampico (Puerto Mexico) and return.

Panama Canal Coastwise to Ecuador.

Trip 10 days. First class $100.
Weekly sailings.
Cristobal, Buenaventura, Tumaco, (Esmeraldas, Bahia de Caraquez), Manta, Guayaquil, and return. Occasional stops at Puerto Bolivar, La Libertad, Machalilla, Manglar Alto.
Officials advise, "We are not able to prearrange interport passage on these boats inasmuch as it can never be determined in advance whether space will be available on one or the other sailings."

Puerto Rico service.

Sailings every 28 days. Local service only, ships proceed to Europe without passengers. Interline service between San Juan, San Pedro, Santo Domingo, Jacmel, Aux Cayes, Kingston, Santiago de Cuba, Port au Prince, St. Marc, Gonaïves, Cape Haitian, Puerto Plata, Kingston, Port au Prince, Puerto Plata.

Freighters and cargo boats with limited accommodations from Hamburg and Bremen to: South America West Coast via Panama Canal; Chile via Straits of Magellan; North Brazil; North China and Japanese ports via Suez; Dutch East Indies; New Guinea via South Seas Ports; Australia via Cape of Good Hope; and Madeira and Canary Islands.

Freight Cabin service from Buenos Aires and Rio de Janeiro to Capetown and Durban.

Also operate first-class de luxe express steamers transatlantic and in other services.

HARRISON LINE, Dock House, Bilter Street, London, England.

London to Caribbean.
Trip 50 days, £76 round voyage.
Monthly sailings.
London, Antigua, St. Kitts, Barbados, Grenada, Trinidad, Demerara, return with stops at Windward and Leeward Islands as inducements offer.

The freighters of this line operating to Gulf ports do not currently carry passengers.

HEAD LINE, McLean Kennedy Ltd., Montreal, Canada.

Transatlantic.
Trip 12 days. $70 one way, $135 round voyage.
Carrying 10 passengers. Sailings about 18 per year.
From Montreal during summer. From St. John, N.B., in winter.
Montreal or St. John, to Dublin or Belfast. Passengers must disembark at first Irish port.
Unaccompanied women not booked.

HOLLAND AMERICA LINE, 29 Broadway, New York, N.Y.

Pacific Coast to Europe via Panama Canal.
Four weeks and up from California, longer from North

Pacific coast. Fares $242–$337, depending on vessel and service; room with bath, 10 per cent. additional. Two sailings monthly.

From Pacific coast: Portland, Seattle, Vancouver, Victoria, San Francisco, Los Angeles, Cristobal (Hamilton, Bermuda), Liverpool, London, Southampton, Rotterdam. (Not all sailings reach all ports.) Returning via Swansea, Bermuda, Jamaica, Curaçao, Colombia, Cristobal. (Joint service with Royal Mail Lines.)

Cuba, Mexico and Gulf to Holland.

Trip 18–26 days, fare $105 one way, $188 round trip. Sailings monthly.

From Gulf: New Orleans, Galveston, Houston, Tampico, Vera Cruz, Havana, Rotterdam.

Transatlantic from New York, Norfolk, Baltimore to Holland.

Trip 11–16 days, fare $97.50 one way, $180.00 round trip. About fourteen sailings monthly.

From the Atlantic coast: ships sail direct from and to most ports.

Ships: 16,000–17,000 tons displacement. Six to twenty-five passengers. Ships: M.V. Delftdyk, Damsterdyk, Bilderdyk, Breedijk, Binnedyk, Maasdam, Edam, Leerdam, and others.

Carrying 5–6 passengers on the Breedijk type of vessel, 25 passengers on the Maasdam type vessels.

Physician usually carried on M.V. Delftdyk and Damsterdyk.

No women or children alone are carried on the smaller boats. Lady traveling alone will not be booked on the Gulf boats.

Swimming pools.

HOLLAND AUSTRALIA LINE, 405 Lexington Ave., New York, N.Y.

Holland to Australia, around Africa.

Trip 55 days one way. Hamburg–Sydney £59. Monthly sailings.

Ships: 13,000–17,000 tons displacement; 10–20 passengers.

Hamburg, Rotterdam, Antwerp (Lisbon), Genoa, Leghorn, Port Said, Suez, Karachi, Bombay, Alleppey, Fremantle, Adelaide, Melbourne, Sydney. Ships return in about 15 days, via Durban, Dakar, Dunkirk and Antwerp.

Round trip 12½ per cent. discount.

Passengers making round voyage can stay on same ship if loading permits, paying approximately $3.00 per day.

HOLLAND EAST ASIA LINE, 405 Lexington Ave., New York, N.Y. 681 Market Street, San Francisco, Calif.

Holland to East Asiatic Ports.

Three months; £111 round trip. Monthly sailings.

SHIPS: 16,000–17,000 tons displacement; 12 passengers.

Ports: Antwerp, Hamburg, Rotterdam, Genoa, Port Said, Colombo, Singapore, Manila, Hong Kong, Shanghai, Dairen, Yokohama, Nagoya, Osaka, Kobe, Shanghai, Foochow, Hong Kong, Manila, Singapore, Penang, Colombo, Aden, Port Said, Genoa, Antwerp, Rotterdam, Amsterdam, Hamburg.

Swimming pools.

HORN LINE, Hamburg, Germany.

Germany to Caribbean.

Two months round voyage to Curaçao; $414 round voyage. Operates over two routes, sailings monthly on northern route reaching Kingston; three times monthly on southern route.

HOULDER LINE, 53 Leadenhall Street, London, England.

Transatlantic from London to South America.
Weekly sailings.

SHIPS: 8,000–9,000 tons. First-class passengers only.

London, Liverpool, to Montevideo and Buenos Aires.

Many steamers have rooms with private bath. Doctor and stewardess are usually carried.

HUDSON'S BAY COMPANY, Winnipeg, Manitoba, Canada.

To the Arctic.

Trip 95 days. $650. Limited accommodations.

One sailing per year.

ICE-BREAKER: *R.M.S. Nascopie.*

Sailing about July 1 from Montreal.

Ports: Halifax, Sydney, Montreal, Hebron, Labrador, Port Burwell, N.W.T., Lake Harbour, Stupart's Bay, Sugluk West, Cape Dorset, Wolstenholme, Southampton Islands, Cape Smith, Port Harrison, Churchill.

Passengers can take train back from Churchill about August 9. If space is available passengers can be booked for last portion of voyage joining ship at Churchill.

Churchill, Chesterfield Inlet, Wolstenholme, Lake Harbour, Thule (Greenland), Craig Harbour, Arctic Bay, Fort Ross, Pond's Inlet, Clyde, Pangnirtung, Port Burwell, Halifax.

Montreal to Churchill, $300. Churchill to Halifax, $350. This route reaches within 800 miles of the North Pole.

Mackenzie River Routes.

By rail from Edmonton, Canada.

River boats from Waterways, Canada.

Weekly service May 12 to September 22 to Fort Smith; 3 days one way.

Weekly from June 9 to Goldfields, Sask., from Waterways; 2 days one way.

Two sailings, Waterways to Stoney Rapids; 4 days one way.

From Fort Smith to Outpost Island and Yellowknife a weekly service will be operated from June 9 connecting with service from Waterways; 3 days. One sailing will go through to Snowdrift and Fort Reliance; 11 nights from Waterways.

Three sailings (June 9, July 14, August 11) from Waterways to Fort Wrigley. The June sailing will connect with a single sailing on the Liard River to Fort Nelson. The June and August sailings will continue to Aklavik. Waterways to Aklavik 16 nights, to Fort Wrigley 9 nights, to Fort Nelson 21 nights.

Ports: Waterways, Fort McKay, Poplar Point, Chippewyon, Fitzgerald (portage of sixteen miles by motor car, truck and tractor between Fort Fitzgerald and Fort Smith). Fort Smith, Fort Resolution, Fort Simpson, Fort Wrigley, Fort Norman, Fort Good Hope, Arctic Red River, Fort McPherson, Aklavik.

(Vessels occasionally run through to Tuktoyaktuk.)

Fares: Round trip. (Including meals and berths.) Fort Smith $50. Fort Resolution, about 10 days, $90. Fort Rae, about 14 days on Great Slave Lake route, $140. Fort Norman, 20 days, $200. Aklavik, 32 days, $325.

Waterways to Fort Nelson 21 days each way, fare $72 plus berth and meal charges. Meals $75 to $125 according to vessel. Berths: Steamships $1.75 per night; motor vessels $1.00 per night.

Peace River Route.

Rail to Peace River Town, Canada.

Fort Vermillion Chutes to Hudson's Hope.

Trip 245 miles to Hudson's Hope from Peace River Town. Sailings May 10 and September 13. 4 days upstream. Fare $14 plus meals and berth charges.

Ports this route: Peace River, Dunvegan, Rolla Landing, Taylor, Fort St. John, Alexanders Landing, Cache Creek, Halfway, Ardills Landing, Hudson's Hope.

Sailing 11 times in season (Tuesdays at 5 P.M.) for Fort Vermillion (three sailings continue to Fort Vermillion Chutes). Two nights en route to either terminus, fare to Fort Vermillion $7.00, to Fort Vermillion Chutes $8.50, berths and meals extra in both cases.

Ports this route, downstream on Peace River: Tar Island, White Mud, Cadotte River, Battle River Landing, Carcajou Point, Keg River Landing, Moose Island, Fort Vermillion, Adams Landing, Fort Vermillion Chutes.

Airplane service operates in this territory with mail passengers and express at all seasons of the year. Special tours and routes including air and river boat can be arranged.

HUMPHREY & MacGREGOR, Tampa, Florida.

Gulf to Central America.

Four days for one way trip, fare $20. Return passage available four to eight days after arrival. Round trip booked on the same vessel $35 for the 8–10-day ocean voyage. Fares on other vessels at $5 per day. Sailings usually weekly. The vessels in this service are small motorships and sailing schooners (with auxiliary motor power), engaged in the fruit trade with Central America.

Tampa to Honduras (Roatan, Trujillo, Puerto Castilla, La Cieba), Belize. Occasional sailing vessel to Georgetown, Cayman Islands, B.W.I.

Literature asks that a stamped envelope be enclosed with all inquiries.

Women frequently travel on these ships the agents advise.

SHIPS: *M.S. General Tosta,* 120 tons deadweight. *M.S. Laguna,* 100 tons deadweight.

ICELAND S.S. CO., Copenhagen, Denmark.

Copenhagen to Iceland ports.

First class, 135 kronen; second class, 90 kronen (meals extra).

CARGO-PASSENGER SHIPS.

Hamburg, Hull, Leith to Iceland ports.

First class £6/10; second class, £4/10 (meals extra). One way takes one week.

From Copenhagen and Leith or Hamburg and Hull, to Reykjavik, Isafjord, Akureyri, return to same ports. Many Iceland ports are optional.

INTEROCEAN S.S. CO., 311 California Street, San Francisco, Calif.

Coast to Europe.
Trip 29–40 days from California, $204–$268, one way; $25 extra if booked from Pacific Northwest; 2–3 sailings monthly.
SHIPS: 13,500 tons displacement; 12–15 passengers.
San Francisco to London, Havre, Antwerp, Rotterdam, via Panama Canal.
Some boats omit call at London.
Outdoor swimming pool.

ITALIAN LINE, 386 Post Street, San Francisco, Calif.
624 Fifth Ave., New York, N.Y.

Pacific Coast and Naples.
Trip 38–50 days; $290–$315; sailings monthly.
Vancouver, Seattle, Portland, San Francisco, Los Angeles, La Libertad, Cristobal, Las Palmas, Marseilles, Genoa, Leghorn, Naples. (Optional stops San Jose, Puntarenas, Panama Canal, Palma de Mallorca.)

Also operate vessels carrying first-, second- and third-class passengers transatlantic, Italy to North America, and Italy to East Coast of South America, and Italy to West Coast of South America.

Various Italian steamship companies represented in the United States by the Italian Line operate freight and passenger vessels to all parts of the world. At one time passengers were carried from New York and other Amer-

ican ports including Gulf ports on freighters of various
Italian companies, but with the consolidation of Italian
shipping activities most of this freighter class business from
American ports was eliminated.

JAMAICA BANANA PRODUCERS STEAMSHIP CO., 64 Harbour Street, Kingston, Jamaica.

Jamaica to London-Rotterdam.
Trip 13–14 days; £30 one way, £50 round trip. Single
room slightly higher. Weekly sailings.
About 6,000 tons gross. Twelve passengers.
SHIPS: *Pontos, Jamaica Progress, Jamaica Pioneer, Jamaica Produce,* etc.
Jamaica, London, Rotterdam.
All rooms with bath.
Swimming pool.
Doctor and stewardess on most ships.

JAVA–NEW YORK LINE, 405 Lexington Ave., New York, N.Y.
JAVA–CHINA–JAPAN LINE.

New York to Dutch East Indies via Africa.
Trip 50 days; $300. Fortnightly sailings.
SHIPS: 8,000–11,000 tons, gross; 4–12 passengers.
New York, Belawan-Deli, Singapore, Batavia, Samarang,
Sourabaya and return with Boston first stop in North America. Vessels usually load at New Orleans, Norfolk, Jacksonville and Savannah before departure from New York. Rates
can be quoted on sailings from these ports depending on
time involved.

Occasionally call at Penang, Port Swettenham and Macassar en route to Belawan.

May stop for refueling at Dakar or Capetown. Both outward and return via Cape of Good Hope around Africa.
Reduction for round voyage 10 per cent.

Java-China-Japan line operates frequent sailings — Hong Kong, Batavia, Sourabaya, Macassar, Balik-papan, Manila and Hong Kong. Also operates similar service including stop at Bali.

Java Lines in conjunction with other Netherlands services set up a variety of around-the-world services, as well as other routes extending beyond the service given by one ship.

JOHNSON LINE, 1270 Sixth Ave., New York, N.Y. 2 Pine St., San Francisco, Calif.

Europe to West Coast of South America.
Trip 40–50 days, $190 one way. Monthly sailings. Canal to Valparaiso, $105 one way.
SHIPS: 6,000–10,000 tons; 12 passengers.
Ports: Stockholm, Baltic Ports, Gothenburg, Antwerp, Cuban Ports, Panama Canal (Puerto Colombia, La Guaira), Buenaventura, Guayaquil, Callao, Arica, Antofagasta, Valparaiso.
This company also operates larger A-class boats carrying first-class passengers at slightly higher rates, to the same ports.

Transatlantic from Pacific Coast.
Trip 4–7 weeks. $227–$299. Sailings twice monthly.
SHIPS: 11,500–13,500 tons displacement; 12–30 passengers depending on ship.
Vancouver, Seattle, Portland, San Francisco, and Los Angeles to Central American ports in Guatemala and San Salvador, Panama Canal, Cristobal, Gothenburg, Plymouth, Hull, London.
Swimming pools.

Twice a year: Hawaiian Islands to Europe.

JOHNSON WARREN LINES, 34 Whitehall St., New York, N.Y.

Transatlantic.

Trip 12–16 days. Fare $130 up. Cabin and second class, about every three weeks.

Boston, Halifax, St. John, Liverpool.

KEENE LINE, 208 West 8th Street, Los Angeles, Calif.

Passenger service has been suspended on this line.

KERR–SILVER LINE, 17 Battery Place, New York, N.Y.

New York around Africa to Colombo.

Trip 40 days to Beira, $275. 65 days, Singapore to New York, £49.

Sailings generally monthly.

SHIPS: *Silverlarch, Silverash, Silveray, Silverpine, Silverfir, Silverwalnut;* 10,000 tons; 8–12 passengers.

New York to Capetown, Port Elizabeth, East London, Durban, Lourenço Marques, Beira, Singapore, Batavia, Port Swettenham, Belawan-Deli, Penang; return via Colombo, Bombay, other Indian ports, Dakar via South and East Africa to Boston (Halifax), New York.

KHEDIVIAL MAIL SERVICE, care Cunard Line, 25 Broadway, New York, N.Y.

Alexandria to Alexandretta.

Trip 12 days, round voyage, 15. 300 Egyptian pounds.

"A few comfortable cabins are available for saloon passengers on the *Zamalek* and *Zaafaran,* as well as a sheltered deck for deck passengers."

Weekly service.

Ports: Alexandria, Port Said, Jaffa, Haifa, Larnaca, Beirut, Tripoli, Latakia, Mersina, Alexandretta and return.

Also operate first-class, third-class vessels on routes Egypt-Cyprus; Piræus, Alexandria, Malta, Marseilles; and Egypt-Red Sea lines on two routes from Suez to Port Sudan.

KLAVENESS LINE, 310 Sansome, San Francisco, Calif.

Transpacific.
Trip 100 days; $400 round trip. Owners' suite on two ships, 20 per cent. extra.
Sailings monthly.
SHIPS: 8,300 tons. 8–12 passengers.
Portland, San Francisco, Los Angeles to Manila, Hong Kong, Singapore, Belawan-Deli, Batavia, Samarang, Sourabaya, Belawan-Deli, Singapore, Batavia, Samarang, Sourabaya, Macassar (Davao), Cebu, Manila, Hong Kong, Los Angeles, San Francisco, Portland.

KNUTSEN LINE, 311 California St., San Francisco, Calif.

Transatlantic to England via Panama Canal.
Trip 25–40 days. From San Francisco: one way, $204; with bath, $224–$258. About 15 sailings annually.
Vancouver, Seattle, Portland, San Francisco, Los Angeles, Panama Canal, Liverpool, Manchester, Belfast and Glasgow.
Many rooms with bath.
Swimming pools.

KOKUSAI LINE, 1 Broadway, New York, N.Y.

Transpacific to Far East via Panama Canal.
Trip 29–43 days; $180–$200 to Yokohama depending on vessel. Sailings twice monthly.
SHIPS: 10,000–11,000 tons; 8–12 passengers.
New York (Hampton Roads, New Orleans, Galveston), Panama Canal, Los Angeles, Yokohama. Return by Manila, Singapore, Keelung, Kobe, Nagoya, Shimidzu, Yokohama, Los Angeles, Panama Canal, New York.

K.P.M. LINE, Chrysler Building, New York, N.Y.

This company operates a variety of freighters, cargo

boats, and first-class vessels throughout the world. Routes not touching North America include: —

Singapore-Java-Australia; Singapore-Java; Belawan-Deli-Batavia; Bali; Orient-Java-Africa.

LAURITZEN LINE, Seattle, Wash.

This company operates Seattle to Palestine, France, and other places.

Their agent advises: "Presently Lauritzen ships do not cater to passengers. While they have a few accommodations the owners are not interested in quoting for passenger business."

LAMPORT & HOLT LINE LTD., 24 State Street, New York, N.Y. Liverpool, England.

New York to South America.

Trip 70–90 days; $330 round voyage by same ship; $288 round trip return within one year.

Carrying 5–12 passengers. Monthly sailings on two different routes.

Fares are the same to terminal ports on both routes.

Ports reached on both routes include: Pará, Maranham, Ceará, Natal, Cabedello, Pernambuco, Maceio, Bahia, Rio de Janeiro, Santos, Montevideo, Buenos Aires.

This company from time to time has operated freighters without passenger space between New York and other Atlantic Ports and Manchester, England.

From London to South America.

Weekly sailings from London/Liverpool, ships with limited first-class passenger capacity, for Bahia, Rio de Janeiro, Santos, Rio Grande do Sul. Some ships sail to Montevideo and Buenos Aires. Other ports as inducement offers.

Ships being transferred from New York-South America service to London route may make round voyage from New

York to London via River Plate ports. Fares will be quoted when such service is available, rarely oftener than once a year.

LLOYD TRIESTINO, care Italian Line, New York, N.Y.

Operates a variety of services with first class, cargo boats and freighters carrying limited number of passengers throughout the world. These routes do not touch the United States and space can rarely be booked by mail in advance for any specific sailing without considerable expense for cables or delay for mails.

Routes include: Italy-East Africa; South Africa; West-South Africa; Far East; Australian ports.

LUCKENBACH LINE, 120 Wall Street, New York, N.Y.

New York to Pacific Northwest.

New York to Los Angeles, 16–18 days: one way $115, round trip $210. New York to Pacific Northwest, 22–26 days: $130 one way, round trip $240. Sailings weekly; 2–12 passengers.

Ports: Seattle, Portland, San Francisco, Los Angeles, Panama Canal to Brooklyn, Philadelphia, Boston, and return.

Gulf to West Coast.

New Orleans to Seattle and Portland, one way $120–$130; Seattle and return, $215–$235.

New Orleans to Los Angeles and San Francisco, 16–18 days. One way $105–$115, round trip $190–$205. Sailings weekly; 2–12 passengers.

Ports: Houston, Mobile, New Orleans, Panama Canal to Los Angeles, San Francisco, Portland, Seattle, Tacoma.

Space sold to Panama Canal when available.

LYKES BROS. — RIPLEY STEAMSHIP CO., Houston, Texas, New Orleans, La., Galveston, Texas, 17 Battery Place, New York, N.Y.

(Dixie U.K. Line; Dixie Mediterranean Line; Southern States Line; American-Gulf-Orient Line, *see also*.)

Gulf ports to Far East via Panama Canal.
Trip 110–160 days. Return fare is $450; $150 to Honolulu. Sailings as cargo offers.
STEAMERS: 3,550 tons (gross) ; 8–14 passengers.
Houston, Panama Canal (Los Angeles), Honolulu, Kobe, Shanghai, Manila. Some ships stop at Hawaii. May return to North Atlantic ports.
Women must be accompanied.

Gulf ports to South America.
Trip 21–30 days. Fare is $135. Two sailings monthly.
STEAMERS: 3,550 tons (gross); 8–14 passengers.
Houston, Havana, Cristobal, Cartagena, Puerto Colombia, and return.

Houston and Galveston to Caribbean.
Trip 23–28 days. Fare is $135 round trip. Sailings weekly.
STEAMERS: 3,550 tons (gross); 8–14 passengers.
Houston and Galveston or Beaumont and Lake Charles to Port au Prince, San Juan, Aquadilla, Mayaguez and Ponce, with optional stops at the other Haitian, Dominican and Puerto Rican ports.
Room with bath is $20 extra.

MAERSK LINE, 26 Broadway, New York, N. Y.

New York to Far East.
Four months. $450.50–$544 round trip, one way $320–$265.
Sailings fortnightly.
SHIPS: 8,500–11,500 tons deadweight; 3–12 passengers.
New York to Norfolk, Savannah, Panama Canal, Los Angeles, Yokohama, Kobe, Shanghai, Hong Kong, Manila, Cebu, Iloilo, Nagoya (Formosa, Shimidzu), and other ports as cargo offers.

Passengers must provide their own accommodations ashore during stay in Manila. If remaining aboard during period ship loads and/or cruises the islands, $4.00 per day will be charged.

Swimming pool on most ships.

Some vessels have one bath for six passengers, others have bath with every room.

Air conditioning on one ship.

Ladies, traveling alone, may be refused booking on some vessels.

This company owns some of the ships and operates others on charter on this and similar routes.

This line formerly operated transatlantic freighter-passenger service.

Now this company offers around-the-world service in collaboration with HOLLAND–EAST ASIA LINES, a cruise of about 4 months, fare $640–680. Also with K.P.M. and AMERICAN SOUTH AFRICAN LINE, a cruise of 4½ months; fare is $895.

MANCHESTER LINERS, LTD., 34 Whitehall Street, New York, N.Y.

Transatlantic.

Trip 10–17 days. Fare $75–$85. About 60 sailings per year.

SHIPS: *Manchester City, Manchester Exporter, Manchester Regiment,* etc.; 8–10,000 tons; 6–12 passengers.

Montreal, Quebec City, Manchester.

Norfolk, St. John, Liverpool.

Philadelphia, West St. John, Halifax and Manchester.

Monthly from Norfolk. Weekly in summer from Montreal.

MANILA STEAMSHIP CO., Manila, P.I.

Inter-Island service in the Philippines.

Manila to Davao, fare about $39. Weekly sailings.

SHIPS: *S.S. Bisavas, Vizcaya, Venus,* and *Sorsogon.*

Manila to Iloilo, Pulupandan, Cebu, Zamboanga, Davao. Also Manila to Bulan, Tacloban, Catbalogan, Calbayog and Masbate.

On these ships there is cabin class, second, and third. Special reductions for parties and students.

MATSON LINE, 30 Rockefeller Plaza, New York, N.Y.

Transpacific — California to Australia.
Trip 24 days, first class, $397; cabin class, $276.
DE LUXE LINERS.
California to Hawaii, Pago Pago and Australia.

McCORMICK STEAMSHIP COMPANY, 17 Battery Place, New York, N.Y. 461 Market Street, San Francisco, Calif.
(Pacific-Argentine-Brazil Line.)
(Mooremack Gulf Lines. Mooremack Lines.)

California to South America.
Trip 48 days one way; fare $225. About 110 days round trip, fare $475. Room with bath is additional. From Seattle or Portland add $15, from Victoria or Vancouver add $20. Sailings monthly.
SHIPS: 12,500 tons displacement; 10–12 passengers.
San Francisco, Los Angeles, Panama Canal, San Juan (P.R.), Mayaguez, Ponce, Trinidad, Pernambuco, Rio de Janeiro, Santos, Montevideo, Buenos Aires, returning usually via Bahia, Pará on the Amazon, Barbados, Port of Spain, Puerto Colombia, Los Angeles, San Francisco. (South bound may stop at Manzanillo, Mexico and St. Thomas, Virgin Islands; north bound may stop at Curaçao and San Jose, Guatemala.)

California to New York.
About 35 days, fare one way is $120 and up. On some of

the ships there are private baths, slight additional fee. Sailings twice monthly.

SHIPS: 12,500 tons displacement; 10–12 passengers.

New York (sometimes via rail to Philadelphia), Philadelphia, Baltimore, Norfolk, Panama Canal, Los Angeles, San Francisco, Portland, Seattle.

Return usually to New York before Philadelphia.

When stops are made at Puerto Rican ports between California and New York additional charge of $10 is made for the trip.

New York to South America.

Round trip, 65 days (10 days at Buenos Aires at passengers' expense).

Fare $210 one way, round voyage $400. Owners' cabin $40 additional round voyage. Rates higher some sailings.

Sailings twice monthly.

SHIPS: 6–9 passengers.

New York (other Atlantic ports if sufficient inducement offers), Rio de Janeiro, Santos, Montevideo, Buenos Aires. Santos and Bahia on return voyage. Boston and/or New York return terminal.

Swimming pools on ships from California.

This company also represents AMERICAN SCANTIC LINE, freighter and first-class vessels.

AMERICAN CARIBBEAN LINE, formerly operated by this company, discontinued.

MESSAGERIES MARITIMES (FRENCH LINE), 610 Fifth Ave., New York, N.Y.

South Seas.

France to Noumea, 48 days, $350. Sailings every six weeks.

France to Papeete, $162.50 first class, $92.50 second class. Sailings every six weeks.

Cargo ships.

Marseilles, Algiers, Pointe-à-Pître, Fort de France

(Curaçao), Cristobal to Papeete (Raiatea), Suva, Port-Villa, Noumea, and return.

Operate large fleet of first class, cargo and freighter class vessels covering routes: African East Coast and Madagascar; Marseilles to India and Indo China via Suez; to China and Japan via Suez; to Mediterranean.

MITSUI LINE, 15 Moore Street, New York, N.Y.

New York to Yokohama via Panama Canal and West Coast.

Trip 30–50 days, New York to Yokohama, $200. Round trip ten per cent. less. Sailings twice monthly.

SHIPS: 10,000 displacement tons. 6–12 passengers, Yokohama boats; 2–7 passengers, Gulf ports to Japan and China.

New York (Boston, Philadelphia, Baltimore), Jacksonville (Galveston), Panama Canal, Los Angeles (British Columbia), Yokohama, Kobe, Moji; returning, Kobe, Manila, Cebu, Iloilo, Penang, Port Swettenham, Singapore, Hong Kong, Kobe, Nagoya, Shimizo, Yokohama, Los Angeles, Panama, New York, Boston, Philadelphia, Baltimore. (Not all sailings reach all ports.)

Women must be accompanied by male relatives.

Occasional ships from Gulf ports to Japan, 60–90 days, $360 up.

Express Service Yokohama-New York, 30 days, $260 one way.

MOBILE, MIAMI AND GULF S.S. CO. (WATERMAN LINE), Mobile, Ala.

Gulf to Puerto Rico.

Trip 16–21 days; $110 round trip. Sailings weekly.

VESSELS: 6,000 tons; 8–10 passengers.

Tampa, Mobile, New Orleans, San Juan. (Ponce, Mayaguez, Arroyo, Arecibo, and other outports as cargo offers.)

All rooms with private baths.

MOBILE OCEANIC LINE (WATERMAN LINE), Mobile, Ala.

Transatlantic.

Trip 14 days, fare $85, round trip $150.

VESSELS: 12,000 tons; 14 passengers. 3–6 sailings monthly. On smaller boats, 2–4 passengers. These smaller vessels take 21 days.

Mobile to Liverpool. (Havre, Bremen, Rotterdam.) Call at Tampa in winter months.) Returning Manchester (or Avonmouth), (Panama City, Pensacola, Gulfport), Mobile.

Connecting baths with all rooms on the 14-day boats.

MONARCH LINE, P.O. Box 414, Miami, Florida.

Miami-Bahamas.

Miami to Nassau, $15 round trip. Three sailings weekly. Miami to Nassau and out islands of the Bahamas (mail steamer), 12 days, $60 round trip. Sailings fortnightly. Shorter trips, if space is available, 2–12 days at $5 per day.

SHIPS: Miami to Nassau and Bahamas out islands, 12 passengers. *S.S. Monarch of Nassau.* Miami to Nassau, *S.S. Richard Campbell. Monarch of Nassau* is 116 feet long, 186 tons.

Ports: Miami, Nassau, New Providence Island, Arthurs Town, the Bight and Devils Point, Cat Island, Watlings Island, Rum Cay; Clarence Town, Long Island; Bird Rock, Crooked Island; Long Cay, Fortune's Island; Castle Island; Mathews Town; Great Inagua Island, and return.

MOOREMACK LINE, 5 Broadway, New York, N.Y. (*See* McCORMICK S.S. CO.)

MORGAN LINE (SOUTHERN PACIFIC S.S. CO.), 535 Fifth Ave., New York, N.Y.

Coastwise, New York to New Orleans.

For 6 days, $55. Round trip $60 up. Sailings every three weeks.

CARGO VESSEL.

MUNSON STEAMSHIP LINES, West 11th Street, New York, N.Y.

Gulf-Mexican Gulf.
Irregular sailings. *S.S. Munplace,* freighter, small passenger capacity, between New Orleans and Progreso, Yucatan, Mexico.

New York to Miami, Nassau, Havana and return, first-class service.
Round trip, 12 days; all expenses, with rates $125 and up. Sailings twice monthly.
SHIP: *S.S. Munargo.*
New York to Miami, Nassau, Havana and return.

This company also operates de luxe passenger service to South America from New York.

N.Y.K. (JAPAN MAIL), 25 Broadway, New York, N.Y.

Transpacific.
De luxe service transpacific. Other superior class service through Pacific Islands, coast of Japan, Australia, etc. This company has a large number of freight boats but has no facilities for passengers in freighters from either Atlantic or Pacific coast.

NEDERLAND LINE.

See: KERR–SILVER
JAVA–NEW YORK
SILVER–JAVA–PACIFIC
K.P.M.
ROYAL NETHERLANDS LINE

NEWFOUNDLAND CANADA S.S. CO. (FURNESS RED CROSS). Joint Service.
Newfoundland Canada S.S. Co., Halifax, N.S.
Furness Red Cross Line, 34 Whitehall St., New York, N.Y.

Coastwise, New York to St. Pierre.

Round trip, 12 to 14 days, $110. Weekly sailings from New York.

New York to Halifax, St. Pierre, St. Johns, Halifax, New York.

Newfoundland Canada S.S. Co. operates cruise service from Canadian ports in summer months; running this service in winter months.

NEWFOUNDLAND RAILWAY, St. Johns, Newfoundland.

St. Johns to Halifax.

Trip 3–4 days each way. Sailings twice monthly, winter service.

St. Johns, Burin, Fortune, Grand Bank, Halifax.

When freight offers, stops at Harbour Buffet, Marystown, Belleoram, English Harbor, Harbour Breton, Gaultois, Ramea, Burgeo.

St. Johns to Labrador.

13-day round trip. Sailings fortnightly, June to October only.

SHIP: *S.S. Kyle.*

St. Johns to Brigus, Ban Roberts, Harbour Grace, Carbonear, Trinity, Catalina, Wesleyville, Twillingate, St. Anthony, Battle Harbor, Spear Harbor, Port Hope Simpson, Francis Harbor, Fishing Ship Harbor, Ship Harbor, Occasional Harbor, Square Islands, Deard Islands, Snug Harbor, Venison Islands, Hawk's Harbor, Bolster's Rock, Comfort Bight, Frenchman's Island, Punch Bowl, Webbers Cove, Flat Island, Sandy Islands, Batteau, Black Tickle, Spotted Islands, Domino, Red Point, Indian Tickle, Wolf

Islands, Grady, Long Island, Cartwright, Peck's Harbor, George's Island, Indian Island, Rigolet, Indian Harbor, Smokey, White Bears, Emily Harbor, Horse Harbor, Holton, Sloop Cove, Cape Harrison, Ragged Islands, Long Tickle, Iron-Bound Islands, Macovik, Ailik, Turnavik, Hopedale.

Placentia Bay — West Run (every two weeks).

Argentia, Merasheen, Presque, St. Kyran's, Little Paradise (or Paradise), South East Blight (once monthly), Petite-Forte, St. Joseph, Little Harbor, Oderin, Blaine Harbour, Flat Island, Marystown, Burin, Great Burin, Epworth, St. Lawrence, Lawn, (Lord's Cove and Point au Gaul, weather permitting), Lamaline.

Placentia Bay — Bay run.

Every two weeks.

Argentia, Ship Harbour, Iona, Red Islan, Rose à Rue, Kingswell, Harbour-Buffet, Haystack, Spencers Cove, Brule, North Harbour, Sound Island, Woody Island, Bar Haven, Tack's Beach, Davis Cove, Clatise Harbour, St. Leonard's Isle Valen.

South Coast and Fortune Bay.

Every two weeks.

Argentia, Marystown, Burin, St. Lawrence, Fortune, Grand Bank, Garnish, Point Enragee, St. Bernards Bay L'Argent, Little Bay East, Harbour Mille, Terrenceville, English Harbour East, Andersons Cove, Stones Cove, Rencontre East, Lally Cove, Bay de Nord, Pools Cove, Belleoram, St. Jaques, English Harbour West, Mose Ambrose, Coomb's Cove, Millers Passage, Little-Bay West, Jersey Harbour, Harbour Breton, Pass Island, Hermitage, Gaultois, Conne River, Milltown, St. Albans, Pushthrough, Rencontre West, François, Cape La Hune, Ramea, Burgeo, Grand Bruit, La Polle, Rose Blanch, (Burnt Island and Isle du Morte, weather permitting), Port-aux-Basques.

NEW YORK AND CUBA MAIL S.S. CO., 545 Fifth Ave., New York, N.Y.

New York to Havana.
Round trip $110.
Frequent first-class service.

New York to Mexico.
Weekly sailings.

NEW YORK AND PORTO RICO S.S. CO. (PORTO RICO LINE), Foot of Wall Street, New York, N.Y.

Coastwise from New York to Dominican and Puerto Rican ports.

All expenses, 11 days, $120 on the de luxe service, weekly sailings; 17 days, $113 minimum on the cabin steamers, weekly sailings.

New York, San Juan, La Romana, Macoris, Sanchez, Puerto Plata, Azua, Barahona, Mayaguez, Ponce, Arecibo, Aguadilla, Jobos and Guanica. Not all ports on any sailing.

NEW ZEALAND LINES, 26 Beaver Street, New York, N.Y.

England–New Zealand.

About 42 days one way, London to Auckland, £42 one way, return trip £77.

Sailings tourist class 100–300 passengers, 42-day boats about five times annually.

This company also operates cabin-class vessels; one way fare is £74. On first-class vessels, £94. First-class vessels make the trip in about 28 days.

Ports: London, (Jamaica), Curaçao, Panama Canal, Auckland, (Wellington, Lyttleton, Port Chalmers). Some ships continue also to Australian ports.

Ships occasionally stop at Pitcairn Island.

Ships occasionally stop at Suva, Fiji Islands.

NORTH GERMAN LLOYD LINE, 57 Broadway, New York, N.Y.

Pacific coast via Panama Canal to Europe.

Trip 28–33 days, $248–$285 one way from California; $273–$310 one way from Pacific Northwest. Two sailings monthly.

San Francisco via Panama Canal, Antwerp, Bremen, Hamburg (with through bookings to London no extra charge). On return voyage optional stops at La Libertad, Salvador, San Jose de Guatemala.

Also see HAMBURG AMERICAN LINE–NORTH GERMAN LLOYD.

NORTHLAND TRANSPORTATION CO., Pier 5, Seattle, Wash.

Coastwise from Seattle to Alaska.

Trip 12 days; $90 and up; sailings weekly; 54 to 144 passengers.

Seattle to Ketchikan, Wrangell, Petersburg, Juneau and Sitka, and return.

This company may operate Vagabond Summer Cruises to Alaskan ports, 17 to 28 days, fares from $152.

NORWEGIAN AMERICAN LINE, 24 State Street, New York, N.Y.

Operates cabin-class de luxe liner service New York and Boston to Bergen and Oslo sailing twice monthly.

Also has occasional sailing of freighters capable of carrying up to nine passengers each, 12–17 days en route.

Company passenger officials say: "We do not desire to quote any passenger rates on our freighters."

NORWEGIAN LOCAL SERVICES.

The Norwegian Travel Information office at 115 Broad St., New York, does not sell tickets or arrange reservations, but they will supply information on various local Norwegian services. Several 4–8–10- and 12-day cruises from Bergen to the North Cape are available at fares around nine or ten dollars a day (lower in some cases).

O.S.K. LINE (Osaka Syosen Kaisya), 17 Battery Place, New York, N.Y. 621 S. Hope St., Los Angeles, Calif.

Around-the-world.
Trip, 5 months, $712–$784.
This company operates a round-the-world service via the South Atlantic. Passengers are required to pay own hotel and other expenses at Buenos Aires and Kobe while waiting for connecting vessel.

Through arrangements with the United Fruit Company passengers can connect with O.S.K. round-the-world service on sailings from New York.

For routes *see below.*

Japan–South America.
Trip 56 days. Fare is $450, $157 third class.
SHIPS: 7,000–10,000 tons, 38–60 first-class passengers; 13–14 sailings per year.

Route: Kobe, Yokkaichi, Yokohama, Kobe, Hong Kong, Singapore, Colombo, Durban, Cape Town, Rio de Janeiro, Santos, Montevideo (if inducements offer, stops will be made at Shimidzu, Saigon, Port Elizabeth, East London, and Rio Grande do Sul on outward voyages and at Montevideo, Rosario, La Plata, Rio Grand Victoria, Angra dos Reis, Bahia, Pernambuco, Belem, and Havana on homeward voyage).

Return route: Buenos Aires, Santos, Rio de Janeiro, Belem, Cristobal, Balboa, Los Angeles, Yokohama, Kobe.

Japan–Africa–South America.
Trip 65 days, $372 (third class $143). Monthly sailings.
SHIPS: *Arizona Maru, Africa Maru, Arabia Maru, Hawaii Maru, Manila Maru,* etc. 9,000–10,000 tons, 10–29 first-class passengers.

Routes: Yokohama, Nagoya, Osaka, Kobe, Moji, Hong Kong, Singapore, Colombo, Mombasa, Zanzibar, Dar-es-Salaam, Beira, Lourenço Marques, Durban, Port Elizabeth, Capetown, Buenos Aires. (If inducements offer, stops will be made at Saigon, Penang Madras, Tanga, East London, Mossel Bay, Rio de Janeiro and Santos on outward voyage and Port Louis, Dar-es-Salaam, Tanga, Penang and Manila homeward.)

Return route: Buenos Aires, Santos, Rio de Janeiro, Montevideo, Capetown, Port Elizabeth, East London, Durban, Lourenço Marques, Zanzibar, Mombasa, Singapore, Hong Kong, Moji, Kobe, Osaka, Nagoya, Yokohama.

Kobe–Tientsin.

Trip 4 days. First class, 70 yen. Six sailings monthly.

SHIPS: *Choko Maru, Choan Maru, Choju Maru.* 3,000 tons; 34 first-class passengers.

Kobe, Moji, Tientsin.

Pacific Coast to Japan.

Trip 19 days, $218–$240 first class. About 10 sailings per year.

These ships are those of South American-Japanese run.

Japan–Philippines.

Trip 22 days, 185 yen first class (round trip 10 per cent. reduction). Sailings twice monthly.

SHIPS: *Chicago Maru, Mexico Maru, Ganges Maru;* 4,000–6,000 tons.

Ports: Yokohama, Nagoya, Osaka, Kobe, Moji, Nagasaki, Keelung, Takao, Amoy, Manila, Cebu, Davao. May stop at other island ports as inducements offer. Returning, Davao, Cebu, Legaspi, and/or Tabaco, Manila, Takao, Keelung, Kobe, Osaka, (Nagoya), Yokohama.

Japan–Saigon–Bangkok.

Japan to Bangkok, 250 yen.

VESSELS: 4,000–5,500 tons.

Kobe–Dairen.

Ten vessels are maintained in this service, making the run in about 70 hours.

Inland Sea of Japan.

This company operates a variety of services on the Inland Seas of Japan.

FRED OLSEN LINE, 15 Moore Street, New York, N.Y.

Pacific Coast to Europe.

Trip 30 days, San Francisco to England; one way, $215. San Francisco to Norway, one way, $240.

SHIPS: Sailings every three weeks. 15,000 tons displacement. 7–12 passengers.

Vancouver, Victoria, Seattle, Tacoma, Portland, San Francisco via Panama Canal to Liverpool, London, Hull, Bergen, Oslo.

Also first-class services; Norway–England–Canary Islands.

PACIFIC STEAM NAVIGATION CO. (Thomas Cook & Son), New York, N.Y.

Europe to Valparaiso.

This company operates the de luxe steamers *Reina del Pacifico, Orbita,* etc., from British Channel ports to Valparaiso, Chile, via Bermuda, Nassau, Havana and the Panama Canal.

They also maintain two freighter-cargo services, one running via the Panama Canal outward and homeward bound, and the other service operating via Brazil, River Plate, Bahia Blanca, Port Stanley (Faulkland Islands) and the Straits of Magellan outward to Valparaiso, returning via the Panama Canal. Stops on these freighter services are dependent entirely on cargo. Round trip fares are from £60–£75, depending on the vessel. Only limited passenger accommodations are available.

PAN–ATLANTIC S.S. CO., Mobile, Ala. 80 Broad St., New York, N.Y.

Coastwise, New York to Gulf ports — Mobile to Philadelphia.

New York to New Orleans, 7 days $55. Mobile to Philadelphia, 8 days $50. Round trip, 10 per cent. discount. Weekly service, 12 passengers.

SHIPS: *S.S. Topa Topa, Bellingham, Hastings.*

New York, Tampa, New Orleans, south bound. Mobile, Panama City, Fla., Tampa, Philadelphia, north bound.

PANAMA LINE, Panama Railroad Steamship Line, 24 State St., New York, N.Y.

Coastwise, New York to Port au Prince to Cristobal and return.

First class only. One way $100, round trip $175, 8 days each way.

Sailings twice monthly, 175 passengers.

New York, Port au Prince, Cristobal, New York.

Company announces: "It is only during the winter months from December until March that we are in position to take care of outside passengers for the round trip because during the balance of the year our steamers are booked full with our Canal Zone employees and their families travelling to and from the States on annual vacation."

PAQUET STEAMSHIP LINE, 610 Fifth Ave., New York, N.Y.

This company operates two lines from Marseilles, France to Maroc and Senegal. Most of the ships in the service are fast *Paquebots* carrying first-, second- and third-class passengers.

Occasional sailings of cargo type vessels carry a few passengers at *classe unique* fares which are about 50 per cent.

less than first class on *Paquebots* but are 20 per cent. higher than the third-class fares on the fast boats.

PHILIPPINE INTER–ISLAND S.S. CO. (General Agents DOLLAR S.S. CO.), Manila, P.I.

Tour of Island ports.
Tour, 5 days at approximately $50 U.S. currency, plus $3.50 per day for room with bath, and/or $1.00 per day for single cabin. Weekly sailings.

PHILIPPINE STEAM NAVIGATION CO., Manila, P.I.

Inter-island service.
Operates weekly service inter-island.

PORT LINE (COMMONWEALTH & DOMINION LINE LTD.), 638 Fifth Ave., New York, N.Y.

England to New York to Australia.
Trip 30–35 days. New York to Sydney $250; to Fremantle $300; 12–15 sailings annually.

Australian ports to Hull, England, via Cape of Good Hope.
Fare £50–£55 one way.

Around-the-world.
Special rates will be quoted on the round-the-world sailings of this line and for New York to England via Australia.
SHIPS: 12,000 tons; 12 passengers.
England to New York to Australia, New Zealand. Also stop at Fiji Islands.
Doctor on some ships.

PACIFIC ARGENTINE BRAZIL LINE. *See* McCOR-MICK S.S. CO.

PRINCE LINE, 34 Whitehall Street, New York, N.Y.

England to Mediterranean.

England to Jaffa/Haifa, £16–£25, depending on ship and season.

Fortnightly sailings in summer, weekly November to April; 6–12 passengers.

Ports: London, Manchester, Tunis, Malta, Alexandria, Jaffa, Haifa, Beirut, (Famagusta, Cyprus).

Not all ships stop at all ports.

PRINCE LINE–SILVER LINE, JOINT SERVICE.
  Prince Line: 34 Whitehall Street, New York, N.Y.
  Silver Line: 17 Battery Place, New York, N.Y.

Around-the-world.

Trip 150 days; $600.

SHIPS: 10,000 tons. 8–12 passengers. Sailings 26 times a year.

New York, Norfolk, Savannah, Panama Canal, Los Angeles (San Francisco), Manila, Shanghai, Hong Kong, Manila, Cebu, Davao, Macassar, Sourabaya, Samarang, Batavia, Telok Betong, Singapore, Port Swettenham, Belawan-Deli, Penang, Colombo, Dakar, (Halifax), Boston, New York.

RED CROSS LINE. *See* FURNESS LINES — NEW-FOUNDLAND CANADA S.S. CO., LTD.

RED STAR LINE. *See* ARNOLD BERNSTEIN LINE.

ROBIN LINE, Seas Shipping Co., 39 Cortlandt Street, New York, N.Y.

Transatlantic to Africa.

New York to Capetown, $260. Fares increase slightly for other ports, Tanga fare one way being $310. Round trip 10 per cent. reduction. Sailings monthly.

OIL-BURNING TURBINE VESSELS: *Robin Hood, Robin Adair, Robin Goodfellow,* etc. 15,000 tons displacement; 8 passengers.

New York to Capetown, Port Elizabeth, East London, Port Natal, Lourenço Marques, Beira, Mombasa, Dar-es-Salaam, Zanzibar, Tanga.

ROYAL MAIL LINES, 587 Fifth Ave., New York, N.Y.

Liverpool to South America.

One way, 20–23 days. £30–£35 depending on the vessel. Round trip £54–£63. Sailings about once each month. About 12 passengers.

Liverpool to Rio de Janeiro, Santos, Montevideo, Buenos Aires.

London to Haiti.

Fare one way to Haiti £25; round trip, £54. Sailings monthly.

London to Bermuda, Nassau, Jamaica, Haiti.

This company operates a variety of first-class passenger services from London.

ROYAL NETHERLANDS STEAMSHIP CO., 25 Broadway, New York, N.Y.

New York to Amsterdam via Caribbean.

About 32 days outgoing, 30 days on return trip. East bound to Amsterdam, fare is $279. Passenger steamers sailing twice monthly.

New York, Port au Prince, La Guaira, Curaçao, Puerto Cabello, Guanta, Puerto Sucre, Pampatar, Carupano, Trinidad, Demerara, Madeira, Plymouth, Havre, Amsterdam. Stop at Dover on return trip.

A variety of cruises can be planned on this line: 17 days, $175, 31 days, $250, etc.

New York to Madeira.

Round trip, 59 days, $450, including hotel expenses ashore.

New York to Caribbean.

Trip 24 days, fare is $150. Sailings weekly; 12 passengers. Two routes, sailing alternate weeks: —

1. New York to Inagua, Port au Prince, La Guaira, Puerto Cabello, Curaçao, return trip skip Port au Prince and stop at Turk's Island.
2. New York to Turk's Island, Cape Haitian, Port au Paix, Gonaïves, St. Marc, Petit Goave, Miragoane, Jeremie, Aux Cayes, Jacmel, Curaçao, Puerto Cabello, Inagua, New York.

Transatlantic — New York to Kingston to Hamburg.

Trip 31 days, $233 minimum first class. Sailings twice monthly.

PASSENGER VESSELS: first, second and third class, except *M.S. Pericles,* 12-passenger cargo vessel.

New York, Kingston, Puerto Limón, Cristobal, Cartagena, Puerto Colombia, Puerto Cabello, La Guaira, Trinidad, Barbados, Plymouth, Havre, Amsterdam, Hamburg.

When space is available these ships will carry passengers between ports in the Caribbean at varying fares ranging from $10 a day minimum.

South Pacific Line: Hamburg to Chile.

About 50 days. Cabin class ships, $325 one way. Freighters, $240 one way. Two sailings monthly.

Hamburg, Antwerp, Rotterdam, Amsterdam, Curaçao, Cristobal, Buenaventura, Guayaquil, Paita, Pimentel, Pacasmayo, Salaverry, Callao, Mollendo, Arica, Iquique, Tocopilla, Antofagasta, Taltal, Valparaiso, San Antonio, Talcahuano, Corral.

Canal Zone to Valparaiso.

Approximately 18 days. Cabin ships, $144; freighters, $105.

New Orleans to Nicaragua.
Trip 12 days; $117 up; sailings weekly.
New Orleans, Havana, Panama Canal, Puerto Cabeza, New Orleans. May stop at La Ceiba on return trip.

New Orleans to Mexico.
Trip 12 days (five days ashore). Sailings weekly. Round trip $90.
New Orleans to Vera Cruz.

New Orleans to Vera Cruz via Tampico.
Fortnightly sailings; 12 days; $90 round trip.
Limited accommodations.
New Orleans, Tampico, Vera Cruz.

This company also has other frequent sailings of fruit vessels. Some ships may have limited passenger accommodations.
Other routes may include: —
New Orleans to La Ceiba.
New Orleans to Alvaro Obregon, Mexico.
Galveston to Alvaro Obregon, Mexico.

SWEDISH ORIENT LINE, Gothenburg, Sweden.
831 South Olive Street, Los Angeles, Calif.

Carries 4–12 passengers; 3–4 sailings monthly.
This line operates boats with limited space for passengers between Danzig, Scandinavian ports to the Mediterranean and Black Sea ports.

SOUTHERN STATES LINE, 17 Battery Place, New York, N.Y. (LYKES BROS.–RIPLEY S.S. CO.) Whitney Building, New Orleans, La.

Gulf to Europe.
About 21 days; fare is $100 one way; sailings twice or oftener monthly; 2–12 passengers.

Sailings from New Orleans, La., Galveston, Houston.

Passengers embark at last Gulf port except by special arrangement and discharge from first Continental port, unless by special arrangement.

TRANSATLANTIC S.S. CO., 240 Battery, San Francisco, Calif.

Pacific Coast to Australia.

Trip 23–36 days. Fare is $175 from California; $25 extra from Portland, Seattle and Vancouver; sailings monthly; 6–22 passengers.

Vancouver, Portland, Seattle, Los Angeles, San Francisco to Brisbane, Sydney, Newcastle, Melbourne, Adelaide.

UNION STEAMSHIPS LTD. (of British Columbia), Vancouver, B.C.

Coastwise to British Columbia ports from Vancouver.

S.S. *Catala,* weekly for Prince Rupert, Stewart, and Naas River points via way ports as inducements offer. Trip 6 days, $45.

S.S. *Cardena,* weekly for Prince Rupert and Skeena River Canneries via Bella Coola and Ocean Falls. Trip 5 days, $36.

Also operates a variety of one and two day trips out of Vancouver.

UNION STEAMSHIP CO. OF NEW ZEALAND, 230 California St., San Francisco, Calif.

Transpacific to Australia.

SHIPS: 13,500 tons displacement. Six to twelve passengers carried. Sailings every four to six weeks.

San Francisco to Papeete, Tahiti, Rarotonga, Wellington and Sydney.

Also operate Auckland to Suva, Apia and other Islands. Sailings every 3–4 weeks.

UNITED FRUIT CO., Boston, Mass.

New York to Cristobal.
Trip 15 days; $175; weekly.
New York, Havana, Cristobal, Port Limón, Havana, New York.

New York to Jamaica and Panama Canal.
Trip 14 days; $175; weekly.
New York, Kingston, Puerto Colombia, Cartagena, Cristobal, Kingston, New York.

New York to Honduras and Guatemala.
Trip 12 days; $130; 36 sailings per year.
New York, Honduras and Guatemala ports as announced shortly before sailing.

New York to Santiago de Cuba and Santa Marta, Colombia.
Trip 12 days, $130–$150; weekly sailings.
New York (Santiago de Cuba), Santa Marta. Only occasional stops at Santiago.

Philadelphia to Puerto Barrios.
Trip 12 days. $130; weekly.
Philadelphia, Puerto Barrios and return.

New Orleans to Tela.
Trip 16 days, $150; weekly.
New Orleans, Havana, Cristobal, Almirante P.R., Tela, Havana, New Orleans.

New Orleans-Tela.
Trip 7–8 days; $126; weekly.
Every other week on route: New Orleans, Tela, Puerto Barrios, New Orleans. Every other week on route: New Orleans, Puerto Cortes, Puerto Barrios, New Orleans.

From Boston.
Sailings per year 50–60. Fares $9–$12 per day.

Boston to various ports to load bananas.

Ships may return to Boston, or to other ports, including Galveston. Exact routes known one day or two weeks in advance, depending on season.

FREIGHTERS carrying maximum 12 passengers used on most of these trips.

This company operates a large fleet of boats, some carrying 100 or more passengers, others carrying 12 or less. One freighter has 12 cabins, each with private bath. Most of regular runs are ships carrying more than 12 passengers, but some regular sailings are by freighter.

Almost never carry passengers out of Galveston.

UNITED STATES NAVIGATION CO., Inc., 17 Battery Pl., New York, N.Y.

Transatlantic.

Trip 26–29 days; $180 round voyage same ship; $200 round trip, with stopover privileges. One way, eastbound, $90–$95; westbound, $100–$105 (depending on season); 20 sailings per year.

SHIPS: *M.V. Helvig, M.V. Vasaland, M.V. Baghdad;* 5–12 passengers.

New York, London, Hamburg and return, or New York, London, Glasgow and return. Three days in London, one day at other port, returning same ship.

Mediterranean and Levant.

Trip 42–49 days. Round voyage same ship $270–$285. Round trip with stopover privileges, $300. New York to Izmir $160; to Casablanca $90. Monthly sailings.

Ports: New York, Casablanca, Alexandria, Piræus, Istanbul, Izmir, and New York. About one day in each port.

WATERMAN LINE, Mobile, Ala. *See* **MOBILE-OCEANIC** *and* **MOBILE, MIAMI AND GULF S.S. CO.**

WESTFAL–LARSEN LINE, 240 Battery St., San Francisco, Calif.

San Francisco coastwise along South America via Straits of Magellan and return via Panama Canal.
Trip is 120 days round trip from California. Fare is $500. Sailings monthly. Fare is $215 as far as Valparaiso; $250 to Buenos Aires; 5–7 passengers.

San Francisco to such West Coast South American ports as Colombia, Ecuador, Peru, Chile, as cargo offers, through the Straits of Magellan to Montevideo and Buenos Aires where passengers disembark for about two weeks at their own expense. Then continue from Buenos Aires to Santo, Rio de Janeiro, (Bahia, Pará), Port of Spain, Cristobal, and via Panama Canal to Los Angeles and San Francisco with stops at other ports as inducements offer.

S. L. WILLIAMS & CO., 12 Port Royal Street, Kingston, Jamaica, B.W.I.

Kingston to Cayman Islands.
Round trip £5/10.
SHIP: *S.S. Cimboco.* Sailings fortnightly; 15 passengers first class.

One way passage is sold only to visitors willing to deposit sixty pounds with authorities of Cayman Islands on arrival.

This company has occasional small schooners carrying two or more passengers sailing this route.

WEINBERGER BANANA CO., INC., 201 Decatur St., New Orleans, La.

New Orleans to banana ports in Mexico.
Sailings several times a week; 7 days round trip; $50 per person.

Ports and fares subject to variation, as also frequency of sailings.

WILHELMSEN LINE, 17 Battery Place, New York, N.Y.

Transatlantic.
Cruise 2½–3 months. Fare is $250 round trip. (Last Gulf port to Gdynia, fare is $130; Danzig to first Atlantic port, $110.) Sailings monthly.

New Orleans, Galveston, Houston, Savannah (Dunkirk), Oslo, Gothenburg, Copenhagen (Gdynia). Return via Oslo, West Norway, (Boston), Savannah, Havana, Vera Cruz, Tampico to Gulf ports and Savannah.

New York to South America.
Trip 20–30 days, Rio de Janeiro–New York, $130, Buenos Aires $160. (Suites 25 per cent. extra.) Round trip 2½ months $285. Monthly sailings.

New York (Bahia), Rio de Janeiro, Santos (Rio Grande do Sul), Buenos Aires and return.

New York to Far East.
Round trip, 4 months at $600. New York to Japan, $265; Los Angeles to Manila or Japan, $165; Manila to Los Angeles, $195; to San Francisco, $190; Yokohama to New York, $245.

SHIP: 10,000 tons, carries 12 passengers.

New York, Panama, San Pedro (San Francisco), Manila, Hong Kong, Shanghai, Kobe, Yokohama.

Europe to South Africa and Australia.
London to Capetown £35, suite £44; London to Sydney £56, suite £70.

Oslo, Hamburg, Rotterdam, London, Antwerp, Lisbon, Capetown, Durban, Fremantle, Adelaide, Melbourne, Sydney, Brisbane (Dakar on return trip).

South Africa to Australia.
Capetown to Sydney, £39. (Return fares lower in off season.)

Europe to Philippines, China, Japan.
Oslo to Colombo, £40, to Manila, £55, to Japan, £70; return fares vary slightly with season; round trip, 4½ months for £125.

Oslo, Hamburg, Antwerp, Rotterdam and/or London to Lisbon, Barcelona, Marseilles, Port Said, Suez, Port Sudan, Aden, Colombo, Singapore, Manila, Hong Kong, Shanghai, Yokohama, Kobe, North China and return, Cebu, Penang, Oran, Casablanca, Antwerp also stop on return route.

Europe to British India.
About four months. Round trip £80; Oslo to Bombay, £40; to Calcutta, £45. Return fares cheaper off season.

Oslo, Hamburg, Rotterdam, London, Antwerp, Lisbon, Port Said, Suez, Aden, Karachi, Bombay, Madras, Calcutta, Rangoon, and return.

Around-the-world.
Trip 3½ months, for £135.
SHIP: about 10,000 tons; 12 passengers.
Via Port Said and Suez to Yokohama — about 10 days in Japan. Return via Pacific coast, Panama Canal, New York to Europe.
Passenger pays own shore expenses at New York and in Japan awaiting ship.
This route is available in either direction.

ADDENDA

CANADIAN TRAVEL LEAGUE
410 St. Nicholas Street,
Montreal, Canada.
This company has the exclusive booking rights for a number of freighters sailing from Montreal and other Eastern ports. Some of the ships they have under contract make the same route regularly, others are one-time ships, contracted for a single voyage.

It is expected that other companies in other sections will enter this business, relieving freighter operators of the detail of handling correspondence, arranging bookings, answering passenger queries, handling passports and the other details that a steamship line must assume for its passengers.

At press date the Canadian Travel League submitted the following list of services under their contract with sufficient frequency of sailings for them to offer space to prospective passengers: —

Belgium and Holland.

From Montreal (occasionally from Sorel, Three Rivers, and Quebec) to Antwerp and Rotterdam. Weekly sailings; $75, 12–14 days (one way); $145 round trip.

Holland.

From Wahana, Newfoundland to Rotterdam. Frequent sailings; $55, 10 days (one way); $100 round trip.

United Kingdom.

From Montreal (and occasionally from Sorel, Three Rivers, and Quebec) to varying ports, including London, Avonmouth, Liverpool, Manchester, Glasgow, Leith, Newcastle, Hull, Belfast. Exact port declared shortly before sailing. Weekly sailings; $70, 12–14 days (one way); $120 round trip.

United Kingdom.

From Vancouver via Panama Canal to varying ports, including London, Avonmouth, Liverpool, Manchester, Glasgow, Leith, Newcastle, Hull, Belfast. Exact port declared shortly before sailing. Monthly sailings; $125, one month (one way).

Australia.

From Vancouver to various ports in Australia. Irregular service; $125, one month (one way).

PORTUGUESE SERVICES

Empresa Insulana de Navegacao.

S.S. *Lima* sails from Lisbon on the 8th of each month for Porto Santo, Madeira, Santa Maria, St. Miguel, Terceira, Graciosa, St. Jorge, Lages do Pico, and arrive Fayal on the 16th. Returning from Fayal on 16/17th, arrive Lisbon on the 24th. Rate to Fayal, first class $902, second class $583. Cruise first class, $1585. Rates in Portuguese currency.

S.S. *Carvalho Aranjo* sails from Lisbon the 23rd of each month for Madeira, St. Miguel, Terceira, Graciosa, St. Jorge, Caes do Pico, Fayal, Corvo and Flores. Returning from Fayal on 2nd via Caes do Pico, St. Jorge, Graciosa, Terceira, St. Miguel, Madeira, arrive Lisbon on the 8th or 9th. Rates to Flores, first class, $1000, $656. Second cruise first class $1585. Portuguese currency.

Companhia Nacional de Navegacao.
Companhia Colonial de Navegacao.
Sailings about every two weeks from Lisbon to Funchal.
Sailings about every two weeks from Funchal to Lisbon.

Trip takes 2 days each way.

Rate in Escudos; first class 650; second class 430; third class 160.

OFFICES: R. do Institute Virgilio Machado, 14, Lisbon; Rua do Comercio, 85, Lisbon.

Carregadores Acoreanos Line.
From London about every 14 days via Antwerp, Rotterdam, to Oporto and Lisbon.

Outward trip about 24 days. Home-bound trip about 5 days.

STEAMERS: S.S. *Pero d'Alenquer* (2,593 tons), S.S. *Corte Real* (1,972 tons).

From London about every 14 days to Oporto and Lisbon. Returning from Lisbon to London via Madeira and St. Michael's.

Outbound trip about 9 days. Home-bound trip about 25 days. Plymouth, Havre and Hamburg. Round trip about 6 weeks.

STEAMERS: *S.S. San Miguel* (2,112 tons), *Villa Franca* (1,998 tons), *Goncalho Velho* (1,595 tons).

LOCAL SERVICES FROM THE ISLAND OF TRINIDAD

To the British West Indies: —

Sailing vessels ply between Port-of-Spain and: —	Average length of voyage	Standard single fare for deckers	Single fare for special privileges
Grenada	1–1½ days	$2.40	$4.00
St. Vincent	2 days	$2.40	$4.00
Barbados	4 days	$5.00	$7.00
Demerara	7 days	—	—
Antigua	4 days	$5.00	$7.00
Nevis	4–5 days	$5.00	$7.00
St. Lucia	3 days	$5.00	$7.00
Montserrat	4 days	$5.00	$7.00

Agents for the *above* services to the British West Indies are G. A. S. Berkeley & Son, 1 Chacon Street, Port-of-Spain.

To Venezuelan ports: —

Between Port of Spain and: —	Average length of voyage
Guiria	1 day
Tucupita	4–5 days
Ciudad Bolivar	4–5 days

Agents for the *above* services to Venezuelan ports are: —
Mr. Salazar Sucre, 7 Charlotte Street, Port-of-Spain.
Mr. L. Vanososte, 4d Charlotte Street, Port-of-Spain.

Trinidad & Tobago sloop service: —

Average length of voyage	Standard single fare for deckers	Single fare for special privileges
1½ days to Tobago; return overnight	$2.00	$3.00

G. A. S. Berkeley & Son are also agents for this service.

Throughout the world, wherever there is local freight to move, local passengers will be carried. The services from the island of Trinidad are typical of services in the Caribbean, although Trinidad may have more sailing ships off her shores than other islands.

Similar conditions will be found elsewhere. Even into Tampa and Miami, banana boats (sail, helped by engine) oftentimes call, unload and carry a passenger or two off on a voyage.

The Trinidad data is given as a sample, no effort has been made to compile data on such services from a number of ports, because of the possibility of rapid changes in rates, sailings, and other matters, and also because it is hardly likely a great many American readers will want to make the journey from Trinidad to Nevis — 4 days for $5, deck passage, provide your own meals.

ROUTES NOT LISTED

Several times there has been reference to booking aboard a "real" tramp steamer. There is but one way to find these vessels — watch the shipping columns of the daily newspapers in some port city.

Lines and freight agents will deny any chance of any passengers being carried until just before the passenger might be booked. Correspondence will not handle this problem.

A number of Norwegian steamers come into Chicago, for example. Bookings can oftentimes be made, according to those in authority in Chicago, but only when personal application is made to the Captain of the vessel when she is about ready to sail.

The same rule holds true for any and all bookings on lines carrying passengers only when signed on as "crew."